KITCHEN CONFIDENTIAL

K I T C H E N

CONFIDENTIAL

ADVENTURES IN THE CULINARY UNDERBELLY

ANTHONY
BOURDAIN

TED SMART

First published in Great Britain 2000
This edition produced for The Book People Ltd 2002
Hall Wood Avenue, Haydock, St Helens, WA11 9UL

Copyright © 2000 by Anthony Bourdain

The moral right of the author has been asserted

Bloomsbury Publishing Plc, 38 Soho Square, London W1D 3HB

AUTHOR'S NOTE: I have changed the names of some of the
individuals and some of the restaurants that are a part of my story.

A CIP catalogue record is available from the British Library

ISBN 0 7475 5072 7

10 9 8 7 6

Typeset by Hewer Text Ltd, Edinburgh
Printed in Great Britain by Clays Ltd, St Ives plc

ACKNOWLEDGMENTS

Portions of this book have appeared previously elsewhere: much of the 'From Our Kitchen To Your Table' and a few other stray bits of business appeared in *The New Yorker*, under the title, 'Don't Eat Before Reading This'. The 'Mission to Tokyo' section appeared first in *Food Arts*, and readers of my short story for Canongate Books' *Rover's Return* collection will see that the fictional protagonist in my contribution, 'Chef's Night Out' had a humiliating experience on a busy broiler station much like my own.

I'd also like to thank Joel Rose, to whom I owe everything . . . Karen Rinaldi and Panio Gianopoulos at Bloomsbury USA. Jamie Byng, David Remnick, the evil Stone Brothers (Rob and Web), Tracy Westmoreland, José de Meireilles and Philippe Lajaunie, Steven Tempel, Michael Batterberry, Kim Witherspoon, Sylvie Rabineau, David Fiore, Scott Bryan, and my ass-kicking crew at Les Halles: Franck, Eddy, Isidoro, Carlos, Omar, Angel, Bautista and Janine.

Cooks Rule.

To Nancy

CONTENTS

CONTENTS

DESSERT

COFFEE AND A CIGARETTE

x

APPETIZER

A NOTE FROM THE CHEF

DON'T GET ME WRONG: I *love* the restaurant business. Hell, I'm still *in* the restaurant business – a lifetime, classically trained chef who, an hour from now, will probably be roasting bones for demi-glace and butchering beef tenderloins in a cellar prep kitchen on lower Park Avenue.

I'm not spilling my guts about everything I've seen, learned and done in my long and checkered career as dishwasher, prep drone, fry cook, grillardin, saucier, sous-chef and chef because I'm angry at the business, or because I want to horrify the dining public. I'd still *like* to be a chef, too, when this thing comes out, as this life is the only life I really know. If I need a favor at four o'clock in the morning, whether it's a quick loan, a shoulder to cry on, a sleeping pill, bail money, or just someone to pick me up in a car in a bad neighborhood in the driving rain, I'm definitely *not* calling up a fellow writer. I'm calling my sous-chef, or a former sous-chef, or my saucier, someone I work with or have worked with over the last twenty-plus years.

No, I want to tell you about the dark recesses of the restaurant underbelly – a subculture whose centuries-old militaristic hierarchy and ethos of 'rum, buggery and the lash' make for a mix of unwavering order and nerve-shattering chaos – because I find it all quite comfortable, like a nice warm bath. I can move around easily in this life. I speak the language. In the small, incestuous community of chefs and cooks in New York City, I know the people, and in my kitchen, I know how to behave (as opposed to

3

in real life, where I'm on shakier ground). I want the professionals who read this to enjoy it for what it is: a straight look at a life many of us have lived and breathed for most of our days and nights to the exclusion of 'normal' social interaction. Never having had a Friday or Saturday night off, always working holidays, being busiest when the rest of the world is just getting out of work, makes for a sometimes peculiar world-view, which I hope my fellow chefs and cooks will recognize. The restaurant lifers who read this may or may not like what I'm doing. But they'll know I'm not lying.

I want the readers to get a glimpse of the true joys of making really good food at a professional level. I'd like them to understand what it feels like to attain the child's dream of running one's own pirate crew – what it feels like, looks like and smells like in the clatter and hiss of a big city restaurant kitchen. And I'd like to convey, as best I can, the strange delights of the language, patois and death's-head sense of humor found on the front lines. I'd like civilians who read this to get a sense, at least, that this life, in spite of everything, can be *fun*.

As for me, I have always liked to think of myself as the Chuck Wepner of cooking. Chuck was a journeyman 'contender', referred to as the 'Bayonne Bleeder' back in the Ali–Frazier era. He could always be counted on to last a few solid rounds without going down, giving as good as he got. I admired his resilience, his steadiness, his ability to get it together, to take a beating like a man.

So, it's not Superchef talking to you here. Sure, I graduated CIA, knocked around Europe, worked some famous two-star joints in the city – damn good ones, too. I'm not some embittered hash-slinger out to slag off my more successful peers (though I will when the opportunity presents itself). I'm usually the guy they call in to some high-profile operation when the first chef turns out to be a psychopath, or a mean, megalomaniacal drunk. This book is about street-level cooking and its practitioners. Line cooks are the heroes. I've been hustling a nicely paid living out of this life for a long time – most of it in the heart of Manhattan, the 'bigs' – so I know a few things. I've still got a few moves left in me.

Of course, there's every possibility this book *could* finish me in the business. There will be horror stories. Heavy drinking, drugs, screwing in the dry-goods area, unappetizing revelations about bad food-handling and unsavory industry-wide practices. Talking about why you probably shouldn't order fish on a Monday, why those who favor well-done get the scrapings from the bottom of the barrel, and why seafood frittata is *not* a wise brunch selection won't make me any more popular with potential future employers. My naked contempt for vegetarians, sauce-on-siders, the 'lactose-intolerant' and the cooking of the Ewok-like Emeril Lagasse is not going to get me my own show on the Food Network. I don't think I'll be going on ski weekends with André Soltner anytime soon or getting a back rub from that hunky Bobby Flay. Eric Ripert won't be calling me for ideas on tomorrow's fish special. But I'm simply *not* going to deceive anybody about the life as I've seen it.

It's all here: the good, the bad and the ugly. The interested reader might, on the one hand, find out how to make professional-looking and -tasting plates with a few handy tools – and on the other hand, decide *never* to order the moules marinières again. *Tant pis*, man.

For me, the cooking life has been a long love affair, with moments both sublime and ridiculous. But like a love affair, looking back you remember the happy times best – the things that drew you in, attracted you in the first place, the things that kept you coming back for more. I hope I can give the reader a taste of those things and those times. I've never regretted the unexpected left turn that dropped me in the restaurant business. And I've long believed that good food, good eating is all about risk. Whether we're talking about unpasteurized Stilton, raw oysters or working for organized crime 'associates', food, for me, has always been an adventure.

FIRST COURSE

FOOD IS GOOD

MY FIRST INDICATION THAT food was something other than a substance one stuffed in one's face when hungry – like filling up at a gas station – came after fourth-grade elementary school. It was on a family vacation to Europe, on the *Queen Mary*, in the cabin-class dining room. There's a picture somewhere: my mother in her Jackie O sunglasses, my younger brother and I in our painfully cute cruisewear, boarding the big Cunard ocean liner, all of us excited about our first transatlantic voyage, our first trip to my father's ancestral homeland, France.

It was the soup.

It was *cold*.

This was something of a discovery for a curious fourth-grader whose entire experience of soup to this point had consisted of Campbell's cream of tomato and chicken noodle. I'd eaten in restaurants before, sure, but this was the first food I really noticed. It was the first food I enjoyed and, more important, remembered enjoying. I asked our patient British waiter what this delightfully cool, tasty liquid was.

'Vichyssoise,' came the reply, a word that to this day – even though it's now a tired old warhorse of a menu selection and one I've prepared thousands of times – still has a magical ring to it. I remember everything about the experience: the way our waiter ladled it from a silver tureen into my bowl, the crunch of tiny chopped chives he spooned on as garnish, the rich, creamy taste

9

of leek and potato, the pleasurable shock, the surprise that it was cold.

I don't remember much else about the passage across the Atlantic. I saw *Boeing Boeing* with Jerry Lewis and Tony Curtis in the *Queen*'s movie theater, and a Bardot flick. The old liner shuddered and groaned and vibrated terribly the whole way – barnacles on the hull was the official explanation – and from New York to Cherbourg, it was like riding atop a giant lawn-mower. My brother and I quickly became bored, and spent much of our time in the 'Teen Lounge', listening to 'House of the Rising Sun' on the jukebox, or watching the water slosh around like a contained tidal wave in the below-deck salt-water pool.

But that cold soup stayed with me. It resonated, waking me up, making me aware of my tongue, and in some way, preparing me for future events.

My second pre-epiphany in my long climb to chefdom also came during that first trip to France. After docking, my mother, brother and I stayed with cousins in a small seaside town near Cabourg, a bleak, chilly resort area in Normandy, on the English Channel. The sky was almost always cloudy; the water was inhospitably cold. All the neighborhood kids thought I knew Steve McQueen and John Wayne personally – as an American, it was assumed we were all pals, that we hung out together on the range, riding horses and gunning down miscreants – so I enjoyed a certain celebrity right away. The beaches, while no good for swimming, were studded with old Nazi blockhouses and gun emplacements, many still bearing visible bullet scars and the scorch of flamethrowers, and there were tunnels under the dunes – all very cool for a little kid to explore. My little French friends were, I was astonished to find, allowed to have a cigarette on Sunday, were given watered *vin ordinaire* at the dinner table, and best of all, they owned Vélo Solex motorbikes. *This* was the way to raise kids, I recall thinking, unhappy that my mother did not agree.

So for my first few weeks in France, I explored underground

passageways, looking for dead Nazis, played miniature golf, sneaked cigarettes, read a lot of Tintin and Astérix comics, scooted around on my friends' motorbikes and absorbed little life-lessons from observations that, for instance, the family friend Monsieur Dupont brought his mistress to some meals and his wife to others, his extended brood of children apparently indifferent to the switch.

I was largely unimpressed by the food.

The butter tasted strangely 'cheesy' to my undeveloped palate. The milk – a staple, no, a mandatory ritual in '60s American kiddie life – was undrinkable here. Lunch seemed always to consist of sandwich au jambon or croque-monsieur. Centuries of French cuisine had yet to make an impression. What I noticed about food, French style, was what they *didn't* have.

After a few weeks of this, we took a night train to Paris, where we met up with my father, and a spanking new Rover Sedan Mark III, our touring car. In Paris, we stayed at the Hôtel Lutétia, then a large, slightly shabby old pile on Boulevard Haussmann. The menu selections for my brother and me ex-panded somewhat, to include steak-frites and steak haché (hamburger). We did all the predictable touristy things: climbed the Tour Eiffel, picnicked in the Bois de Boulogne, marched past the Great Works at the Louvre, pushed toy sailboats around the fountain in the Jardin de Luxembourg – none of it much fun for a nine-year-old with an already developing criminal bent. My principal interest at this time was adding to my collection of English translations of Tintin adventures. Hergé's crisply drafted tales of drug-smuggling, ancient temples, and strange and far-away places and cultures were *real* exotica for me. I prevailed on my poor parents to buy hundreds of dollars-worth of these stories at W. H. Smith, the English bookstore, just to keep me from whining about the deprivations of France. With my little short-shorts a permanent affront, I was quickly becoming a sullen, moody, difficult little bastard. I fought constantly with my brother, carped about everything, and was in every possible way a drag on my mother's Glorious Expedition.

My parents did their best. They took us everywhere, from restaurant to restaurant, cringing, no doubt, every time we insisted on steak haché (with ketchup, no less) and a 'Coca.' They endured silently my gripes about cheesy butter, the seemingly endless amusement I took in advertisements for a popular soft drink of the time, Pschitt. 'I want shit! I want shit!' They managed to ignore the eye-rolling and fidgeting when they spoke French, tried to encourage me to find something, anything, to enjoy.

And there came a time when, finally, they *didn't* take the kids along.

I remember it well, because it was such a slap in the face. It was a wake-up call that food could be important, a challenge to my natural belligerence. By being denied, a door opened.

The town's name was Vienne. We'd driven miles and miles of road to get there. My brother and I were fresh out of Tintins and cranky as hell. The French countryside, with its graceful, tree-lined roads, hedgerows, tilled fields and picture-book villages provided little distraction. My folks had by now endured weeks of relentless complaining through many tense and increasingly unpleasant meals. They'd dutifully ordered our steak haché, crudités variées, sandwich au jambon and the like long enough. They'd put up with our grousing that the beds were too hard, the pillows too soft, the neck-rolls and toilets and plumbing too weird. They'd even allowed us a little watered wine, as it was clearly the French thing to do – but also, I think, to shut us up. They'd taken my brother and me, the two Ugliest Little Americans, everywhere.

Vienne was different.

They pulled the gleaming new Rover into the parking lot of a restaurant called, rather promisingly, La Pyramide, handed us what was apparently a hoarded stash of Tintins . . . *and then left us in the car!*

It was a hard blow. Little brother and I were left in that car for over three hours, an eternity for two miserable kids already bored out of their minds. I had plenty of time to wonder: *What could be so great inside those walls?* They were eating in there. I knew that. And it was certainly a Big Deal; even at a witless age nine, I could recognize the nervous anticipation, the excitement, the near-reverence with which my beleaguered parents had approached this hour. And I had the Vichyssoise Incident still fresh in my mind. Food, it appeared, could be *important*. It could be an event. It had secrets.

I know now, of course, that La Pyramide, even in 1966, was the center of the culinary universe. Bocuse, Troisgros, *everybody* had done their time there, making their bones under the legendarily fearsome proprietor, Ferdinand Point. Point was the Grand Master of cuisine at the time, and La Pyramide was Mecca for foodies. This was a pilgrimage for my earnestly francophile parents. In some small way, I got that through my tiny, empty skull in the back of the sweltering parked car, even then.

Things changed. *I* changed after that.

First of all, I was furious. Spite, always a great motivating force in my life, caused me to become suddenly adventurous where food was concerned. I decided then and there to outdo my foodie parents. At the same time, I could gross out my still uninitiated little brother. I'd show *them* who the gourmet was!

Brains? Stinky, runny cheeses that smelled like dead man's feet? Horsemeat? Sweetbreads? Bring it on!! Whatever had the most shock value became my meal of choice. For the rest of that summer, and in the summers that followed, I ate *everything*. I scooped gooey Vacherin, learned to love the cheesy, rich Normandy butter, especially slathered on baguettes and dipped in bitter hot chocolate. I sneaked red wine whenever possible, tried fritures – tiny whole fish, fried and eaten with persillade – loving that I was eating heads, eyes, bones and all. I ate ray in beurre noisette, saucisson à l'ail, tripes, rognons de veau (kidneys), boudin noir that squirted blood down my chin.

And I had my first oyster.

Now, *this* was a truly significant event. I remember it like I remember losing my virginity – and in many ways, more fondly.

August of that first summer was spent in La Teste de Buch, a tiny oyster village on the Bassin d'Arcachon in the Gironde (Southwest France). We stayed with my aunt, Tante Jeanne, and my uncle, Oncle Gustav, in the same red tile-roofed, white stuccoed house where my father had summered as a boy. My Tante Jeanne was a frumpy, bespectacled, slightly smelly old woman, my Oncle Gustav, a geezer in coveralls and beret who smoked hand-rolled cigarettes until they disappeared onto the tip of his tongue. Little had changed about La Teste in the years since my father had vacationed there. The neighbors were still all oyster fishermen. Their families still raised rabbits and grew tomatoes in their backyards. Houses had two kitchens, an inside one and an outdoor 'fish kitchen'. There was a hand pump for drinking water from a well, and an outhouse by the rear of the garden. Lizards and snails were everywhere. The main tourist attractions were the nearby Dune of Pyla (Europe's Largest Sand Dune!) and the nearby resort town of Arcachon, where the French flocked in unison for *Les Grandes Vacances*. Television was a Big Event. At seven o'clock, when the two national stations would come on the air, my Oncle Gustav would solemnly emerge from his room with a key chained to his hip and ceremoniously unlock the cabinet doors that covered the screen.

My brother and I were happier here. There was more to do. The beaches were warm, and closer in climate to what we knew back home, with the added attraction of the ubiquitous Nazi blockhouses. There were lizards to hunt down and exterminate with readily available *pétards*, firecrackers which one could buy legally (!) over-the-counter. There was a forest within walking distance where an actual hermit lived, and my brother and I spent hours there, spying on him from the underbrush. By now I could read and enjoy comic books in French and of course I was eating – *really* eating. Murky brown soupe de poisson, tomato salad, moules marinières, poulet basquaise (we were only a few miles from the Basque country). We made day trips to Cap Ferret, a wild, deserted and breathtakingly magnificent Atlantic beach with big rolling waves, taking along baguettes and saucissons and wheels of cheese, wine and Evian (bottled water was at that time unheard of back home). A few miles west was Lac Cazaux, a fresh-water lake where my brother and I could rent *pédalo* watercraft and pedal our way around the deep. We ate gaufres, delicious hot waffles, covered in whipped cream and powdered sugar. The two hot songs of that summer on the Cazaux jukebox were 'Whiter Shade of Pale' by Procol Harum, and 'These Boots Were Made for Walkin'' by Nancy Sinatra. The French played those two songs over and over again, the music punctuated by the sonic booms from French air force jets which would swoop over the lake on their way to a nearby bombing range. With all the rock and roll, good stuff to eat and high-explosives at hand, I was reasonably happy.

So, when our neighbor, Monsieur Saint-Jour, the oyster fisherman, invited my family out on his *pinasse* (oyster boat), I was enthusiastic.

At six in the morning, we boarded Monsieur Saint-Jour's small wooden vessel with our picnic baskets and our sensible footwear. He was a crusty old bastard, dressed like my uncle in ancient denim coveralls, espadrilles and beret. He had a leathery, tanned and windblown face, hollow cheeks, and the tiny broken blood vessels on nose and cheeks that everyone seemed to have from drinking so much of the local Bordeaux. He hadn't fully briefed his guests on what was involved in these daily travails. We put-putted out to a buoy marking his underwater oyster *parc*, a fenced-off section of bay bottom, and we sat . . . and sat . . . and sat, in the roaring August sun, waiting for the tide to go out. The idea was to float the boat over the stockaded fence walls, then sit there until the boat slowly sank with the water level, until it rested on the *bassin* floor. At this point, Monsieur Saint-Jour, and his guests presumably, would rake the oysters, collect a few good specimens for sale in port, and remove any parasites that might be endangering his crop.

There was, I recall, still about two feet of water left to go before the hull of the boat settled on dry ground and we could walk about the *parc*. We'd already polished off the Brie and baguettes and downed the Evian, but I was still hungry, and characteristically said so.

Monsieur Saint-Jour, on hearing this – as if challenging his American passengers – inquired in his thick Girondais accent, if any of us would care to try an oyster.

My parents hesitated. I doubt they'd realized they might actually have to *eat* one of the raw, slimy things we were currently floating over. My little brother recoiled in horror.

But I, in the proudest moment of my young life, stood up smartly, grinning with defiance, and volunteered to be the first.

And in that unforgettably sweet moment in my personal history, that one moment still more alive for me than so many of the other 'firsts' which followed – first pussy, first joint, first day in high school, first published book, or any other thing – I attained glory. Monsieur Saint-Jour beckoned me over to the gunwale, where he leaned over, reached down until his head nearly disappeared underwater, and emerged holding a single silt-encrusted oyster, huge and irregularly shaped, in his rough, clawlike fist. With a snubby, rust-covered oyster knife, he popped the thing open and handed it to me, everyone watching now, my little brother shrinking away from this glistening, vaguely sexual-looking object, still dripping and nearly alive.

I took it in my hand, tilted the shell back into my mouth as instructed by the by now beaming Monsieur Saint-Jour, and with one bite and a slurp, wolfed it down. It tasted of seawater . . . of brine and flesh . . . and somehow . . . of the future.

Everything was different now. Everything.

I'd not only survived – I'd *enjoyed*.

This, I knew, was the magic I had until now been only dimly and spitefully aware of. I was hooked. My parents' shudders, my little brother's expression of unrestrained revulsion and amazement only reinforced the sense that I had, somehow, become a man. I had had an *adventure*, tasted forbidden fruit, and everything that followed in my life – the food, the long and often stupid and self-destructive chase for *the next thing*, whether it was drugs or sex or some other new sensation – would all stem from this moment.

I'd learned something. Viscerally, instinctively, spiritually – even in some small, precursive way, sexually – and there was no turning back. The genie was out of the bottle. My life as a cook, and as a chef, had begun.

Food had *power*.

It could inspire, astonish, shock, excite, delight and *impress*. It had the power to please me . . . and others. This was valuable information.

For the rest of that summer, and in later summers, I'd often slip off by myself to the little stands by the port, where one could buy brown paper bags of unwashed, black-covered oysters by the dozen. After a few lessons from my new soul-mate, blood brother and bestest buddy, Monsieur Saint-Jour – who was now sharing his after-work bowls of sugared *vin ordinaire* with me too – I could easily open the oysters by myself, coming in from behind with the knife and popping the hinge like it was Aladdin's cave.

I'd sit in the garden among the tomatoes and the lizards and eat my oysters and drink Kronenbourgs (France was a wonderland for under-age drinkers), happily reading *Modesty Blaise* and the *Katzenjammer Kids* and the lovely hard-bound *bandes dessinées* in French, until the pictures swam in front of my eyes, smoking the occasional pilfered Gitane. And I still associate the taste of oysters with those heady, wonderful days of illicit late-afternoon buzzes. The smell of French cigarettes, the taste of beer, that unforgettable feeling of doing something I shouldn't be doing.

I had, as yet, no plans to cook professionally. But I frequently look back at my life, searching for that fork in the road, trying to figure out where, exactly, I *went bad* and became a thrill-seeking, pleasure-hungry sensualist, always looking to shock, amuse, terrify and manipulate, seeking to fill that empty spot in my soul with something new.

I like to think it was Monsieur Saint-Jour's fault. But of course, it was me all along.

FOOD IS SEX

IN 1973, UNHAPPILY IN love, I graduated high school a year early so I could chase the object of my desire to Vassar College – the less said about that part of my life, the better, believe me. Let it suffice to say that by age eighteen I was a thoroughly undisciplined young man, blithely flunking or fading out of college (I couldn't be bothered to attend classes). I was angry at myself and at everyone else. Essentially, I treated the world as my ashtray. I spent most of my waking hours drinking, smoking pot, scheming, and doing my best to amuse, outrage, impress and penetrate anyone silly enough to find me entertaining. I was – to be frank – a spoiled, miserable, narcissistic, self-destructive and thoughtless young lout, badly in need of a good ass-kicking. Rudderless and unhappy, I went in with some friends on a summer share in Provincetown, Cape Cod. It was what my friends were doing and that was enough for me.

Provincetown was (and is) essentially a small Portuguese fishing village all the way out on the fish-hooked tip of the Cape. During the summer months, however, it became Times Square/Christopher Street-by-the-Sea. This was the '70s, remember, so factor that in when you conjure up the image of a once quaint New England port town, clogged with tourists, day-trippers, hippies, drifters, lobster poachers, slutty chicks, dopers, refugees from Key West, and thousands upon thousands of energetically cruising gay men. For a rootless young man with sensualist inclinations, it was the perfect getaway.

19

Unfortunately, I needed money. My on-again-off-again girl-friend spun pizza for a living. My room-mates, who had sum-mered in P-town before, had jobs waiting for them. They cooked, washed dishes, waited tables – usually at night – so we all went to the beaches and ponds each morning, smoked pot, sniffed a little coke, dropped acid and sunbathed nude, as well as indulging in other healthy teenage activities.

Tired of my drain on the household finances, one annoyed and practical room-mate hooked me up with a dishwashing gig at the restaurant where she waited tables. Dishwashers (sudbusters, aka pearl divers) were the most transient breed in the seasonal restaurant business, so when one goofball failed to show up for work for two days, I was in. It was my introduction to the life – and at first, I did not go happily.

Scrubbing pots and pans, scraping plates and peeling moun-tains of potatoes, tearing the little beards off mussels, picking scallops and cleaning shrimp did not sound or look attractive to me. But it was from these humble beginnings that I began my strange climb to chefdom. Taking that one job, as dishwasher at the Dreadnaught, essentially pushed me down the path I still walk to this day.

The Dreadnaught was – well, you've eaten there, or someplace like it: a big, old, ramshackle driftwood pile, built out over the water on ancient wooden pylons. In bad weather, the waves would roll under the dining-room floor and thud loudly against the sea wall. Grey wood shingles, bay windows, and inside, the classic Olde New Englande/Rusty Scupper/Aye Matey/Cap'n Whats's decor: hanging fishnets, hurricane lamps, buoys, nau-tical bric-a-brac, the bars fashioned from halved lifeboats. Call it Early Driftwood.

We served fried clams, fried shrimp, fried flounder, fried scallops, French fries, steamed lobsters, a few grilled and broiled steaks, chops and fish fillets to the mobs of tourists who'd pour into town each week between the 4th of July and Labor Day.

I was surprisingly happy in my work. The Dreadnaught management were an aged, retiring and boozy lot who stayed out of the kitchen most of the time. The waitresses were attractive and cheerful, free with drinks for the kitchen and with their favors as well.

And the cooks?

The cooks *ruled*.

There was Bobby, the chef, a well-toasted, late-thirtyish ex-hippie who, like a lot of people in P-town, had come for vacation years back and stayed. He lived there year-round, cheffing in the summer, doing roofing and carpentry and house-sitting during the off-season. There was Lydia, a half-mad, matronly Portuguese divorcee with a teenage daughter. Lydia made the clam chowder for which we were somewhat famous, and during service dished out the vegetables and side dishes. She drank a lot. There was Tommy, the fry cook, a perpetually moving surfer dude with electric blue eyes, who even when there was nothing to do, rocked back and forth like an elephant to 'keep up the momentum'. There was Mike, an ex-con and part-time methedrine dealer, who worked salad station.

In the kitchen, they were like gods. They dressed like pirates: chef's coats with the arms slashed off, blue jeans, ragged and faded headbands, gore-covered aprons, gold hoop earrings, wrist cuffs, turquoise necklaces and chokers, rings of scrimshaw and ivory, tattoos – all the decorative detritus of the long-past Summer of Love.

They had style and swagger, and they seemed afraid of nothing. They drank everything in sight, stole whatever wasn't nailed down, and screwed their way through floor staff, bar customers and casual visitors like nothing I'd ever seen or imagined. They carried big, bad-ass knives, which they kept honed and sharpened to a razor's edge. They hurled dirty sauté pans and pots across the kitchen and into my pot sink with casual accuracy. They spoke their own peculiar dialect, an unbelievably profane patois of countercultural jargon and local Portugee slang, delivered with ironic inflection, calling each other, for instance, 'Paaahd' for 'Partner' or 'Daahlin' for 'Darling'. They looted the place for everything it was worth, stocking up well in advance for the lean months of the off-season. A couple of nights a week, the chef would back his Volkswagen van up to the kitchen door and load whole sirloin strips, boxes of frozen shrimp, cases of beer, sides of bacon into the cargo area. The speed racks over each station – containing bottles of cooking wine, oil, etc. for easy access during service – were always loaded with at least two highball glasses per cook; Lydia liked to call them 'summertime coolers', usually strong Cape Codders, Sea Breezes or Greyhounds. Joints were smoked in the downstairs walk-in, and cocaine – always available, though in those days *very* expensive and still considered a rich man's drug – was everywhere. On payday everyone in the kitchen handed money back and forth in a Byzantine rondelay of transactions as the cooks settled up the previous week's drug debts, loans and wagers.

I saw a lot of bad behavior that first year in P-town. I was impressed. These guys were master criminals, sexual athletes, compared to my pitiful college hijinks. Highwaymen rogues, buccaneers, cut-throats, they were like young princes to me, still only a lowly dishwasher. The life of the cook was a life of *adventure*, looting, pillaging and rock-and-rolling through life with a carefree disregard for all conventional morality. It looked pretty damn good to me on the other side of the line.

But if there was one moment where I saw clearly what I wanted, it was at the end of that summer.

I'd moved up a bit by now. Mike had gone missing on a meth jag and I had been promoted to the salad station plating shrimp cocktails, cracking oysters and cherrystone clams, mixing canned lobster meat with mayonnaise and filling champagne glasses with strawberries and whipped cream.

The Dreadnaught line was a long, narrow affair: a cold station by the exit door to the parking lot, a double-decker lobster steamer where we'd kill off the 1½ and 2-pounders by the dozen, stacking them up like cordwood before slamming shut the heavy metal doors and turning the wheel, giving them the steam. Then came a row of deep-fryers, a range, a big Garland pull-out broiler, a few more burners, and finally a brick hearth for charcoal grilling, all of this bordered by the usual pass-through on the other side – wooden cutting board/counter with sunken steam table, and below that, the low-boy reach-in refrigerators for reserve supplies. By the far-end open hearth, where Bobby, the chef, worked, was a Dutch door, the top half kept open so incoming tourists could get a peek at some lobsters or steaks grilling as they entered and get in the mood.

One weekday, a large wedding party arrived, fresh from the ceremony: bride, groom, ushers, family and friends. Married up-Cape, the happy couple and party had come down to P-town for the celebratory dinner following, presumably, a reception. They were high when they arrived. From the salad station at the other end of the line, I saw a brief, slurry exchange between Bobby and some of the guests. I noticed particularly the bride, who at one point leaned into the kitchen and inquired if any of us 'had any hash'. When the party moved on into the dining room, I pretty much forgot about them.

We banged out meals for a while, Lydia amusing us with her usual patter, Tommy dunking clams and shrimp into hot grease, the usual ebb and flow of a busy kitchen. Then the bride reappeared at the open Dutch door. She was blonde and good-looking in her virginal wedding white, and she spoke closely with the chef for a few seconds; Bobby suddenly grinned from ear to ear, the sunburned crow's-feet at the corners of his eyes growing more pronounced. A few moments later she was gone again, but Bobby, visibly trembling, suddenly said, 'Tony! Watch my station,' and promptly scooted out the back door.

Ordinarily, this alone would have been a momentous event. To be allowed to work the busy broiler station, to take the helm – even for a few minutes – was a dream come true. But curiosity got the better of all of us remaining in the kitchen. We had to look.

There was a fenced-off garbage stockade right outside the window by the dishwasher, that concealed the stacked trash and cans of edible waste the restaurant sold to a pig farm up-Cape, from the cars in the parking lot. Soon, all of us – Tommy, Lydia, the new dishwasher and I – were peering through the window, where in full view of his assembled crew, Bobby was noisily rear-ending the bride. She was bent obligingly over a 55-gallon drum, her gown hiked up over her hips. Bobby's apron was up, resting over her back as he pumped away furiously, the young woman's eyes rolled up into her head, mouth whispering, 'Yess, yess . . . good . . . good . . .'

While her new groom and family chawed happily on their flounder fillets and deep-fried scallops just a few yards away in the Dreadnaught dining room, here was the blushing bride, getting an impromptu send-off from a total stranger.

And I knew then, dear reader, for the first time: I wanted to be a chef.

FOOD IS PAIN

I DON'T WANT YOU to think that everything up to this point was about fornication, free booze and ready access to drugs. I should recall for you the delights of Portuguese squid stew, of Wellfleet oysters on the halfshell, New England clam chowder, of greasy, wonderful, fire-red chorizo sausages, kale soup, and a night when the striped bass jumped right out of the water and onto Cape Cod's dinner tables.

There was, in 1974, no culinary culture that I was aware of. In P-town in particular, there were not, as there are today, any star chefs – school-trained, name-on-the-jacket characters whose names and utterances were tossed around by foodies, photos swapped like baseball cards. There were no catch-phrases like 'Bam!' and 'Let's kick it up a notch!' bandied about on television for a credulous public like there are today. These were early times in American food. Squid was considered a 'garbage fish', practically given away at the docks. Tuna was sold mainly as cat-food, or to canneries, and to a few enterprising Japanese who were thought to 'confuse things' with the high prices they paid. Monkfish was yet to be called *lotte* and make its appearance on Manhattan dinner tables. Most fish in P-town was slapped boneless and skinless onto sizzle-platters, drizzled with clarified butter and paprika and then broiled to death. The parsley sprig and the lemon wedge were state-of-the art garnishes. Our few culinary heroes at the Dreadnaught were admired more for their studliness on the line – meaning number of dinners served each night, amount of pain and heat endured, total number of wait-resses screwed, cocktails consumed without visible effect. These were stats we understood and appreciated.

There was Jimmy Lester, the Broiler King, whom we thought a lot of. He'd worked for years at a nearby steakhouse and was famous for the remarkable number of steaks and chops he could handle at one time on his big roll-out broiler. Jimmy had 'moves', meaning he spun and twirled and stabbed at meat with considerable style and grace for a 220-pound man. He was credited with coming up with 'the bump' – a bit of business where a broiler man with both hands full of sizzle-platters or plates knocks the grill back under the flames with his hip. We liked that.

The mishandling of food and equipment with panache was always admired; to some extent, this remains true to this day. Butchers still slap down prime cuts with just a little more force and noise than necessary. Line cooks can't help putting a little English on outgoing plates, spinning them into the pass-through with reverse motion so they curl back just short of the edge. Oven doors in most kitchens have to be constantly tightened because of repeatedly being kicked closed by clog-shod feet. And all of us dearly love to play with knives.

The boys across the street were considered to be a champion-ship team, the perfect example of the culinary ideals of the time. Mario's Restaurant was a hugely successful Southern Italian joint and the Mario crew were feared and respected because they did more covers, by a few hundred each night, than almost anyone else in town. It was fairly sophisticated stuff for the time: whole legs of veal were actually butchered on the premises, stocks were made from real bones (not commercial base), sauces were made from scratch with quality ingredients – and the Mario crew were the loudest, crudest, most bad-ass bunch of cookies in town. When they'd swing by the Dreadnaught for a few pops after work, they made our ragtag bunch of part-time roofers feel small. They were richer, more confident, and moved with even more swagger and style than our motley crew of oddballs and amateurs. They moved in a pack, with their own dialect – a high-pitched, ultra-femme, affected drawl, salted with terms from eighteenth-century English literature and Marine Corps drill instructor-speak – a lush, intimidating, sardonic secret language, which was much imitated.

'You, sir, are a loathsome swine. Too damn ignorant to pour piss from a boot! Your odor offends me and my shell-like ear gapeth to hear thy screams of pain. I *insist* you avert your face and serve me a libation before I smite your sorry ass with the tip of my boot – you sniveling little cocksucker!'

They had women's names for each other, a jarring thing to hear as they were all huge, ugly-looking and wild-eyed, with muscles and scars and doorknocker-sized earrings. They looked down on outsiders, frequently communicated with only a glance or a smile, and moved through the streets and bars and back alleys of P-town like Titans. They had more coke, better weed, bigger gold, prettier women. They loved rubbing our noses in it.

'How many?' they'd ask after a busy Saturday night.

'Oh . . . one-fifty, two hundred,' Bobby would reply, fluffing the number a little.

'We did . . . what? How many was it, Dee Dee, daahlin?' the Mario chef would ask casually, 'Four-fifty? Five?'

'Six, I think,' Dimitri, the Mario pasta man, would reply – a man who would later play a major part in my career.

'Yes . . . six. Slow night, I dare say. Pathetic, don't you know. Pig-dogs must have eaten their mung elsewhere tonight. Dairy Queen, probably.'

And then there was Howard Mitcham. Howard was the sole 'name chef' in town. Fiftyish, furiously alcoholic, and stone-deaf – the result of a childhood accident with fireworks – Howard could be seen most nights after work, holding up the fishermen's bars or lurching about town, shouting incomprehensibly (he liked to sing as well). Though drunk most of the time, and difficult to understand, Howard was a revered elder statesman of Cape Cod cookery, a respected chef of a very busy restaurant, and the author of two very highly regarded cookbooks: *The*

Provincetown Seafood Cookbook and *Creole, Gumbo and All That Jazz* – two volumes I *still* refer to, and which were hugely influential for me and my budding culinary peers of the time.

He had wild, unruly white hair, a gin-blossomed face, a boozer's gut, and he wore the short-sleeved, snap-button shirt of a dishwasher. Totally without pretension, both he and his books were fascinating depositories of recipes, recollections, history, folklore and illustrations, drawing on his abiding love for humble, working-class ethnic food of the area.

Howard *loved* seafood. *All* seafood. Unlike most of us, he knew what to do with it. He loved the less popular fishes of the day, using tuna, squid, mackerel, bluefish and salt cod to great advantage. His signature dish was haddock amandine, and people would drive for hours from Boston to sample it. He was the first chef I knew to appreciate fully the local Portugee cuisine: the spicy cumin-scented squid stews, the linguica-laden kale soups, the coupling of fish and pork sausages. And he was a strident advocate for the mystical powers of the Quahog, that humble, slightly tough local clam.

Once each summer, Howard and friends – mostly artists, local fishermen, writers and drunks – would throw a party called the John J. Gaspie Memorial Clambake, in honor of a departed fisherman friend. It was a major social event for P-town's year-round residents, and for those of us who worked the season in the restaurant business. Howard and friends would dig pits in the beach and drop shiny new trash cans into the holes, then fill them with quahogs, lobsters, codfish, vegetables, potatoes and corn, allowing them to simmer over glowing coals buried deep in the sand while everyone drank themselves silly.

To us at the Dreadnaught, Howard was a juju man, an oracle who spoke in tongues. We might not have understood Howard, but we understood his books, and while it was hard to reconcile his public behavior with the wry, musical, and lovingly informative tone of his writings, we knew enough to respect the man for what he knew and for what he could do. We saw someone who loved *food*, not just the life of the cook. Howard showed us how to cook for *ourselves*, for the pure pleasure of eating, not just for the tourist hordes.

Howard showed us that there was hope for us as cooks. That food could be a calling. That the stuff itself was something we could actually be *proud of*, a reason to live. And that stuck with some of us from those early frontier days. He influenced a lot of my friends. I read a Molly O'Neill column in the *New York Times Magazine* recently, in which she was describing the delights of Portuguese-influenced Cape Cod food like white beans, kale and chorizo, and I *knew* she'd eaten the old man's food, and probably read his books too. Without his name being mentioned, Howard's reach had extended across the decades to my Sunday paper – and I was glad of it.

There was another inspiring moment: a rough, choppy, moonlit night on the water, and the Dreadnaught's manager looked out the window suddenly to spy thousands of tiny baitfish breaking the surface, rushing frantically toward shore. He knew what that meant, as did everyone else in town with a boat, a gaff and a loaf of Wonderbread to use as bait: the stripers were running!

Thousands of the highly prized, relatively expensive striped bass were, in a rare feeding frenzy, suddenly there for the taking. You had literally only to throw bread on the water, bash the tasty fish on the head with a gaff and then haul them in. They were taking them by the hundreds of pounds. Every restaurant in town was loading up on them, their parking lots, like ours, suddenly a Coleman-lit staging area for scaling, gutting and wrapping operations. The Dreadnaught lot, like every other lot in town, was suddenly filled with gore-covered cooks and dishwashers, laboring under flickering gaslamps and naked bulbs to clean, wrap and freeze the valuable white meat. We worked for hours with our knives, our hair sparkling with snowflake-like fish scales, scraping, tearing, filleting. At the end of the night's work, I took home a 35-pound monster, still twisted with rigor. My room-mates were smoking weed when I got back to our little place on the beach and, as often happens on such occasions, were hungry. We had only the bass, some butter and a lemon to work with, but we cooked that sucker up under the tiny home broiler and served it on aluminum foil, tearing at it with our fingers. It was a bright, moonlit sky now, a mean high tide was lapping at the edges of our house, and as the windows began to shake in their frames, a smell of white spindrift and salt saturated the air as we ate. It was the freshest piece of fish I'd ever eaten, and I don't know if it was due to the dramatic quality the weather was beginning to take on, but it hit me right in the brainpan, a meal that made me feel better about things, made *me* better for eating it, somehow even *smarter*, somehow . . . It was a protein rush to the cortex, a clean, three-ingredient high, eaten with the hands. Could anything be better than that?

As the season came to an end, the regular crew began to fade away, off to work ski resorts in Colorado, charter boats in the Caribbean, restaurants and crab-shacks in Key West. After Labor Day, I got my chance to move up for the last few weeks before the Dreadnaught closed for the year. I worked the fry station, dunking breaded clams and shrimp into hot oil for a while, racked up a serious body count of lobsters on the double-decker steamer, and finally was moved up yet again to do a few shifts on the mighty broiler. I cannot describe to you the sheer pleasure, the *power* of commanding that monstrous, fire-breathing iron and steel furnace, bumping the grill under the flames with my hip the way I'd seen Bobby and Jimmy do it. It was tremendous. I couldn't have felt happier – or more powerful in the cockpit of an F-16. I ruled the world for a few short weeks, and I was determined to make that station my own the following season.

Sadly, things didn't turn out as planned. The next summer, Mario bought our faltering restaurant. Mario was kind enough to allow those of us who'd worked there the previous year to audition for our old jobs with a few shifts in his kitchen. I was thrilled by the opportunity, and headed up to P-town that April filled with hope and confidence, *certain* I'd make the cut, land that top-tier broiler job, the big money, the gig that would surely make me one of the pirate elite, an ass-kicking, throat-slitting stud who could lord it over the salad men and fry cooks and prep drones at less successful restaurants.

I pulled into town, I remember, wearing – God help me – a spanking-new light blue Pierre Cardin seersucker suit. The shoes, too, were blue. Here I was, hitchhiking into a town that for all intents and purposes was a downscale, informal Portuguese fishing village and artists' colony, a town where people dressed unpretentiously in work clothes – denims, army surplus, old khakis – and in some deranged, early '70s bout of disco-inspired hubris, I chose to make my entrance in gull-wing shouldered Robert Palmer-wear, just itching to show the local yokels how we did it in New York City.

They were pounding veal in the kitchen when I arrived; the whole crew, on every available horizontal surface, banging on veal cutlets for scallopine with heavy steel mallets. The testosterone level was high, very high. These guys were the A-Team, and they knew it. Everybody knew it. The floor staff, the managers, even Mario seemed to walk on eggs around them, as if one of them would suddenly lunge through the bars of their cage and take a jagged bite. I alone was too stupid to see how over my head I was among these magnificent cooking machines. I'd served a few hundred meals, at a relaxed pace, in a not very busy joint, in the off-season. These guys drilled out four, five, six hundred fast-paced, high-end meals a *night*!

It was Friday, an hour before service, when I was introduced to Tyrone the broiler man, whom I'd be trailing. Looking back, I can't remember Tyrone as being anything less than 8 feet tall, 400 pounds of carved obsidian, with a shaved head, a prominent silver-capped front tooth, and the ubiquitous fist-sized gold hoop earring. While his true dimensions were probably considerably more modest, you get the picture: he was *big*, black, hugely muscled, his size 56 chef's coat stretched across his back like a drumhead. He was a gargantua, a black Viking, Conan the Barbarian, John Wayne and the Golem all rolled into one. But unintimidated as only the ignorant can be, I started shooting my stupid mouth off right away, regaling my new chums with highly exaggerated versions of my adventures at the old Dreadnaught – what bad boys *we* had been. I blathered on about New York, trying to portray myself as some street-smart, experienced, even slightly dangerous professional gun-for-hire of the cooking biz.

They were, to be charitable to myself, not impressed. Not that this deterred me in the slightest from yapping on and on. I ignored all the signs. All of them: the rolling eyes, the tight smiles. I plunged on, oblivious to what was happening in the kitchen right around me; the monstrous amounts of food being loaded into low-boys and reach-ins for mise-en-place. I missed the determined sharpening of knives, the careful arranging and folding of side towels in kitty-cornered stacks, the stockpiling of favorite pans, ice, extra pots of boiling water, back-up supplies of everything. They were like Marines digging in for the siege at Khe Sanh, and I registered nothing.

I should have seen this well-practiced ritual for what it was, understood the level of performance here in Marioland, appreciated the experience, the time served together which allowed these hulking giants to dance wordlessly around each other in the cramped, heavily manned space behind the line without ever colliding or wasting a movement. They turned from cutting board to stove-top with breathtaking economy of movement, they hefted 300-pound stockpots onto ranges, tossed legs of veal around like pullets, blanched hundreds of pounds of pasta, all the while indulgently enduring without comment my endless self-aggrandizing line of witless chatter. I should have understood this femme/convict patois, this business with the women's names, the arcane expressions, seen it for what it was: the end result of *years* working together in a confined space under extreme pressure. I should have understood. But I didn't.

An hour later the board was filled with more dinner orders than I'd ever seen in my life.

Ticket after ticket kept coming in, one on top of the other, waiters screaming, tables of ten, tables of six, four-tops, more and more of them coming, no ebb and flow, just a relentless, incoming, nerve-shattering gang-rush of orders. And the orders were all in *Italian*! I couldn't even *understand* most of the dupes, or what these waiters were screaming at me. The seasoned Mario cooks had an equally impenetrable collection of code names for each dish, making it even more difficult to make sense of it all. There were cries of 'Ordering!' and 'Pick up!' every few seconds, and 'Fire!', more food going out, more orders coming in, the squawk of an intercom as an upstairs bartender called down for food. Flames 3 feet high leaped out of pans, the broiler was crammed with a slowly moving train of steaks, veal chops, fish fillets, lobsters. Pasta was blanched and shocked and transferred in huge batches into steaming colanders, falling everywhere, the floor soon ankle-deep in spaghetti alla chitarra, linguine, garganelli, taglierini, fusilli. The heat was horrific. Sweat flowed into my eyes, blinding me as I spun in place.

I struggled and sweated and hurried to keep up the best I could, Tyrone slinging sizzle-platters under the broiler, and me, ostensibly helping out, getting deeper and deeper into the weeds with every order. On the rare occasions when I could look up at the board, the dupes now looked like cuneiform or Sanskrit – indecipherable.

I was losing it. Tyrone, finally, had to help the helper.

Then, grabbing a sauté pan, I burned myself.

I yelped out loud, dropped the pan, an order of osso bucco milanese hitting the floor, and as a small red blister raised itself on my palm, I foolishly – oh, so foolishly – asked the beleaguered Tyrone if he had some burn cream and maybe a Band-Aid.

This was quite enough for Tyrone. It went suddenly very quiet in the Mario kitchen, all eyes on the big broiler man and his hopelessly inept assistant. Orders, as if by some terrible and poetically just magic, stopped coming in for a long, horrible moment. Tyrone turned slowly to me, looked down through bloodshot eyes, the sweat dripping off his nose, and said, 'Whachoo want, white boy? Burn cream? *A Band-Aid?*'

Then he raised his own enormous palms to me, brought them up real close so I could see them properly: the hideous constellation of water-filled blisters, angry red welts from grill marks, the old scars, the raw flesh where steam or hot fat had made the skin simply roll off. They looked like the claws of some monstrous science-fiction crustacean, knobby and calloused under wounds old and new. I watched, transfixed, as Tyrone – his eyes never leaving mine – reached slowly under the broiler and, with one naked hand, picked up a glowing-hot sizzle-platter, moved it over to the cutting board, and set it down in front of me.

He never flinched.

The other cooks cheered, hooted and roared at my utter humiliation. Orders began to come in again and everyone went back to work, giggling occasionally. But I knew. I was *not* going to be the Dreadnaught's broiler man this year – *that* was for damn sure. (They ended up kicking me back down to prep, one step above dishwasher on the food chain.) I had been shown up for the loudmouthed, useless little punk that I was. I was, I learned later, a *mal carne*, meaning 'bad meat' in Italian, referred to as 'Mel' for weeks after. I had been identified as a pretender, and an obnoxious one at that.

I slunk home that night in my blue Pierre Cardin suit as if it was sackcloth and ashes. I had not yet found a summer rental, so I was sleeping over the walk-in in the back room at Spiritus Pizza. My torment, my disgrace was complete.

After a few days of sulking and self-pity, I slowly, and with growing determination, began to formulate a plan, a way to get back at my tormentors. I would go to school, at the Culinary Institute of America – they were the best in the country and certainly none of these P-town guys had been there. I would apprentice in France. I would endure anything: evil drunk chefs, crackpot owners, low pay, terrible working conditions; I would let sadistic, bucket-headed French sous-chefs work me like a

Sherpa . . . *but I would be back*. I would do whatever was necessary to become as good as, or better than, this Mario crew. I would have hands like Tyrone's and I would break loudmouth punks like myself over the wheel like they'd broken me.

I'd show them.

INSIDE THE CIA

BURNING WITH A DESIRE for vengeance and vindication, I applied myself to gaining entry to the Culinary Institute of America in Hyde Park, New York. My Vassar friends – those who remained on speaking terms with me after two years of truly disgusting behavior on my part – thought I was out of my mind, but then they thought that anyway. I'm sure that there was a collective sigh of relief on Vassar's rolling, green, well-tended campus that I would no longer be around to cadge free drinks, steal drugs, make pointedly cruel remarks and generally lower the level of discourse. My idols of that time had been, all too predictably, Hunter Thompson, William Burroughs, Iggy Pop and Bruce Lee; I had had, for some time, a romantic if inaccurate view of myself as some kind of hyperviolent, junkie Byron. My last semester at Vassar, I'd taken to wearing nunchakus in a strap-on holster and carrying around a samurai sword – that should tell you all you need to know. The most romantic thing I *had* done in two years was to chop down about an acre of Vassar's lilacs one night with my sword, so that I could fill my girlfriend's room with the blossoms.

CIA was a bit of a departure. I'd love to tell you it was tough getting in. There *was* a long waiting list. But I reached out to a friend of a friend who'd donated some heavy bucks to the school and owned a well-known restaurant in New York City, and about two weeks after filling out my application I was in. I was an enrolled student at an institution where everyone wore identical white uniforms, funny paper hats and actually *had* to attend class. Like I said, it was a bit of a departure. But I was ready.

CIA is located in the buildings and grounds of a former Jesuit monastery on a Hudson River clifftop, a short cab ride from Poughkeepsie. In my buttoned-up chef's coat, check pants, neckerchief and standard-issue leatherette knife roll-up, I arrived determined but full of attitude.

My knives set me apart right away. I had my by now well-worn high-carbon Sabatiers rolled in with the cheap school-supply junk: hard-to-sharpen Forschner stainless steel, peeler, parisienne scoop, paring knife and slicer. I was older than most of my fellow students, many of whom were away from home for the first time. Unlike them, I lived off campus, in Pough-keepsie with the remnants of my Vassar pals. I'd actually worked in the industry – and I'd had sex with a woman. These were not the cream of the crop, my fellow culinarians. It was 1975 and CIA was still getting more than their share of farm boys, bed-wetters, hicks, flunk-outs from community colleges and a few misfits for whom CIA was preferable to jail or juvenile detention. Hopeless in the kitchen, happy in their off-hours to do little more than build pyramids of beer cans, they were easy marks for a hard case like myself. I nearly supported myself during my two years in Hyde Park playing seven-card stud, Texas hold-em, no-peek and acey-deucey. I felt no shame or guilt taking their money, selling them beat drugs or cheating at cards. They were about to enter the restaurant industry; I figured they might as well learn sooner rather than later. If the Mario crew ever got hold of some of these rubes, they'd have the fillings out of their teeth.

It was very easy going for me. The first few months at CIA were spent on stuff like: 'This is the chef's knife. This is the handle. This is the blade,' as well as rote business on sanitation. My food sanitation instructor, an embittered ex-health inspector (judging from the scars on his face, the last honest man in that trade), regaled us with stories of pesticide-munching super rats, the sex lives of bacteria and the ever-present dangers of unseen filth.

I took classes in food-handling, egg cookery, salads, stocks, soups, basic knifework. But after spending way too many hours deep in the bowels of Marioland, peeling spuds, making gallons of dressings, chopping vegetables and so on, I knew this stuff in my bones.

Of course, my stocks in class always tasted far better than my classmates'. No one could figure out how I coaxed such hearty flavor out of a few chicken bones, or made such wonderful fish fumet with fish racks and shrimp shells, all in the limited time available. Had my instructors given me a pat-down before class they might have learned my secret: two glassine envelopes of Minor's chicken and lobster base inside my chef's coat, for that little extra kick. They never figured it out.

The CIA of 1975 was very different from the four-year professional institution it is today. Back then, the desired end-product seemed to be future employees at a Hilton or Restaurant Associates corporate dining facility. A lot of time was spent on food destined for the steam table. Sauces were thickened with roux. Escoffier's heavy, breaded, soubised, glacéed and over-sauced dinosaur dishes were the ideal. Everything, it was implied, *must* come with appropriate starch, protein, vegetable. Nouvelle cuisine was practically unheard of. Reductions? No way. Infusions? Uh-uh. We're talking two years of cauliflower in Mornay sauce, saddle of veal Orloff, lobster thermidor, institutional favorites like chicken Hawaiian, grilled ham steak with pineapple ring and old-style lumbering classics like beef Wellington. The chef/instructors were largely, it seemed, burn-outs from the industry: bleary-eyed Swiss, Austrian and French ex-cronies, all ginblossoms and spite – along with some motivated veterans of major hotel chains, for whom food was all about cost per unit.

But it was fun. Pulled sugar, pastillage work, chaud-froids, ice-carving. You don't see a lot of that in the real world, and there were some really talented, very experienced old-school

Euro-geezers at CIA who passed on to their adoring students the last of a dying style. Charcuterie class was informative and this old style was well suited to learning about galantines and ballottines and socles and pâtés, rillettes, sausage-making and aspic work. Meat class was fun; learning the fundamentals of butchering, I found for the first time that constant proximity to meat seems to inspire black humor in humans. My meat instructor would make hand puppets out of veal breast and his lamb demo/sexual puppet show was legendary. I have since found that almost everybody in the meat business is funny – just as almost everyone in the fish business is not.

They'd let us practice our knife work on whole legs of beef, my novice butcher class-mates and I absolutely destroying thousands of pounds of meat; we were the culinary version of the Manson Family. Fortunately, the mutilated remains of our efforts were – as was all food at CIA – simply passed along to another class, where it was braised, stewed or made into soup or grinding meat . . . before ending up on our tables for dinner. They had figured out this equation really well. All students were either cooking for other students, serving other students or being fed by other students – a perfect food cycle, as we devoured our mistakes and our successes alike.

There were also two restaurants open to the general public, but a few fundamentals were in order before the school trusted us with inflicting our limited skills on the populace.

Vegetable Cookery was a much-feared class. The terrifying Chef Bagna was in charge, and he made the simple preparing of vegetables a rigorous program on a par with Parris Island. He was an Italian Swiss, but liked to use a German accent for effect, slipping quietly up behind students mid-task, and screaming questions at the top of his lungs.

'Recite for me . . . *schnell!* How to make pommes dauphinoisee!!'

Chef Bagna would then helpfully provide misleading and incorrect clues, 'Zen you add ze *onions*, ya?' He would wait for his flustered victim to fall into his trap, and then shriek,

'*Nein! Nein!* Zere is *no* onions in ze potatoes dauphinoise!' He was a bully, a bit of a sadist and a showman. But the man knew his vegetables, and he knew what pressure was. Anyone who couldn't take Chef Bagna's ranting was *not* going to make it in the outside world, much less make it through the penultimate CIA class: Chef Bernard's 'E Room'.

Another class, Oriental Cookery, as I believe it was then called, was pretty funny. The instructor, a capable Chinese guy, was responsible for teaching us the fundamentals of both Chinese *and* Japanese cooking. The Chinese portion of the class was terrific. When it came time to fill us in on the tastes of Japan, however, our teacher was more interested in giving us an extended lecture on the Rape of Nanking. His loathing of the Japanese was consuming. In between describing the bayoneting of women, children and babies in World War II, he'd point at a poster of a sushi/sashimi presentation on the wall, and say in his broken, heavily accented English, 'That a raw a fish. You wanna eat that? Hah! Japanese *shit*!' Then he'd go back into his dissertation on forced labor, mass executions, enslavement, hinting darkly that Japan would pay, sooner or later, for what it had done to his country.

The joke went that everyone gained 5 pounds in baking class. I could see what they meant. It was held in the morning, when everyone was starving, and after a few hours of hard labor, hefting heavy sacks of flour, balling and kneading dough, loading giant deck and windmill ovens with cinnamon buns, croissants, breads and rolls for the various school-operated dining rooms, the room would fill with the smell. When the finished product started coming out of the ovens, the students would fall on it, slathering the still-hot bread and buns with gobs of butter, tearing it apart and shoveling it in their faces. Brownies, pecan diamonds, cookies, profiteroles – around 10 percent of the stuff disappeared into our faces and our knife rolls before it was loaded into proof racks and packed off to its final destinations. It was not a pretty sight, all these pale, gangly, pimpled youths, in a frenzy of hunger and sexual frustration, shredding bread. It was like *Night of the Living Dead*, everyone seemed always to be chewing.

If there was an Ultimate Terror, a man who fit all of our ideas of a Real Chef, a monstrous, despotic, iron-fisted Frenchman who ruled his kitchen like President for Life Idi Amin, it was Chef Bernard. The final class before graduation was the dreaded yet yearned-for 'E Room', the Escoffier Room, an open-to-the-public, three-star restaurant operated for profit by the school. Diners, it was said, made reservations *years* in advance. Here, classic French food was served à la carte, finished and served off guéridons by amusingly inept students. Our skipper, the mighty septuagenarian Chef Bernard, had, it was rumored, *actually worked with Escoffier himself*. His name was mentioned only in whispers; students were aware of his unseen presence for months before entering his kitchen.

'Wait till "E Room",' went the ominous refrain, 'Bernard's gonna have your ass for breakfast.'

Needless to say, the pressure, the fear and the anticipation in the weeks before Escoffier Room were palpable.

It was an open kitchen. A large window allowed customers to watch the fearsome chef as he lined up his charges for inspection, assigned the day's work stations, reviewed the crimes and horrors and disappointments of the previous night's efforts. This was a terrifying moment, as we all dreaded the soufflé station, the one station where one was assured of drawing the full weight of Chef Bernard's wrath and displeasure. The likelihood of a screw up was highest here, too. It was certain that at least *one* of your à la minute soufflés would, under real working conditions, fail to rise, rise unevenly, collapse in on itself – in some way fail to meet our leader's exacting standards. Students would actually tremble with fear before line-up and work assignments, praying, 'Not me, Lord. Not today . . . please, not the soufflé station.'

If you screwed up, you'd get what was called the 'ten minutes'. In full view of the gawking public and quavering comrades, the offending soufflé cook would be called forward to stand at attention while the intimidating old French master would look down his Gallic shnozz and unload the most withering barrage of scorn any of us had ever experienced.

'You are a shit chef!' he would bellow. 'I make two cook like you in the *toilette* each morning! You are deezgusting! A *shoe-maker*! You have destroyed my life! . . . You will *never* be a chef! You are a *disgrace*! Look! Look at this *merde . . . merde . . . merde*!' At this point, Bernard would stick his fingers into the offending object and fling bits of it on the floor. 'You *dare* call this cuisine! This . . . this is grotesque! An abomination! You . . . you should kill yourself from shame!'

I had to hand it to the old bastard, though, he was fair. *Everyone* got ten minutes. Even the girls, who would, sad to say, invariably burst into tears thirty seconds into the chef's tirade. He did not let their tears or sobs deter him. They stood there, shaking and heaving for the full time while he ranted and raved and cursed heaven and earth and their ancestors and their future progeny, breaking them down like everybody else, until all that remained was a trembling little bundle of nerves with an un-naturally red face in a white polyester uniform.

One notable victim of Chef Bernard's reign of terror was a buddy of mine – also much older than the other students – who had just returned from Vietnam. He'd served in combat with an artillery unit and returned stateside to attend the CIA under the GI Bill and had made it through the whole program, had only *four days* to go before graduation, but when he saw that in a day or two *his* number would be up and *he*, without question, would be working the dreaded soufflé station, he folded under the pressure. He went AWOL, disappearing from Hyde Park for-ever. Boot camp and the Viet Cong had not been as bad as Chef Bernard's ten minutes, I guess.

When my time came to stand there in front of my fellow students, and all the world, and get *my* ten minutes, I was ready. I could see Chef Bernard looking deep into my eyes as he began his standard tirade, could see him recognize a glimmer of *something* familiar somewhere in there. I did the convict thing.

The louder and more confrontational the authority figure got, the more dreamy and relaxed I became. Bernard saw it happening. I may have been standing at rigid attention, and saying all the right things, '*Oui*, Chef! *Non*, Chef!' at all the right moments, and showing the right respect, but he could see, perhaps in my dead fish-eye gaze, that he wasn't getting anywhere with me. I think the old bastard might have even smiled a little bit, halfway through. There seemed to be a twinkle of amusement in his eyes as he finally dismissed me with feigned disgust. He knew, I think, that I had *already* been humiliated. He looked in my eyes and saw, perhaps, that Tyrone and the Mario crew had done his work for him. I liked Chef Bernard and respected him. I enjoyed working under him. But the fat bastard didn't scare me. And he knew it. He could have smacked me upside the head with a skillet and I would have smiled at him through broken teeth. He saw that, I think – and it ruined all the fun.

He was actually nice to me after that. He'd let me stand and watch him decorate the voiture each night, a task he reserved for himself: the glazing and garnishing of a hot roast in a rolling silver display cart. He layered on his blanched leeks and carved tomato roses like a brain surgeon, humming quietly to himself, aware, I think, that soon they wouldn't be doing much of this anymore.

My final proud accomplishment at CIA was the torpedoing of a dangerous folly being planned for the graduation ceremonies. The event was planned for the Great Hall, the former chapel in the main building. An idea was being floated by some of my class-mates – all over-zealous would-be pastry chefs – to create a display of pastillage, marzipan, chocolate sculpture and wedding cakes to wow and amaze our loved ones as they were herded into the ceremony. I'd *seen* the kind of work an over eager pâtissier can do – I'd seen their *instructor*'s work – and most of it was awful, as so much pastry and garde-manger work is when the chef starts thinking he's an artist rather than a craftsman. I'd seen a much admired commemorative cake, depicting Nixon, painted in chocolate on a pastillage cameo, communicating by telephone with the Apollo astronauts in their space module, also chocolate on pastillage. I did not want my friends and family to have to gaze upon a horror like that.

I didn't want to be a killjoy. To dampen the enthusiasm at this proud and happy event by being a naysayer and a cynic was too close to what I'd been at Vassar, and those days, I liked to think, were behind me. I was sneakier in my strategy to put an end to this outrage. I submitted my own earnest proposal, requesting that I be allowed to contribute a *pièce montée* to the festivities, even going so far as to submit a sketch of my proposed project:

It would be a life-sized tallow sculpture, depicting a white-toqued baby Jesus, with knife and steel in his tiny hands, held by an adoring Madonna. Needless to say, my beef-fat Madonna horrified the graduation committee. Rather than offend my disturbingly sincere, if quirky, religious beliefs, they scotched the whole display. An animal-fat Sistine Chapel was not something they wanted all those parents and dignitaries to see. And who knows what could happen if they opened the door for me? What other demented expressions of personal hell might wind up lining the Great Hall?

The ensuing ceremony was thus spared the prospect of decomposing aspics depicting Moses parting the Red Sea, or melting wedding cakes. A few days later, I had my diploma. I was now a graduate of the best cooking school in the country – a valuable commodity on the open market – I had field experience, a vocabulary and a criminal mind.

I was a danger to myself and others.

THE RETURN OF MAL CARNE

MY TRIUMPHANT RETURN TO Provincetown – halfway through the program at CIA – came the following summer. Newly invigorated with obscure cooking terms, *The Professional Chef* and the *Larousse Gastronomique* under my arm, and my head filled with half-baked ideas and a few techniques I'd seen and maybe even tried a few times, I rejoined my old comrades at the Dreadnaught, to much curiosity and amusement. A little knowledge can be dangerous *and* annoying . . . but I had actually learned some useful things. I'd been working in the city weekends while at school, I could work a station without embarrassing myself, and I was enthusiastic about my new, if modest, skills. I was determined to outwork, outlast and in every way impress my old tormentors at Mario's.

Dimitri, the pasta man, was years older than I was. Then in his early thirties, running to fat, with chunky-framed glasses and a well-tended handlebar moustache, he was markedly different from his fellow cooks at Mario's. Born in the USA of a Russian father and a German mother, he was the only other cook in P-town who'd been to cooking school – in his case, a hotel school in Switzerland. Though he claimed to have been expelled for demonstrating the Twist in that institution's dining hall, I always doubted this version of events. He became the second great influence in my career.

A mama's boy, loner, intellectual, voracious reader and gourmand, Dimitri was a man of esoteric skills and appetites:

a gambler, philosopher, gardener, fly-fisherman, fluent in Russian and German as well as having an amazing command of English. He loved antiquated phrases, dry sarcasm, military jargon, regional dialect, and the *New York Times* crossword puzzle – to which he was hopelessly addicted.

It was from Dimitri's fertile mind that much of what I'd come to know as Mariospeak had originated. Brainy, paranoid, famously prone to sulking, he both amused and appalled his co-workers with his many misadventures, his affected mannerisms and his tendency to encounter tragicomic disaster. Fond of hyperbole and dramatic over-statement, Dimitri had distinguished himself after a particularly unpleasant breakup with a girlfriend by shaving his head completely bald. This would have been, in itself, a rather bold statement of self-loathing and grief, but Dimitri pushed matters to the extreme; the story went that he had no sooner revealed his snow-white skull to the world than he went to the beach, got drunk and sat there, roasting his never-before-exposed-to-the-sun scalp to the July ultraviolets. When he returned to work the next day, not only was he jarringly bald, but his head was a bright strawberry-red, blistered and oozing skullcap of misery. No one talked to him until his hair grew back.

Dimitri saw himself, I think, as a Hemingwayesque, hard-boozing raconteur Renaissance man, but he was completely under the thumb of his mother, a severe, equally brilliant gynecologist, whose daily calls to the Mario kitchen were much imitated.

'Alloo? Is Dih-mee-tree zere?'

We'd met before, of course, the previous year, when he'd known me, no doubt, as 'Mel'. But I was a broiler man now, a CIA student, a curiosity. It was permissible for Dimitri to talk to me. It was like Hunt and Liddy meeting; the world would probably have been a better place had it never happened, but a lot of fun was had by all.

Dimitri was scared of the outside world. He lived year-round at the tip of the Cape, and he liked to fancy himself a townie. He did a damn good imitation of a local Portuguese fisherman accent, too. But Dimitri was – as the Brits say – quite the other thing. We'd have drinks after knocking off at our respective restaurants and try to outdo each other with arcane bits of food knowledge and terminology. Dimitri, like me, was a born snob, so it was only natural that when our lord and master, Mario, decided on two employees to cater his annual garden party, he selected his two would-be Escoffiers, the Dimitri and Tony Show.

Our early efforts were, in the cold light of day, pretty crude and laughable. But nobody else in town was doing pâté en croûte or galantines in aspic, or elaborate chaud-froid presentations. Mario tasked his most pretentious cooks with an important mission, and we were determined not to let him down – especially as it allowed us time off from our regular kitchen chores and all the overtime we needed. We threw ourselves into the task with near-fanatical once-in-a-lifetime zeal and prodigious amounts of cocaine and amphetamines.

As a fly-fisherman, Dimitri made his own lures; this obsessive eye for detail carried over to his food. For Mario's garden party, we spent days together in a walk-in refrigerator, heads filled with accelerants, gluing near-microscopic bits of carved and blanched vegetables onto the sides of roasts and poached fishes and fowls with hot aspic. We must have looked like crazed neurologists, using tweezers, bamboo skewers and bar straws to cut and affix garnishes, laboring straight through the night. Covered with gelée, sleepless after forty-eight hours in the cooler, we lost all perspective, Dimitri at one point obsessing over a tiny red faux mushroom in one corner of a poached salmon, muttering to himself about the distinctive white dots on the hood of the *Amanita muscara* or psilocybin mushroom, while he applied dust-sized motes of cooked egg white for 'authenticity'. He buried all sorts of horticultural in-jokes in his work – already insanely detailed Gardens of Eden made of leek strips, chives, scallions, paper-thin slices of carrots and peppers. He created jungle tableaux on the sides of hams that he considered, 're-miniscent of Rousseau's better efforts' or 'Gauguin-like'. When I jokingly suggested Moses parting the Red Sea on the side of a striped bass, Dimitri got a faraway look on his face and immediately suggested a plan.

'The Israelites, in the foreground . . . we can use straws to cut the olives and egg whites for their eyes. But the Egyptians pursuing in the *background* . . . we can cut their eyes with bar straws, you know, the zip-stix! So they're *smaller*, you see! For *perspective*!' I had to physically restrain him from attempting this tableau.

We had been under refrigeration for three days straight when we finally collapsed in the Dreadnaught's cocktail lounge at 4 A.M., unshaven, dirty and crazed. We woke up a few hours later, covered with flies attracted by the tasty, protein-rich gelée that covered us from head to toe.

The garden party was, to be modest, a smashing success. No one in dowdy old Provincetown had ever seen anything like it. We became instantly notorious, and we made the most of it, printing up business cards for a planned catering venture called Moonlight Menus. The cards, commissioned from a local artist, depicted us sneering in toques. We proceeded to hand these things out to local businessmen, telling them blithely that not only did we not need, or even *want* their business, but they couldn't *possibly* afford us, as we were easily the most expensive and *exclusive* caterers on the entire Cape! Two highly trained specimens like us had more than enough business, thank you very much.

There was, of course, no business. But the strategy worked. In the coke-soaked final weeks of 1975 P-town, there were plenty of local businessmen eager to impress their friends with an elaborate end-of-season bash. And we were only too happy to encourage them in even grander pretensions, filling their heads with names and dishes we'd culled from my *Larousse* (few of which we'd actually attempted) and quoting staggering prices. We knew well how much these people were paying for cocaine – and that the more coke cost, the more people wanted it. We applied the same marketing plan to our budding catering operation, along with a similar pricing structure, and business was suddenly very, very good.

In no time, we were able to leave our regular jobs at the Dreadnaught and Mario's, lording it over our old co-workers in brand-new Tony Lama boots, and brandishing shiny new Wusthoff knives when we dropped by for a quick visit and a gloat.

Our customers were restaurateurs, coke dealers, guys who ran fast boats out to motherships off Hyannis and Barnstable to offload bales of marijuana. We catered weddings, parties, private dinners for pizza magnates, successful leather and scrimshaw merchants. All the while, I filled Dimitri's head with the idea that what we were doing here, we could do back in New York – only *bigger* and *better*.

Ah, those heady days of happy delusion, spirited argument, grandiose dreams of glory and riches. We did not aspire to be the new Bocuses. No, that wasn't enough. Jacked up on coke and vodka, we wanted nothing less than to be like Carême, whose enormous *pièces montées* married the concepts of architecture and food. Our work would literally tower over the work of our contemporaries: Space Needles, Towers of Babel, Parthenons of forcemeat-stuffed pastry, carefully constructed New Babylons of barquettes, vol-au-vents, croquembouches . . . the very words excited and challenged us to reach higher and higher.

We had some successes – and some failures.

A steamship round (a whole roast leg of beef on the bone) sounded like a good idea; it was, after all, big. Until we overcooked it. An all-Chinese meal we did was so overloaded with dried Szechuan peppers that we could hear the muffled wails of pain from the next room. And I recall with horror a *blue* wedding cake, layers of turquoise-colored buttercream and sponge cake, decorated with fruit that looked more like Siegfried and Roy's beach house than anything Carême ever did. But we did have some notable successes as well. Provincetown's first Crown Roast of Veal with Mushroom Duxelle Stuffing and Black Truffle–Studded Madeira Sauce for one – and our mighty Coliseum of Seafood Blanquette.

The client was a restaurant owner, and we oversold ourselves somewhat. Committed to our pastry terrordome, we soon found that there wasn't a mold quite large enough for this ambitious effort. What we wanted was a tasty yet structurally sound 'coliseum' of pastry crust into which we could pour about 5 gallons of seafood stew. And we wanted the whole thing to be covered by a titanic pastry dome, perhaps with a tiny pastry figure from antiquity, like Ajax or Mercury, perched on top.

We didn't know if the thing could be done. Other than old engravings from *Larousse* we'd never even seen anything like what we were attempting. There was no suitable spring-form mold, something we could line with foil and fill with beans and then blind-bake. We couldn't cook it together with the blanquette; it would never hold. The bubbling velouté suspending our medley of fish and shellfish and wild mushrooms would make the walls too soft. And the dough: what crust could support the weight of 5 gallons of molten stew?

As game time approached, we were getting worried. We set up our operations center in our client's restaurant kitchen and promptly bivouacked to a bar for some serious strategizing.

In the end – as it so often does – it came down to Julia. Julia Child's recipes have little snob appeal, but they also tend to work. We took a recipe for dough from her book on French cooking, and after rubbing the *outside* of a large lobster steamer with shortening, stretched and patched our dough around and over it. It was exactly the opposite of the prevailing wisdom; fortunately, we didn't know that at the time. For our dome, we used the top of the pot, and the same principle, laying our dough *over* the outside of the round lid and baking it until firm.

When we finally slid the things off – very carefully, I can tell you – Dimitri was characteristically pessimistic. Would it *hold*? He didn't think so. It was a lot of stew we were planning on pouring into this thing, and Dimitri was convinced it would crumble at the table mid-meal, boiling hot fish and lavalike velouté rushing onto the laps of the terrified guests. There would be terrible burns involved, he guessed, 'genital scarring . . .

lawsuits . . . total disgrace'. Dimitri cheered himself up by suggesting that should the unthinkable happen, we were obliged, like Japanese naval officers, to take our own lives. 'Or like Vatel,' he submitted, 'he ran himself on his sword over a late fish delivery. It's the *least* we could do.' In the end we agreed that should our Coliseum of Seafood Blanquette fall, we'd simply walk quietly out the door and into the bay to drown ourselves.

Party time came and we were ready – we hoped.

First there were hors d'oeuvres: microscopic canapés of smoked salmon, cucumber and caviar; Dimitri's chicken liver mousse with diced aspic; little barquettes of something or other; deviled eggs with fish roe; a lovely pâté en croûte with center garnishes of tongue, ham, pistachio and black truffles, and an accompanying sauce Cumberland I'd lifted right out of my CIA textbook. Our crown roast was no problem. It was the blanquette that filled our hearts with dread and terror.

But God protects fools and drunks, and we were certainly both foolish and drunk much of the time.

Things went brilliantly. Our coliseum's walls held!

The crown roast, decorated with little frilly panties on each gracefully outward-arching rib bone, looked and tasted sensational. We were given a standing ovation by the dazzled guests and grateful client.

When we next showed up at our old kitchens for our weekly gloat, our heads were too big to fit in P-town's doors. We were already planning on hunting bigger game. We had newer, more sophisticated, even richer victims in mind for our learn-as-we-go operation. In New York.

SECOND COURSE

WHO COOKS?

WHO'S COOKING YOUR FOOD anyway? What strange beasts lurk behind the kitchen doors? You see the chef: he's the guy without the hat, with the clipboard under his arm, maybe his name stitched in Tuscan blue on his starched white chef's coat next to those cotton Chinese buttons. But who's actually cooking your food? Are they young, ambitious culinary school grads, putting in their time on the line until they get their shot at the Big Job? Probably not. If the chef is anything like me, the cooks are a dysfunctional, mercenary lot, fringe-dwellers motivated by money, the peculiar lifestyle of cooking and a grim pride. They're probably not even American.

Line cooking done well is a beautiful thing to watch. It's a high-speed collaboration resembling, at its best, ballet or modern dance. A properly organized, fully loaded line cook, one who works clean, and has 'moves' – meaning economy of movement, nice technique and, most important, speed – can perform his duties with Nijinsky-like grace. The job requires character – and endurance. A good line cook never shows up late, never calls in sick, and works through pain and injury.

What most people don't get about professional-level cooking is that it is not at all about the best recipe, the most innovative presentation, the most creative marriage of ingredients, flavors and textures; that, presumably, was all arranged long before you sat down to dinner. Line cooking – the real business of preparing the food you eat – is more about consistency, about mindless, unvarying repetition, the same series of tasks performed over and over and over again in exactly the same way. The last thing a chef wants in a line cook is an innovator, somebody with ideas of his own who is going to mess around with the chef's recipes and presentations. Chefs require blind, near-fanatical loyalty, a strong back and an automaton-like consistency of execution under battlefield conditions.

A three-star Italian chef pal of mine was recently talking about why he – a proud Tuscan who makes his own pasta and sauces from scratch daily and runs one of the best restaurant kitchens in New York – would never be so foolish as to hire any Italians to cook on his line. He greatly prefers Ecuadorians, as many chefs do: 'The Italian guy? You screaming at him in the rush, "Where's that risotto?! Is that fucking risotto ready yet? Gimme that risotto!" . . . and the Italian . . . he's gonna *give it to you* . . . An Ecuadorian guy? He's gonna just turn his back . . . and stir the risotto and keep cooking it *until it's done the way you showed him*. That's what I want.'

I knew just what he meant. Generally speaking, American cooks – meaning, born in the USA, possibly school-trained, culinarily sophisticated types who know before you show them what *monter au beurre* means and how to make a béarnaise sauce – are a lazy, undisciplined and, worst of all, high-maintenance lot, annoyingly opinionated, possessed of egos requiring constant stroking and tune-ups, and, as members of a privileged and wealthy population, unused to the kind of 'disrespect' a busy chef is inclined to dish out. No one understands and appreciates the American Dream of hard work leading to material rewards better than a non-American. The Ecuadorian, Mexican, Dominican and Salvadorian cooks I've worked with over the years make most CIA-educated white boys look like clumsy, sniveling little punks.

In New York City, the days of the downtrodden, underpaid illegal immigrant cook, exploited by his cruel masters, have largely passed – at least where quality line cooks are concerned. Most of the Ecuadorians and Mexicans I hire from a large pool –

a sort of farm team of associated and often related former dishwashers – are very well-paid professionals, much sought after by other chefs. Chances are they've worked their way up from the bottom rung; they remember well what it was like to empty out grease traps, scrape plates, haul leaking bags of garbage out to the curb at four o' clock in the morning. A guy who's come up through the ranks, who knows every station, every recipe, every corner of the restaurant and who has learned, first and foremost, *your* system above all others is likely to be more valuable and long-term than some bed-wetting white boy whose mom brought him up thinking the world owed him a living, and who thinks he actually knows a few things.

You want loyalty from your line cooks. Somebody who wakes up with a scratchy throat and slight fever and thinks it's okay to call in sick is not what I'm looking for. While it's necessary for cooks to take pride in their work – it's a good idea to let a good cook stretch a little now and again with the occasional contribution of a special or a soup – this is still the army. Ultimately, I want a salute and a 'Yes, sir!'. If I want an opinion from my line cooks, *I*'ll provide one. Your customers arrive expecting the same dish prepared the same way they had it before; they don't want some budding Wolfgang Puck having fun with kiwis and coriander with a menu item they've come to love.

There are plenty of exceptions, of course. I have a few Americans in my traveling road show, a few key people whom I tend to hire over and over as I move from place to place. The relationship between chef and sous-chef can be a particularly intimate one, for instance, and it's nice to have someone with a similar background and world-view when you're going to spend almost every waking hour together. Women line cooks, however rare they might be in the testosterone-heavy, male-dominated world of restaurant kitchens, are a particular delight. To have a tough-as-nails, foul-mouthed, trash-talking female line cook on your team can be a true joy – and a civilizing factor in a unit where conversation tends to center around who's got the bigger balls and who takes it in the ass.

I've been fortunate enough to work with some really studly women line cooks – no weak reeds these. One woman, Sharon, managed to hold down a busy sauté station while seven months pregnant – and still find time to provide advice and comfort to a romantically unhappy broiler man. A long-time associate, Beth, who likes to refer to herself as the 'Grill Bitch', excelled at putting loudmouths and fools into their proper place. She refused to behave any differently than her male co-workers: she'd change in the same locker area, dropping her pants right alongside them. She was as sexually aggressive, and as vocal about it, as her fellow cooks, but unlikely to suffer behavior she found demeaning. One sorry Moroccan cook who pinched her ass found himself suddenly bent over a cutting board with Beth dry-humping him from behind, saying, 'How do *you* like it, bitch?' The guy almost died of shame – and never repeated that mistake again.

Another female line cook I had the pleasure of working with arrived at work one morning to find that an Ecuadorian pasta cook had decorated her station with some particularly ugly hard-core pornography of pimply-assed women getting penetrated in every orifice by pot-bellied guys with prison tattoos and back hair. She didn't react at all, but a little later, while passing through the pasta man's station, casually remarked. 'José, I see you brought in some photos of the family. Mom looks good for her age.'

Mise-en-place is the religion of all good line cooks. Do *not* fuck with a line cook's 'meez' – meaning their set-up, their carefully arranged supplies of sea salt, rough-cracked pepper, softened butter, cooking oil, wine, back-ups and so on. As a cook, your station, and its condition, its state of readiness, is an extension of your nervous system – and it is profoundly upsetting if another cook or, God forbid, a *waiter* – disturbs your precisely and carefully laid-out system. The universe is in order when your station is set up the way you like it: you know where to find everything with your eyes closed, everything you need during the course of the shift is at the ready at arm's reach, your defenses are deployed. If you let your mise-en-place run down, get dirty and disorganized, you'll quickly find yourself spinning in place and calling for back-up. I worked with a chef who used to step behind the line to a dirty cook's station in the middle of the rush to explain why the offending cook was falling behind. He'd press his palm down on the cutting board, which was littered with peppercorns, spattered sauce, bits of parsley, breadcrumbs and the usual flotsam and jetsam that accumulates quickly on a station if not constantly wiped away with a moist side-towel. 'You see this?' he'd inquire, raising his palm so that the cook could see the bits of dirt and scraps sticking to his chef's palm, 'That's what the inside of your head looks like now. *Work clean*!'

Working clean, constantly wiping and cleaning, is a desirable state of affairs for the conscientious line cook. That chef was right: messy station equals messy mind. This explains why side-towels are hoarded like gold by good line cooks. When the linen order arrives, the smart cookies fall onto it voraciously, stashing stacks of the valuable objects anywhere they can hide them. One cook I knew would load them above the acoustic tile in the ceiling above his station, along with his favorite tongs, favorite non-stick pans, slotted spoons, and anything else he figured he needed on his station and didn't want another cook to get. I'm sure that years later, though that restaurant has changed hands many times since, future generations of cooks are still finding stashes of fluffy, clean side-towels.

It's not just clean that you value in a side-towel – it's *dry*. It's nice, wiping the rim of a plate with a slightly moist one, but try grabbing a red-hot sauté pan handle with a wet towel, and you'll learn fast why a fresh stack of dry towels is a necessity. Some traditional European kitchens still issue two towels per cook at the beginning of the shift: one to work with while the other dries on the oven handle. This strikes me as criminally parsimonious. I like a tall stack, conveniently located over my station, in neatly folded, kitty-cornered, easy-to-grab fashion, and I don't ever want to run out. I'll rip through twenty of them in the course of an eight-hour service period, and if it costs my masters a few bucks extra, tough. I'm not burning my hand or wiping grease on my nice plates because they're too mean to shell out for a few more rented towels.

What exactly is this mystical mise-en-place I keep going on about? Why are some line cooks driven to apoplexy at the pinching of even a few grains of salt, a pinch of parsley? Because it's *ours*. Because we set it up the way we want it. Because it's like our knives, about which you hear the comment: 'Don't touch my dick, *don't touch my knife*.'

A fairly standard mise-en-place is a pretty extensive list. A typical one would be composed of, for instance:

kosher or sea salt
crushed black peppercorns (hand-crushed – *not* ground in the blender)
ground white pepper
fresh breadcrumbs
chiffonade parsley
blended oil in wine bottle with speed pourer
extra virgin olive oil
white wine
brandy
chervil tops in ice water for garnish
chive sticks or chopped chives
tomato concasseé
caramelized apple sections
garlic confit
chopped or slivered garlic
chopped shallots
softened butter
favorite ladles, spoons, tongs, pans, pots
all sauces, portioned fish, meat, menu items, specials and back-ups conveniently positioned for easy access

Being set up properly, trained and coordinated is not nearly enough. A good line cook has to be able to remain clear-headed,

organized and reasonably even-keeled during hectic and stressful
service periods. When you've got thirty or forty or more tables
all sitting down at the same time and ordering different items
with different temperatures, the stuff has to come up together;
the various stations – sauté, garde-manger, broiler, middle –
have to assemble a party of ten's dinner at the same moment.
You can't have one member of a party's Dover sole festering in
the window by the sauté station while the grill guy waits for a
rack of lamb to hit medium-rare. It's got to come up together!
Your hero line cook doesn't let the screaming, the frantic cries of
'Is it ready yet?', the long and potentially confusing list of
donenesses all working at the same time throw him. He's got
to keep all those temperatures straight in his head, remembering
which steak goes with what. He's got to be able to tune out the
howls of outrage from the chef, the tiny, gibbering annoyances
from the floor, the curses and questions and prompts from his
co-workers: 'Ready on seven? *Via*! Let's go! *Vamos*! Coming up
on *seven*!'

The ability to 'work well with others' is a must. If you're a
sauté man, your grill man is your dance partner, and chances
are, you're spending the majority of your time working in a hot,
uncomfortably confined, submarine-like space with him. You're
both working around open flame, boiling liquids with plenty of
blunt objects at close hand – and you both carry knives, lots of
knives. So you had better get along. It will not do to have two
heavily armed cooks duking it out behind the line over some
perceived insult when there are vats of boiling grease and razor-
sharp cutlery all around.

So who the hell, exactly, *are* these guys, the boys and girls in
the trenches? You might get the impression from the specifics of
my less than stellar career that all line cooks are wacked-out
moral degenerates, dope fiends, refugees, a thuggish assortment
of drunks, sneak thieves, sluts and psychopaths. You wouldn't
be too far off base. The business, as respected three-star chef
Scott Bryan explains it, attracts 'fringe elements', people for
whom something in their lives has gone terribly wrong. Maybe

they didn't make it through high school, maybe they're running away from something – be it an ex-wife, a rotten family history, trouble with the law, a squalid Third World backwater with no opportunity for advancement. Or maybe, like me, they just like it here. They're comfortable with the rather relaxed and informal code of conduct in the kitchen, the elevated level of tolerance for eccentricity, unseemly personal habits, lack of documentation, prison experience. In most kitchens, one's freakish personal proclivities matter little if at all. Can you keep up? Are you ready for service? Can I count on you to show up at work tomorrow, to not let the side down?

That's what counts.

I can break down line cooks into three subgroups.

You've got your Artists: the annoying, high-maintenance minority. This group includes specialists like pâtissiers (the neurologists of cooking), sous-chefs, butchers, garde-manger psychos, the occasional saucier whose sauces are so ethereal and perfect that delusions of grandeur are tolerated.

Then there are the Exiles: people who just can't make it in any other business, could never survive a nine-to-five job, wear a tie or blend in with civilized society – and their comrades, the Refugees, usually émigrés and immigrants for whom cooking is preferable to death squads, poverty or working in a sneaker factory for 2 dollars a week.

Finally, there are the Mercenaries: people who do it for cash and do it well. Cooks who, though they have little love or natural proclivity for cuisine, do it at a high level because they are paid well to do it – and because they are professionals. Cooking is a *craft*, I like to think, and a good cook is a craftsman – *not* an artist. There's nothing wrong with that: the great cathedrals of Europe were built by craftsmen – though not designed by them. Practicing your craft in expert fashion is noble, honorable and satisfying. And I'll generally take a stand-up mercenary who takes pride in his professionalism over an artist any day. When I hear 'artist', I think of someone who doesn't think it necessary to show up at work on time. More often than not their efforts, convinced as they are of their own genius, are geared more to giving themselves a hard-on than satisfying the great majority of dinner customers. Personally, I'd prefer to eat food that tastes good and is an honest reflection of its ingredients, than a 3-foot-tall caprice constructed from lemon grass, lawn trimmings, coconuts and red curry. You could lose an eye trying to eat that. When a job applicant starts telling me how Pacific Rim-job cuisine turns him on and inspires him, I see trouble coming. Send me another Mexican dishwasher anytime. I can teach *him* to cook. I *can't* teach character. Show up at work on time six months in a row and we'll talk about red curry paste and lemon grass. Until then, I have four words for you: 'Shut the fuck up.'

FROM OUR KITCHEN TO YOUR TABLE

I SAW A SIGN the other day outside one of those Chinese-Japanese hybrids that are beginning to pop up around town, advertising 'Discount Sushi'. I can't imagine a better example of Things To Be Wary Of in the food department than bargain sushi. Yet the place had customers. I wonder, had the sign said 'Cheap Sushi' or 'Old Sushi', if they'd still have eaten there.

Good food and good eating are about risk. Every once in a while an oyster, for instance, will make you sick to your stomach. Does this mean you should stop eating oysters? No way. The more exotic the food, the more adventurous the serious eater, the higher the likelihood of later discomfort. I'm not going to deny myself the pleasures of morcilla sausage, or sashimi, or even ropa vieja at the local Cuban joint just because sometimes I feel bad a few hours after I've eaten them.

But there are some general principles I adhere to, things I've seen over the years that remain in mind and have altered my eating habits. I may be perfectly willing to try the grilled lobster at an open-air barbecue shack in the Caribbean, where the refrigeration is dubious and I can see with my own eyes the flies buzzing around the grill (I mean, how often am I in the Caribbean? I want to make the most of it!), but on home turf, with the daily business of eating in restaurants, there are some definite dos and don'ts I've chosen to live by.

I never order fish on Monday, unless I'm eating at Le Bernardin – a four-star restaurant where I *know* they are buying their fish directly from the source. I know how old most seafood is on Monday – about four to five days old!

You walk into a nice two-star place in Tribeca on a sleepy Monday evening and you see they're running a delicious sounding special of Yellowfin Tuna, Braised Fennel, Confit Tomatoes and a Saffron Sauce. Why not go for it? Here are the two words that should leap out at you when you navigate the menu: 'Monday' and 'Special'.

Here's how it works: the chef of this fine restaurant orders his fish on Thursday for delivery Friday morning. He's ordering a pretty good amount of it, too, as he's not getting another delivery until Monday morning. All right, *some* seafood purveyors make Saturday deliveries, but the market is closed Friday night. *It's the same fish from Thursday!* The chef is hoping to sell the bulk of that fish – your tuna – on Friday and Saturday nights, when he assumes it will be busy. He's assuming also that if he has a little left on Sunday, he can unload the rest of it then, as seafood salad for brunch, or as a special. Monday? It's merchandizing night, when whatever is left over from the weekend is used up, and hopefully sold for money. Terrible, you say? Why doesn't he throw the leftover tuna out? The guy can get deliveries on *Monday*, right? Sure, he can . . . but what is preventing his seafood purveyor from thinking exactly the same way? The seafood vendor is emptying out *his* refrigerator, too! But the Fulton Street fish market is *open* on Monday morning, you say!! He can get *fresh*! I've been to the Fulton Street market at three o'clock on Monday morning, friends, and believe me, it does *not* inspire confidence. Chances are good that that tuna you're thinking of ordering on Monday night has been kicking around in the restaurant's reach-ins, already cut and held with the mise-en-place on line, commingling with the chicken and the salmon and the lamb chops for four days, the reach-in doors swinging open every few seconds as the line cooks plunge their fists in, blindly feeling around for what they need. These are not optimum refrigeration conditions.

This is why you don't see a lot of codfish or other perishable items as a Sunday or Monday night special – they're not sturdy enough. The chef *knows*. He anticipates the likelihood that he might still have some fish lying around on Monday morning – and he'd like to get money for it without poisoning his customers.

Seafood is a tricky business. Red snapper may only cost a chef $4.95 a pound, but that price includes the bones, the head, the scales and all the stuff that gets cut and thrown away. By the time it's cut, the actual cost of each piece of cleaned fillet costs the chef more than *twice* that amount, and he'd greatly prefer to sell it than toss it in the garbage. If it still smells okay on Monday night – you're eating it.

I don't eat mussels in restaurants unless I know the chef personally, or have seen, with my own eyes, how they store and hold their mussels for service. I love mussels. But in my experience, most cooks are less than scrupulous in their handling of them. More often than not, mussels are allowed to wallow in their own foul-smelling piss in the bottom of a reach-in. *Some* restaurants, I'm sure, have special containers, with convenient slotted bins, which allow the mussels to drain while being held – and maybe, just maybe, the cooks at these places pick carefully through every order, mussel by mussel, making sure that *every* one is healthy and alive before throwing them into a pot. I haven't worked in too many places like that. Mussels are too easy. Line cooks consider mussels a gift; they take two minutes to cook, a few seconds to dump in a bowl, and ba-da-bing, one more customer taken care of – now they can concentrate on slicing the damn duck breast. I have had, at a very good Paris brasserie, the misfortune to eat a single bad mussel, one treacherous little guy hidden among an otherwise impeccable group. It slammed me shut like a book, sent me crawling to the bathroom shitting like a mink, clutching my stomach and projectile vomiting. I prayed that night. For many hours. And, as you might assume, I'm the worst kind of atheist. Fortunately, the French have liberal policies on doctor's house calls and affordable health care. But I do not care to repeat that experience. No thank you on the mussels. If I'm hungry for mussels, I'll pick the good-looking ones out of *your* order.

How about seafood on Sunday? Well . . . sometimes, but never an obvious attempt to offload aging stuff, like seafood salad vinaigrette or seafood frittata, on a brunch menu. Brunch menus are an open invitation to the cost-conscious chef, a dumping ground for the odd bits left over from Friday and Saturday nights or for the scraps generated in the normal course of business. You see a fish that would be much better served by quick grilling with a slice of lemon, suddenly all dressed up with vinaigrette? For 'en vinaigrette' on the menu, read 'preserved' or 'disguised'.

While we're on brunch, how about hollandaise sauce? Not for me. Bacteria *love* hollandaise. And hollandaise, that delicate emulsion of egg yolks and clarified butter, *must* be held at a temperature not too hot nor too cold, lest it break when spooned over your poached eggs. Unfortunately, this lukewarm holding temperature is also the favorite environment for bacteria to copulate and reproduce in. Nobody I know has *ever* made hollandaise to order. Most likely, the stuff on your eggs was made hours ago and held on station. Equally disturbing is the likelihood that the butter used in the hollandaise is melted table butter, heated, clarified, and strained to get out all the bread-crumbs and cigarette butts. Butter is expensive, you know. Hollandaise is a veritable petri-dish of biohazards. And how long has that Canadian bacon been ageing in the walk-in any-way? Remember, brunch is only served once a week – on the weekends. Buzzword here, 'Brunch Menu'. Translation? 'Old, nasty odds and ends, and 12 dollars for two eggs with a free Bloody Mary'. One other point about brunch. Cooks hate brunch. A wise chef will deploy his *best* line cooks on Friday and Saturday nights; he'll be reluctant to schedule those same cooks early Sunday morning, especially since they probably went out after work Saturday and got hammered until the wee hours. Worse, brunch is demoralizing to the serious line cook. Nothing makes an aspiring Escoffier feel more like an army commissary cook, or Mel from Mel's Diner, than having to slop out eggs over easy with bacon and eggs Benedict for the Sunday brunch crowd. Brunch is punishment block for the 'B'-Team cooks, or where the farm team of recent dishwashers learn their chops. Most chefs are off on Sundays, too, so supervision is at a minimum. Consider that before ordering the seafood frittata.

I *will* eat bread in restaurants. Even if I *know* it's probably been recycled off someone else's table. The reuse of bread is an industry-wide practice. I saw a recent news exposé, hidden camera and all, where the anchor was *shocked* . . . *shocked* to see unused bread returned to the kitchen and then sent right back onto the floor. Bullshit. I'm sure that some restaurants explicitly instruct their Bengali busboys to throw out all that unused bread – which amounts to about 50 percent – and maybe some places actually do it. But when it's busy, and the busboy is crumbing tables, emptying ashtrays, refilling water glasses, making espresso and cappuccino, hustling dirty dishes to the dishwasher – and he sees a basket full of untouched bread – most times he's going to use it. This is a fact of life. This doesn't bother me, and shouldn't surprise you. Okay, maybe once in a while some tubercular hillbilly has been coughing and spraying in the general direction of that bread basket, or some tourist who's just returned from a walking tour of the wetlands of West Africa sneezes – you might find that prospect upsetting. But you might just as well avoid air travel, or subways, equally dodgy environments for airborne transmission of disease. Eat the bread.

I *won't* eat in a restaurant with filthy bathrooms. This isn't a hard call. They let you *see* the bathrooms. If the restaurant can't be bothered to replace the puck in the urinal or keep the toilets and floors clean, then just imagine what their refrigeration and work spaces look like. Bathrooms are relatively easy to clean. Kitchens are not. In fact, if you see the chef sitting unshaven at the bar, with a dirty apron on, one finger halfway up his nose, you can assume he's not handling your food any better behind closed doors. Your waiter looks like he just woke up under a bridge? If management allows him to wander out on the floor looking like that, God knows what they're doing to your shrimp!

'Beef Parmentier'? 'Shepherd's pie'? 'Chili special'? Sounds like leftovers to me. How about swordfish? I like it fine. But my seafood purveyor, when he goes out to dinner, won't eat it. He's seen too many of those 3-foot-long parasitic worms that riddle the fish's flesh. You see a few of these babies – and we all do – and you won't be tucking into swordfish anytime soon.

Chilean sea bass? Trendy. Expensive. More than likely frozen. This came as a surprise to me when I visited the market recently. Apparently the great majority of the stuff arrives frozen solid, still on the bone. In fact, as I said earlier, the whole Fulton Street market is not an inspiring sight. Fish is left to sit, un-iced, in leaking crates, in the middle of August, right out in the open. What isn't bought early is sold for cheap later. At 7 A.M. the Korean and Chinese buyers, who've been sitting in local bars *waiting* for the market to be near closing, swoop down on the over-extended fishmonger and buy up what's left at rock-bottom prices. The next folks to arrive will be the cat-food people. Think about that when you see the 'Discount Sushi' sign.

'Saving for well-done' is a time-honored tradition dating back to cuisine's earliest days: meat and fish cost money. Every piece of cut, fabricated food must, ideally, be sold for three or even four times its cost in order for the chef to make his 'food cost percent'. So what happens when the chef finds a tough, slightly skanky end-cut of sirloin, that's been pushed repeatedly to the back of the pile? He can throw it out, but that's a total loss, representing a three-fold loss of what it cost him per pound. He can feed it to the family, which is the same as throwing it out. Or he can 'save for well-done' – serve it to some rube who *prefers* to eat his meat or fish incinerated into a flavorless, leathery hunk of carbon, who won't be able to tell if what he's eating is food or flotsam. Ordinarily, a proud chef would hate this customer, hold him in contempt for destroying his fine food. But not in this case. The dumb bastard is *paying for the privilege of eating his garbage*! What's not to like?

Vegetarians, and their Hezbollah-like splinter-faction, the vegans, are a persistent irritant to any chef worth a damn. To me, life without veal stock, pork fat, sausage, organ meat, demi-glace, or even stinky cheese is a life not worth living. Vegetarians are the enemy of everything good and decent in the human spirit, an affront to all I stand for, the pure enjoyment of food. The body, these waterheads imagine, is a temple that should not be polluted by animal protein. It's healthier, they insist, though every vegetarian waiter I've worked with is brought down by any *rumor* of a cold. Oh, I'll accommodate them, I'll rummage around for *something* to feed them, for a 'vegetarian plate', if called on to do so. Fourteen dollars for a few slices of grilled eggplant and zucchini suits my food cost fine. But let me tell you a story.

A few years back, at a swinging singles joint on Columbus Avenue, we had the misfortune to employ a sensitive young man as a waiter who, in addition to a wide and varied social life involving numerous unsafe sexual practices, was something of a jailhouse lawyer. After he was fired for incompetence, he took it on himself to sue the restaurant, claiming that a gastro-intestinal problem, caused apparently by amoebas, was a result of his work there. Management took this litigation seriously enough to engage the services of an epidemiologist, who obtained stool samples from *every* employee. The results – which I was privy to – were enlightening to say the least. The waiter's strain of amoebas, it was concluded, was common to persons of his lifestyle, and to many others. What was interesting were the results of our Mexican and South American prep cooks. These guys were *teeming* with numerous varieties of critters, none of which, in their cases, caused illness or discomfort. It was explained that the results in our restaurant were no different from results at any other restaurant and that, particularly amongst my recently arrived Latino brethren, this sort of thing is normal – that their systems are used to it, and it causes them no difficulties at all. Amoebas, however, are transferred most easily through the handling of raw, uncooked vegetables, particularly during the washing of salad greens and leafy produce. So think about that next time you want to exchange deep tongue kisses with a vegetarian.

I'm not even going to talk about blood. Let's just say we cut ourselves a lot in the kitchen and leave it at that.

Pigs are filthy animals, say some, when explaining why they deny themselves the delights of pork. Maybe they should visit a chicken ranch. America's favorite menu item is also the most likely to make you ill. Commercially available chickens, for the most part (we're not talking about kosher and expensive free-range birds), are loaded with salmonella. Chickens are dirty. They eat their own feces, are kept packed close together like in a rush-hour subway, and when handled in a restaurant situation are most likely to infect other foods, or cross-contaminate them. And chicken is boring. Chefs see it as a menu item for people who don't know what they want to eat.

Shrimp? All right, if it looks fresh, smells fresh, and the restaurant is busy, guaranteeing turnover of product on a regular basis. But shrimp toast? I'll pass. I walk into a restaurant with a mostly empty dining room, and an unhappy-looking owner staring out the window? I'm not ordering shrimp.

This principle applies to anything on a menu actually, especially something esoteric and adventurous like, say, bouillabaisse. If a restaurant is known for steak, and doesn't seem to be doing much business, how long do you think those few orders of clams and mussels and lobster and fish have been sitting in the refrigerator, waiting for someone like you to order it? The key is rotation. If the restaurant is busy, and you see bouillabaisse flying out the kitchen doors every few minutes, then it's probably a good bet. But a big and varied menu in a slow, half-empty place? Those less popular items like broiled mackerel and calves' liver are kept mouldering in a dark corner of the reach-in because they look good on the menu. You might not actually want to eat them. Look at your waiter's face. He knows. It's another reason to be polite to your waiter: he could save your life with a raised eyebrow or a sigh. If he likes you, maybe he'll stop you from ordering a piece of fish he knows is going to hurt you. On the other hand, maybe the chef has ordered him, under pain of death, to move that codfish before it begins to *really* reek. Observe the body language, and take note.

Watchwords for fine dining? Tuesday through Saturday. Busy. Turnover. Rotation. Tuesdays and Thursdays are the best nights to order fish in New York. The food that comes in Tuesday is fresh, the station prep is new, and the chef is well rested after a Sunday or a Monday off. It's the real start of the new week, when you've got the goodwill of the kitchen on your side. Fridays and Saturdays, the food is fresh, but it's busy, so the chef and cooks can't pay as much attention to your food as they – and you – might like. And weekend diners are universally viewed with suspicion, even contempt, by both cooks and waiters alike; they're the slackjaws, the rubes, the out-of-town-ers, the well-done-eating, undertipping, bridge-and-tunnel pre-theater hordes, in to see *Cats* or *Les Miz* and never to return. Weekday diners, on the other hand, are the home team – potential regulars, whom all concerned want to make happy. Rested and ready after a day off, the chef is going to put his best foot forward on Tuesday; he's got his best-quality product coming in and he's had a day or two to think of creative things to do with it. He *wants* you to be happy on Tuesday night. On Saturday, he's thinking more about turning over tables and getting through the rush.

If the restaurant is clean, the cooks and waiters well groomed, the dining room busy, everyone seems to actually *care* about what they're doing – not just trying to pick up a few extra bucks between head-shots and auditions for *Days of Our Lives* – chances are you're in for a decent meal. The owner, chef and a bored-looking waiter sitting at a front table chatting about soccer scores? Plumber walking through the dining room with a toilet snake? Bad signs. Watch the trucks pull up outside the restaurant delivery entrance in the morning if you're in the neighborhood. Reputable vendors of seafood, meat and pro-duce? Good sign. If you see sinister, unmarked step-vans, off-loading all three at once, or the big tractor trailers from one of the national outfits – you know the ones, 'Servicing Restaurants and Institutions for Fifty Years' – remember what institutions they're talking about: cafeterias, schools, prisons. Unless you *like* frozen, portion-controlled 'convenience food'.

Do all these horrifying assertions frighten you? Should you stop eating out? Wipe yourself down with antiseptic towelettes every time you pass a restaurant? No way. Like I said before, your body is *not* a temple, it's an amusement park. Enjoy the ride. Sure, it's a 'play you pay' sort of an adventure, but you knew that already, every time you ever ordered a taco or a dirty-water hot dog. If you're willing to risk some slight lower GI distress for one of those Italian sweet sausages at the street fair, or for a slice of pizza you just *know* has been sitting on the board for an hour or two, why not take a chance on the good stuff? All the great developments of classical cuisine, the first guys to eat sweetbreads, to try unpasteurized Stilton, to discover that snails actually taste *good* with enough garlic butter, these were daredevils, innovators and desperados. I don't know who figured out that if you crammed rich food into a goose long enough for its liver to balloon up to more than its normal body weight you'd get something as good as foie gras – I believe it was those kooky Romans – but I'm very grateful for their efforts. Popping raw fish into your face, especially in pre-refrigeration days, might have seemed like sheer madness to some, but it turned out to be a pretty good idea. They say that Rasputin used to eat a little arsenic with breakfast every day, building up resistance for the day that an enemy might poison him, and that sounds like good sense to me. Judging from accounts of his death, the Mad Monk wasn't fazed at all by the stuff; it took repeated beatings, a couple of bullets, and a long fall off a bridge into a frozen river to finish the job. Perhaps we, as serious diners, should emulate his example. We are, after all, citizens of the world – a world filled with bacteria, some friendly, some not so friendly. Do we really want to travel in hermetically sealed popemobiles through the rural provinces of France, Mexico and the Far East, eating only in Hard Rock Cafés and McDonald's? Or do we want to eat without fear, tearing into the local stew, the humble taqueria's mystery meat, the sincerely offered gift of a lightly grilled fish head? I know what I want. I want it all. I want to try everything once. I'll give you the benefit of the doubt, Señor Tamale Stand Owner, Sushi-chef-san, Monsieur Bucket-head. What's that feathered game bird, hanging on the porch, getting riper by the day, the body nearly ready to drop off? I want some.

I have no wish to die, nor do I have some unhealthy fondness for dysentery. If I *know* you're storing your squid at room temperature next to a cat box, I'll get my squid down the street, thank you very much. I will continue to do my seafood eating on Tuesdays, Wednesdays and Thursdays, because I know better, because I can wait. But if I have one chance at a full-blown dinner of blowfish gizzard – even if I have not been properly introduced to the chef – and I'm in a strange, Far Eastern city and my plane leaves tomorrow? I'm going for it. You only go around once.

HOW TO COOK LIKE THE PROS

UNLESS YOU'RE ONE OF us already, you'll probably never cook like a professional. And that's okay. On my day off, I rarely want to eat restaurant food unless I'm looking for new ideas or recipes to steal. What I want to eat is home cooking, somebody's – *anybody*'s – mother's or grandmother's food. A simple pasta pomodoro made with love, a clumsily thrown-together tuna casserole, roast beef with Yorkshire pudding, all of this is pure exotica to me, even when I've been neck-deep all day in filet mignon and herb-infused oils and all the bits of business we do to distinguish restaurant food from what you get at home. My mother-in-law would always apologize before serving dinner when I was in attendance, saying, 'This must seem pretty ordinary for a *chef* . . .' She had no idea how magical, how reassuring, how pleasurable her simple meat loaf was for me, what a delight even lumpy mashed potatoes were – being, as they were, blessedly devoid of truffles or truffle oil.

But you don't want to know this. What you'd like to know is how to make your next dinner party look as though you've got the Troisgros family chained to the stove in your home kitchen. Maybe you're curious about the tricks, the techniques, the few simple tools that can make your plates look as if they've been prepared, assembled and garnished by cold-blooded professionals.

Let's talk about tools first. What do we have in *our* kitchens that you probably don't? The joke is that many of our stock items – herb oils, crushed spices, chiffonaded parsley, puréed starches and veggies – are often made with home-model equipment, just like yours. I may have a 25-quart professional Hobart mixer and an ultra-large Robot-Coupe, but chances are I used a home blender to make that lovely roast red pepper coulis dotted with bright green basil oil drizzled around your plate. So, what do you absolutely need?

You need, for God's sake, **a decent chef's knife.** No con foisted on the general public is so atrocious, so wrongheaded, or so widely believed as the one that tells you you need a full set of specialized cutlery in various sizes. I wish sometimes I could go through the kitchens of amateur cooks everywhere just throwing knives out from their drawers – all those medium-size 'utility' knives, those useless serrated things you see advertised on TV, all that hard-to-sharpen stainless-steel garbage, those ineptly designed slicers – not one of the damn things could cut a tomato. Please believe me, here's all you will ever need in the knife department: ONE good chef's knife, as large as is comfortable for your hand. Brand name? Okay, most talented amateurs get a boner buying one of the old-school professional high-carbon stainless knives from Germany or Austria, like a Henkel or Wusthof, and those *are* fine knives, if heavy. High carbon makes them slightly easier to sharpen, and stainless keeps them from getting stained and corroded. They look awfully good in the knife case at the store, too, and you send the message to your guests when flashing a hundred-dollar hunk of Solingen steel that you take your cooking seriously. But do you really *need* something so heavy? So expensive? So difficult to maintain (which you probably won't)? Unless you are really and truly going to spend fifteen minutes every couple of days working that blade on an oiled carborundum stone, followed by careful honing on a diamond steel, I'd forgo the Germans.

Most of the professionals I know have for years been retiring their Wusthofs and replacing them with the lightweight, easy-to-sharpen and relatively inexpensive vanadium steel Global knives, a very good Japanese product which has – in addition to its many other fine qualities – the added attraction of *looking* really cool.

Global makes a lot of knives in different sizes, so what do you *need*? One chef's knife. This should cut just about anything you might work with, from a shallot to a watermelon, an onion to a sirloin strip. Like a pro, you should use the tip of the knife for the small stuff, and the area nearer the heel for the larger. This isn't difficult; buy a few rutabagas or onions – they're cheap – and practice on them. Nothing will set you apart from the herd quicker than the ability to handle a chef's knife properly. If you need instruction on how to handle a knife without lopping off a finger, I recommend Jacques Pépin's *La Technique*.

Okay, there *are* a couple of other knives you might find useful. I carry a **flexible boning knife**, also made by the fine folks at Global, because I fillet the occasional fish, and because with the same knife I can butcher whole tenderloins, bone out legs of lamb, French-cut racks of veal and trim meat. If your butcher is doing all the work for you you can probably live without one. A **paring knife** comes in handy once in a while, if you find yourself tournéeing vegetables, fluting mushrooms and doing the kind of microsurgery that my old pal Dimitri used to excel at. But how often do you do that?

A genuinely useful blade, however, and one that is increasingly popular with my cronies in the field, is what's called an **offset serrated knife**. It's basically a serrated knife set into an ergonomic handle; it looks like a 'Z' that's been pulled out and elongated. This is a truly cool item which, once used, becomes indispensable. As the handle is not flush with the blade, but raised away from the cutting surface, you can use it not only for your traditional serrated blade needs – like slicing bread, thick-skinned tomatoes and so on – but on your full line of vegetables, spuds, meat and even fish. My sous-chef uses his for just about everything. F. Dick makes a good one for about twenty-five bucks. It's stainless steel, but since it's serrated it doesn't really matter; after a couple of years of use, if the teeth start to wear down, you just buy yourself another one.

Knives are obvious. What other toys are in the professionals' bag of tricks? Numero uno – the indispensable object in most chefs' shtick – is the simple **plastic squeeze bottle**. May be you've seen Bobby Flay on TV artfully drizzling sauce around a plate with one of these – the man's been making Mexican food look like haute cuisine for years with these things. Sure, it's just ancho pepper mayonnaise he's squirting all over that fish, but it *looks* like . . . well . . . *abstract, man*!!! No big deal acquiring these things, they're essentially the same objects you see at roadside hot-dog stands, loaded with mustard and ketchup. Mask a bottom of a plate with, say, an emulsified butter sauce, then run a couple of concentric rings of darker sauce – like demi-glace, or roast pepper purée – around the plate, and pay attention here, folks, now drag a **toothpick** through the rings or lines, and you'll see that all the fuss is about nothing. It should take you about half an hour of dicking around with a couple of squeeze bottles and your toothpick to grab the concept fully. This same gag is used by pastry chefs to swirl chocolate or raspberry sauce through crème anglaise and allows them to charge you another three bucks a plate for two seconds of work that you could easily train a chimp to do.

But . . . but Chef, you say . . . how do they make the food so *tall*? How can *I* make *my* breast of chicken and mashed potatoes tower like a fully engorged priapus over my awed and cowering guests? The answer is yet another low-tech item: the **metal ring**. A thin metal ring, or cut-down section of PVC pipe, about an inch and a half to two inches tall and varying inches across, is the backbone of pretentious food presentation. Just spoon your mashed potatoes in here – or better, *pipe* the spuds in with a **pastry bag** – and you are in business. Just pile it high, slip off the collar, stack your vegetable, deposit your chicken on top of that, and you're halfway to making that fuzzy little Emeril your bitch. Jam a gaufrette potato into the mashed, maybe a sprig of fresh herb, or a nice pile of ultra-thin julienne of fried leeks that you've cut with your new Global, and you're talking *tall*.

Gaufrette wha'? That's French for waffle-cut, and what we're talking about here is a potato chip. You can do that. All you need is what's called a **mandoline**, a vertically held slicer with various blade settings. They make some very cheap, very effective ones in Japan these days, so it's not a major investment. One of these bad boys can help you make those slick-looking, perfectly uniform julienned and bâtonnet-cut veggies you thought they cut by hand last time you ate out – and it cranks out lovely waffle cuts with a twist of the wrist. Dauphinoise potatoes cut to identical thickness? No sweat. You didn't think they actually cut those with a *knife*, did you?

All right, the mandolin won't cut meat, and it certainly won't make paper-thin slices of prosciutto. You need a professional rotary cold-cut slicer for that, like they have at the deli. The home versions suck. But I highly recommend, if presenting sausage or meat on a buffet, that you slip the neighborhood deli guy a few bucks to slice what you need before you arrange it on platters. It makes all the difference in the world. Or if you have a few extra bucks, read the back of the paper for notices of restaurant auctions. As you've probably gathered by now, restaurants go out of business *all the time*, and have to sell off their equipment quickly and cheaply before the marshals do it for them. I know people who buy whole restaurants this way, in what's called a turnkey operation, and in a business with a failure rate of over 60 percent they often do very well. You can buy all sorts of professional quality stuff. I'd recommend **pots and pans** as a premium consideration if scavenging this way. Most of the ones sold for home use are dangerously flimsy, and the heavyweight equipment sold for serious home cooks is almost always overpriced. **Stockpots, saucepans, thick-bottomed sauté pans** are nice things, even necessary things to have, and there's no reason to buy new and no reason to pay a lot – just wait for that new tapas place on the corner to go out of business, then make your move.

Let me stress that again: **heavyweight**. A thin-bottomed saucepan is useless for anything. I don't care if it's bonded with copper, hand-rubbed by virgins, or fashioned from the same material they built the stealth bomber out of. If you like scorched sauces, carbonized chicken, pasta that sticks to the bottom of the pot, burnt breadcrumbs, then be my guest. A proper sauté pan, for instance, should cause serious head injury if brought down hard against someone's skull. If you have any doubts about which will dent – the victim's head or your pan – then throw that pan right in the trash.

A **non-stick sauté pan** is a thing of beauty. Crêpes, omelettes, a delicately browned fillet of fish or tender skate wing? You need a nice thick non-stick pan, and *not* one with a thin veneer of material that peels off after a few weeks. And when you buy a non-stick, treat it nice. *Never* wash it. Simply wipe it clean after each use, and *don't* use metal in it, use a wooden spoon or ceramic or non-metallic spatula to flip or toss whatever you're cooking in it. You don't want to scratch the surface.

I don't want to oversimplify here. Obviously, if you have no sense of taste or texture, and no eye for color or presentation – hell, if you can't cook at *all* – then all the equipment in the world ain't gonna help you. But if you can throw together a decent meal, can read a cookbook, well then, you can do a lot better if you spend some time playing with the toys I've mentioned.

There are also some ingredients that separate food at home from food in a restaurant – stuff that *we* in a professional kitchen have on hand that you probably don't – and I'll tell you now which of these make all the difference in the world.

Shallots. You almost never see this item in a home kitchen, but out in the world they're an essential ingredient. Shallots are one of the things – a basic prep item in every mise-en-place – which make restaurant food taste different from your food. In my kitchen we use nearly 20 *pounds* a day. You should always have some around for sauces, dressings and sauté items.

Butter. I don't care what they tell you they're putting or not putting in your food at your favorite restaurant, chances are, you're eating a ton of butter. In a professional kitchen, it's almost always the first and last thing in the pan. We sauté in a mixture of butter and oil for that nice brown, caramelized color, and we finish nearly every sauce with it (we call this *monter au beurre*); that's why my sauce tastes richer and creamier and mellower than yours, why it's got that nice, thick, opaque consistency. Believe me, there's a big crock of softened butter on almost every cook's station, and it's getting a heavy workout. Margarine? That's not food. I Can't Believe It's Not Butter? I can. If you're planning on using margarine in *anything*, you can stop reading now, because I won't be able to help you. Even the Italians – you know, those crafty Tuscans – spout off about getting away from butter, and extol the glories of olive oil (and it *is* glorious), but pay a surprise visit to the kitchen of that three-star Northern Italian, and what's that they're sneaking into the pasta? And the risotto? The veal chop? Could it be? Is it . . . why, I can't believe it IS butter!!

Roasted garlic. Garlic is divine. Few food items can taste so many distinct ways, handled correctly. Misuse of garlic is a crime. Old garlic, burnt garlic, garlic cut too long ago, garlic that has been tragically smashed through one of those abominations, the garlic press, are all disgusting. Please, treat your garlic with respect. Sliver it for pasta, like you saw in *Goodfellas*, don't burn it. Smash it, with the flat of your knife blade if you like, but *don't* put it through a press. I don't know what that junk is that squeezes out the end of those things, but it ain't garlic. And try roasting garlic. It gets mellow and sweeter if you roast it whole, still on the clove, to be squeezed out later when it's soft and brown. Try a Caesar dressing, for instance, with a mix of fresh, raw garlic for bite, and roasted for background, and you'll see what I mean. Nothing will permeate your food more irrevocably and irreparably than burnt or rancid garlic. Avoid at all costs that vile spew you see rotting in oil in screwtop jars. Too lazy to peel fresh? You don't deserve to eat garlic.

Chiffonaded parsley. Big deal, right? Restaurants *garnish* their food. Why shouldn't you? And parsley tastes good, too. Just *don't* chop it in a machine, please. Dip the picked sprigs in cold water, shake off excess, allow to dry for a few minutes, and *slice* the stuff, as thinly as you can, with that sexy new chef's knife I inspired you to buy. I promise you, sprinkled over or around your plate it'll give your chow that striking professional touch it's been missing.

Stock. Stock is the backbone of good cooking. You need it – and you don't have it. I have the luxury of 30-quart stockpots, a willing prep crew, readily available bones and plenty of refrigeration space. Does this mean you should subject your guests to a sauce made from nasty commercial bases or salty canned broth? Make stock already! It's easy! Just roast some bones, roast some vegetables, put them in a big pot with water and reduce and reduce and reduce. Make a few months' worth, and when it's reduced enough strain it and freeze it in small containers so you can pull it from the freezer as needed. Life without stock is barely worth living, and you will never attain demi-glace without it.

Demi-glace. There are a lot of ways to make demi-glace, but I recommend you simply take your already reduced meat stock, add some red wine, toss in some shallots and fresh thyme and a bay leaf and peppercorns, and slowly, slowly simmer it and reduce it again until it coats a spoon. Strain. Freeze this stuff in an ice-cube tray, pop out a cube or two as needed, and you are in business – you can rule the world. And remember, when making a sauce with demi-glace, don't forget to *monter au beurre.*

Chervil, basil tops, chive sticks, mint tops, etc. What does it take, for chrissakes?! A nice sprig of chervil on top of your chicken breast? A healthy-looking basil top decorating your pasta? A few artfully scattered chive sticks over your fish? A mint top nestled in a dollop of whipped cream, maybe rubbing up against a single raspberry? Come *on*! Get in the game here! It takes so little to elevate an otherwise ordinary-looking plate. You need zero talent to garnish food. So why not do it? And how about a sprig of fresh herb – thyme or rosemary? You can use the part not needed for garnish to maybe actually *flavor* your food. That dried sawdust they sell in the cute little cans at the super market? You can throw that, along with the spice rack, right in the garbage. It all tastes like a stable floor. Use fresh! Good food is very often, even *most* often, simple food. Some of the best cuisine in the world – whole roasted fish, Tuscan-style, for instance – is a matter of three or four ingredients. Just make sure they're *good* ingredients, *fresh* ingredients, and then *garnish* them. How hard is that?

Example: here's a very popular dish I used to serve at a highly regarded two-star joint in New York. I got thirty-two bucks an order for it and could barely keep enough in stock, people liked it so much. Take one fish – a red snapper, striped bass, or dorade – have your fish guy remove gills, guts and scales and wash in cold water. Rub inside and out with kosher salt and crushed black pepper. Jam a clove of garlic, a slice of lemon and a few sprigs of fresh herb – say, rosemary and thyme – into the cavity where the guts used to be. Place on a lightly oiled pan or foil and throw the fish into a very hot oven. Roast till crispy and cooked through. Drizzle a little basil oil over the plate – you know, the stuff you made with your blender and then put in your new squeeze bottle? – sprinkle with chiffonaded parsley, garnish with basil top . . . See?

OWNER'S SYNDROME

AND OTHER MEDICAL ANOMALIES

TO WANT TO OWN a restaurant can be a strange and terrible affliction. What causes such a destructive urge in so many otherwise sensible people? Why would anyone who has worked hard, saved money, often been successful in other fields, want to pump their hard-earned cash down a hole that statistically, at least, will almost surely prove dry? Why venture into an industry with enormous fixed expenses (rent, electricity, gas, water, linen, maintenance, insurance, license fees, trash removal, etc.), with a notoriously transient and unstable workforce, and highly perishable inventory of assets? The chances of ever seeing a return on your investment are about one in five. What insidious spongiform bacteria so riddles the brains of men and women that they stand there on the tracks, watching the lights of the oncoming locomotive, knowing full well it will eventually run them over? After all these years in the business, I still don't know.

The easy answer, of course, is ego. The classic example is the retired dentist who was always told he threw a great dinner party. 'You should open a restaurant,' his friends tell him. And our dentist believes them. He wants to get in the business – not to make money, not really, but to swan about the dining room signing dinner checks like Rick in *Casablanca*. And he'll have plenty of chance to sign dinner checks – when the deadbeat friends who told him what a success he'd be in the restaurant business keep coming by looking for freebies. All these original geniuses will be more than happy to clog up the bar, sucking down free drinks, taking credit for this bold venture – until the place starts running into trouble, at which point they dematerialize, shaking their heads at their foolish dentist who just didn't seem up to the job.

Maybe the dentist is having a mid-life crisis. He figures the Bogie act will help pull the kind of chicks he could never get when he was yanking molars and scraping plaque. You see a lot of this ailment – perfectly reasonable, even shrewd businessmen, hitting their fifties, suddenly writing checks with their cock. And they are not entirely misguided in this; they probably *will* get laid. The restaurant business does have somewhat relaxed mores about casual sex, and there are a number of amiably round-heeled waitresses, most of them hopelessly untalented aspiring actresses for whom sexual congress with older, less attractive guys is not entirely unfamiliar.

Unsurprisingly, a retired dentist who starts a restaurant for the sex, or to be told he's marvelous, is totally unprepared for the realities of the business. He's completely blindsided when the place doesn't start making money immediately. Under-capitalized, uneducated about the arcane requirements of new grease traps, frequent refrigeration repairs, unforeseen equipment replacement, when business drops, or fails to improve, he panics, starts looking for the quick fix. He thrashes around in an escalating state of agitation, tinkering with concept, menu, various marketing schemes. As the end draws near, these ideas are replaced by more immediately practical ones: close on Sundays . . . cut back staff . . . shut down lunch. Naturally, as the operation becomes more schizophrenic – one week French, one week Italian – as the poor schmuck tries one thing after another like a rat trying to escape a burning building, the already elusive dining public begins to detect the unmistakable odor of uncertainty, fear and approaching death. And once that distinctive reek begins to waft into the dining room, he may as well lay out petri-dishes of anthrax spores as bar snacks, because there is *no way* the joint is gonna bounce back. It's remarkable how long some of these neophytes hang on after the clouds of doom gather around the place, paying for deliveries COD as if magic will happen – one good weekend, a good review, something will somehow save them.

Like some unseen incubus, this evil cloud of failure can hang over a restaurant long after the operation has gone under, killing any who follow. The cumulative vibe of a history of failed restaurants can infect an address year after year, even in an otherwise bustling neighborhood. You can see it when passersby peer into the front window of the next operator; there's a scowl, a look of suspicion, as if they are afraid of contamination.

Of course there are many, many operators who do well in the restaurant business, who know what they're doing. They know from the get-go what they want, what they are capable of doing well, and exactly how much it's going to cost them at the outset. Most important, they have a fixed idea of how long they're willing to lose money before they pull the plug. Like professional gamblers, a slick restaurateur never changes his betting style. He doesn't bother with magic bullets, changing pricing strategies or menu concepts. With steely resolve, a pro, in the face of adversity, will suck it up and redouble his efforts to make the restaurant what he wanted and planned it to be all along – hoping that the great unwashed will eventually discover it, trust it, learn to love it. These guys know that when you hit the panic button and call in the consultants (read: unemployable chefs, failed restaurateurs who still like to eat for free), or start taking austerity measures like combining waiter/bartender functions on slow lunches – or worst of all, closing early – that they may as well close the doors for good: it's just good money after bad. A smart operator will, when he realizes things haven't worked out, fold up his tent and move on – before he's knocked out of the game for good. One disastrous restaurant venture can drag down an entire string of successful ones, as I have seen many times.

These knuckleheads are even less easy to explain than the

novice owner with a hard-on for waitron nookie. Proven operators, guys with two or three or even more thriving restaurants, guys who've already beaten the odds, who have had and *still* have successful money-making joints, spitting out dough – what makes these guys over-reach? Often, the original flagship operation is a simple, straightforward concept: a bar with decent food, or a simple country Italian restaurant, or a bistro loved for its lack of pretension. But success makes these guys feel invulnerable. They *must* be geniuses, right? They're making money in the restaurant business! So *why not* open a 300-seat interactive Tuscan restaurant/take-out/with merchandising outlet in a high-rent district? Or three more restaurants! Maybe the Hamptons! Miami! The Seaport! Two frat-bar saloons with two Chinese cooks and a large-breasted bartender as overheads have been raking in the dough, so *why not* open up a jazz-club theme restaurant in Times Square? A multistory one with a three-star chef and live music?

The answer is simple. Because it's not what they're good at!

Making money in the bar business? What's wrong with that? You're a lucky man! Stay in the goddamn bar business! Hang on to your money! I can't tell you how many times I've seen cunning, powerful, even wildly successful men fall victim to this kind of delusional power grab, this sudden urge to expand the empire – only to find their personal Stalingrad waiting for them. Some get away with it for a while, and though things aren't exactly rocket-to-the-moon, they aren't going too badly, either: the second place isn't losing money, it looks like it might even make money someday, so why not open two more at the same time? When they finally go to the well once too often, find themselves overextended, have to start ignoring the original operation – the one that made all the money for them in the first place, eventually bleeding it dry – next thing you know, the Russian tanks are rolling through the suburbs, misusing your womenfolk, and Mr Restaurant Genius is holed up in the bunker thinking about eating his gun.

The most dangerous species of owner, however – a true

menace to himself and others – is the one who gets into the business for love. Love for the song stylings of George Gershwin (always wanted a place where they could present the cabaret music they adore), love for the regional cuisine of rural Mexico (and it'll be *authentic*, too! No frozen margaritas!), love of eighteenth-century French antiques (I need a restaurant so people can *see* them, see what good taste I have!), love for that great Bogie film they have all that memorabilia from. These poor fools are the chum of the restaurant biz, ground up and eaten before most people even know they were around. Other operators feed on these creatures, lying in wait for them to fold so they can take over their leases, buy their equipment, hire away their help. Purveyors see these guys coming, rarely extending more than a week's credit from the outset, or demanding bill-to-bill payment. In fact, if you ever have any question about the viability of your operation, ask your fish purveyor: he probably knows better than you. *You* may be willing to take it in the neck for a few hundred thousand dollars, but he isn't. He's got it all figured out as soon as he claps eyes on you and your ludicrous restaurant – exactly how much he's willing to get stiffed for when you suddenly throw in the towel. Chances are it's no more than a week's worth of product.

Given these perils . . . why? Why would anyone want to do it?

Inarguably, a successful restaurant demands that you *live* on the premises for the first few years, working seventeen-hour days, with *total* involvement in every aspect of a complicated, cruel and very fickle trade. You must be fluent in not only Spanish but the Kabbala-like intricacies of health codes, tax law, fire department regulations, environmental protection laws, building code, occupational safety and health regs, fair hiring practices, zoning, insurance, the vagaries and back-alley backscratching of liquor licenses, the netherworld of trash removal, linen, grease disposal. And with every dime you've got tied up in your new place, suddenly the drains in your prep kitchen are backing up with raw sewage, pushing hundreds of gallons of impacted crap into your dining room; your coke-addled chef just called that Asian waitress who's working her way through law school a chink, which ensures your presence in court for the next six months; your bartender is giving away the bar to under-age girls from Wantagh, any one of whom could then crash Daddy's Buick into a busload of divinity students, putting your liquor license in peril, to say the least; the Ansel System could go off, shutting down your kitchen in the middle of a ten-thousand-dollar night; there's the ongoing struggle with rodents and cockroaches, any one of which could crawl across the Tina Brown four-top in the middle of the dessert course; you just bought 10,000 dollars-worth of shrimp when the market was low, but the walk-in freezer just went on the fritz and naturally it's a holiday weekend, so good luck getting a service call in time; the dishwasher just walked out after arguing with the busboy, and they need glasses *now* on table seven; immigration is at the door for a surprise inspection of your kitchen's Green Cards; the produce guy wants a certified check or he's taking back the delivery; you didn't order enough napkins for the weekend – and is that the *New York Times* reviewer waiting for your hostess to stop flirting and notice her?

I have met and worked for the one perfect animal in the restaurant jungle, a creature perfectly evolved for the requirements of surviving this cruel and unforgiving business, a guy who lives, breathes and actually *enjoys* solving little problems like the ones above. He is a man who loves the restrictions, the technical minutiae, the puzzling mysteries of the life as things to be conquered, outwitted, subjugated. He rarely invests his own money, but he always makes money for his partners. He never goes anywhere and never does anything except what he's good at, which is running restaurants. He's good. He's so good that to this day, more than ten years after I stopped working for the man, I *still* wake up every morning at five minutes of six, always before the alarm, and I'm *never* late to work. Why? Because to disappoint the man – not to live up to his shining example of total involvement would be, even now, treason to my trade. I became a real chef – meaning a person capable of organizing, operating and, most important, *leading* a kitchen – because of the man. He taught me everything *really important* I know about the business. He, more than anyone else I encountered in my professional life, transformed me from a bright but druggie fuck-up into a serious, capable and responsible chef. He made me a leader, the combination of good-guy bad-guy the job requires. He's the reason I am never off sick, go to sleep every night running tomorrow's prep lists and menus through my mind. He's also the reason I smoke three packs of cigarettes a day, and know everything there is to know about everyone I work with, why my purveyors cringe when they get my call, and why my wife has to remind me when I get home from work that she's my wife and *not* an employee.

Let's call him Bigfoot.

BIGFOOT

I FIRST MET BIGFOOT while still at CIA. He was then, and remains, a West Village legend, either loved or despised (and frequently both) by generations of bar customers, waiters, bartenders, cooks, chefs and restaurant lifers. I won't give his name, though everyone below 14th Street who reads this will know who I'm talking about. He'll certainly know. He'll call me.

'Hey, Flaco,' he'll say. He calls me Flaco to this day. There was *already* a Tony working for him when he took me on, and as Bigfoot likes an organized operation, he needed a distinct name for me. 'Flaco, I read your book . . .'

'Yess . . .' I'll respond, waiting for the punch line.

'There's a typo on page seventy-seven,' he'll say. 'I don't know a lot about publishing, but . . . it seems to me that . . . maybe someone over there should know how to spell . . .'

Now, the first thing I heard about Bigfoot when I worked for him weekends back in the '70s was that 'he killed a guy'! Whether this is true or not, I have *no* idea. Though I like to consider him a friend and mentor, we have never discussed it – and I have heard, over the years, so many versions from so many unreliable people that I can't vouch for the veracity of even that simple statement. But the point is that this was the first thing I heard about him. That he had killed a guy with his bare hands. And Bigfoot, as you might imagine, is *big*. As he likes to describe himself, 'a big, fat, balding, red-faced Jewboy', which is typically a less than completely fair description. Bigfoot is not an unattractive guy – he looks like an elongated Bruce Willis – but he *is* over 6 foot 4, an ex-college basketball player, with enormous hands, strong shoulders and arms and deceptively quizzical eyes. He likes to play dumb – *loves* to play dumb – and like a sunbathing crocodile, when he makes his move, it's way too late.

'You know . . .' he'd say, 'I'm not a chef . . . and I don't know a lot about food, or cooking . . . so I don't know how to make, say . . . guacamole.' Then he'd shred my recipe and any illusions I might have about him not knowing anything about food, breaking down that preparation ingredient by ingredient, gram by gram, and showing how it could be done faster, better, cheaper. Of course he knew how to make guacamole! He knows to the atom how much of each ingredient goes in for how much eventual yield. He knows where to get the best avocados cheapest, how to ripen them, store them, sell them, merchandize them. He also knows how much fillet you get off every fish that swims, keeps a book on *every* cook who works for him with their individual yield averages for each and every fish they ever cut for him – so he *knows*, when Tony puts a knife to, say, a striped bass, exactly how many portions Tony is likely to get compared to the other cooks. Tony averages 62.5 percent usable yield on red snapper, and Mike averages 62.7 . . . so maybe Mike should cut that fish. As an ex-jock, Bigfoot likes scrupulous stats.

Cunning, manipulative, brilliant, mercurial, physically intimidating – even terrifying – a bully, a yenta, a sadist and a mensch: Bigfoot is all those things. He's also the most stand-up guy I ever worked for. He inspires a strange and consuming loyalty. I try, in my kitchen, to be just like him. I want my cooks to have me inside their heads just like Bigfoot remains in mine. I want them to think that, like Bigfoot, when I look into their eyes, I see right into their very souls.

My first night working for Bigfoot – a man I knew nothing of other than the rumor, and the fact that everyone appeared terrified of him – I knocked a few hundred meals out of his cramped kitchen, finished the evening feeling discouraged, exhausted and resigned never to work in his claustrophobic galley again. But the intercom at the bar rang as I was preparing to slink away, and the bartender gave me a curious look and told me, 'Bigfoot wants you downstairs in the office.' Downstairs, in Bigfoot's lair, the big man looked up at me, complimented me on a fine job, and picking up the phone, summoned a waiter with two snifters of brandy. 'We are pleased with the job you did for us this evening,' he began (Bigfoot loves to use 'we' when talking about the management of his restaurants, though in his domain there is never any 'we'). 'And we'd like you to stay on with us – if that's agreeable. Saturday nights . . . and Sunday brunches.' I can't adequately describe the gratification I felt at having pleased the imposing Bigfoot. Though we quickly agreed that he'd be paying me only 40 bucks a shift, I felt, going home that night, like a million. Bigfoot, you see, had purchased my soul for a snifter of Spanish brandy.

I was not alone in handing over my soul to the man. He retained, among other deeply flawed outcasts who'd inexplicably sworn loyalty oaths and joined up for the duration, a Presidential Guard of blue-uniformed porters whom he had personally trained in the manly arts of refrigeration repair, plumbing, basic metal work, glazing, electrical repair and maintenance. In addition to the usual tasks of cleaning, mopping, toilet-plunging and porter work, Bigfoot porters could lay tile, dig out a foundation, build you a lovely armoire or restore a used reach-in refrigerator to factory specs. Nothing pissed off Bigfoot more than having to pay some high-priced specialist for a job he thought he should be able to do himself.

One day I was sitting at the bar, enjoying an after-work drink, when Bigfoot approached and began giving me an uncharacteristic shoulder massage. I thought this a remarkably kind gesture until he told me that his Presidential Guard was at that moment downstairs tackling the difficult problem of repairing a city-owned sewage pipe. The problem had occurred directly below our walk-in. In typical fashion, Bigfoot had induced his Mexican disciples to hammer straight down through 2 feet of concrete, then, like Colditz escapees, tunnel 25 feet through waste-sodden earth beneath the walk-in, and make a hard-left turn to the site of the break. The big hands gently squeezing my shoulders were trying to determine whether I was thin enough to wriggle around the tight corner – through mud and shit – to help the porters, apparently too well fed to fit.

I couldn't hold it against him for trying. 'That's not my job' was not in the Bigfoot phrase book. Toilet overflows while the chef is at hand? He's going right in with a plunger, and fast. No waiting for the toilet guy – he *is* the toilet guy now. In Bigfoot's army, you fight for the cause, anywhere you are needed. If it's slow in the kitchen, you pick an old sauté pan and scrub the carbon off the bottom. Genteel sensibilities are unwelcome. Lead, follow . . . or get out of the way.

I worked for Bigfoot part-time while I attended CIA, and years later – over ten years later – I washed up on his shores again. It was a low point in my career. I was burnt out from my five-year run in the restaurant netherworld as a not very good chef – in rehab for heroin, still doing cocaine, broke – and reduced to working brunches at a ridiculous mom and pop restaurant in SoHo where they served lion, tiger, hippopotamus braciole and other dead zoo animals. I was determined never to be a chef again, sickened by my last gargantuan operation: a three-kitchen Italian place in the South Street Seaport, where I seemed to have spent most of my time as a convenient hatchet man, waking up every morning with the certain knowledge that today I'd be firing someone again . . . I was spent, desperate, unhappy, with a negligible-to-bad rep, in general a Person Not To Be Hired Or Trusted, when Bigfoot called looking for someone to cook lunches at his new saloon/bistro on 10th Street.

We met, and I must have looked like a rhesus monkey – the one in the perils-of-freebase commercial, cornered up a tree, shunned by his monkey pals, exhibiting erratic, paranoid and hostile behavior. I was rail-thin, shaky, and the first thing I did was ask my old pal Bigfoot if he could lend me 25 bucks until payday. Without hesitation, he reached in his pocket and lent me 200 – a tremendous leap of faith on his part. Bigfoot hadn't laid eyes on me in over a decade. Looking at me, and hearing the edited-for-television version of what I'd been up to in recent years, he must have had every reason to believe I'd disappear with the two bills, spend it on crack, and never show up for my first shift. And if he'd given me the 25 instead of 200, that might well have happened. But as so often happens with Bigfoot, his trust was rewarded. I was so shaken by his baseless trust in me – that such a cynical bastard as Bigfoot would make such a gesture – that I determined I'd sooner gnaw my own fingers off, gouge my eyes out with a shellfish fork and run naked down Seventh Avenue than *ever* betray that trust.

There was order in my life again. In Bigfootland you showed up for work *fifteen minutes* before your shift. Period. Two minutes late? You lose the shift and are sent home. If you're on the train and it looks like it's running late? You get off the train at the next stop, inform Bigfoot of your pending lateness, and then get back on the next train. It's okay to call Bigfoot and say, 'Bigfoot, I was up all night smoking crack, sticking up liquor stores, drinking blood and worshipping Satan . . . I'm going to be a little late.' That's acceptable – once in a very great while. But *after* showing up late, try saying (even if true), 'Uh . . . Bigfoot, I was on the way to work and the President's limo crashed right next to me . . . and I had to pull him out of the car, give him mouth-to-mouth . . . and like I saved the leader of the free world, man!' You, my friend, are fired.

I fondly recall how once, after a long-time waitress arrived back late from vacation, claiming her flight arrived fifteen minutes after scheduled time, Bigfoot called the airport to check her story and then fired her for lying. Treating Bigfoot like an idiot was always a big mistake. He lived for that. In the man's three or so decades in the life, he'd seen and heard every scam, every bullshit story, every trick, deception, ploy and gag that ever existed or that a human mind could conceive – and was always happy to prove that to anyone foolish enough to try. If Bigfoot asked you a question, and you didn't know the answer, he always preferred an 'I dunno' to a long-winded series of qualified statements, speculation and half-truths. You kept Bigfoot informed of your movements. He would never allow himself to fall victim to 'manager's syndrome' – constantly watching the clock, wondering if and when his employees were going to show up. Where Bigfoot ruled, he *knew* when they were showing up: fifteen minutes before start of shift. That's when.

Bigfoot understood – as I came to understand – that *character* is far more important than skills or employment history. And he recognized character – good and bad – brilliantly. He understood, and taught me, that a guy who shows up every day on time, never calls in sick, and does what he said he was going to do, is less likely to fuck you in the end than a guy who has an incredible résumé but is less than reliable about arrival time. Skills can be taught. Character you either have or don't have. Bigfoot understood that there are two types of people in the world: those who do what they say they're going to do – and everyone else. He'd lift ex-junkie sleazeballs out of the gutter and turn them into trusted managers, guys who'd kill themselves rather than misuse one thin dime of Bigfoot receipts. He'd get Mexicans right off the boat, turn them into solid citizens with immigration lawyers, nice incomes and steady employment. But if Bigfoot calls them at four in the morning, wanting them to put in a rooftop patio, they'd better be prepared to roll out of bed and get busy quarrying limestone.

Purveyors hated his guts. They'd peel the labels off the cartons they delivered, out of fear that Bigfoot would simply cut out the middleman and order directly from the source. He was an expert in equipment. I recall him getting a leasing company to guarantee a certain number of cubic feet of ice production from a machine he was contracting for. Two minutes after signing, he had his Presidential Guard measuring and weighing ice. When it turned out that the machine fell short by a few pounds or cubic feet, Bigfoot found himself with *two* new ice machines for the price of one. He loved playing purveyors against each other, driving the price down. Every once in a while, if a meat company, say, promised him the lowest price they could give, he'd have someone call them up, pretending to be their largest account – a 300-seat steakhouse, for instance – and ask for a copy of their last invoice, as theirs had gone missing; could they please fax another one? God help the poor meat guys if Peter Luger was paying two cents less a pound than Bigfoot was.

Nothing made him happier than discovering fraud or deception or even a simple white lie. Once, after years of ordering frozen BeeGee shrimp from a reputable seafood purveyor, Bigfoot discovered a hastily applied label indicating net weight. When it peeled off, he realized the company had, for years, been printing their own fake labels, heat-sealing them over the actual weight printed on the box, and cheating him out of a few ounces of shrimp every 5 pounds. Next time the company sent Bigfoot a bill, he simply sent them a Polaroid photo of the incriminating box, label peeling off to reveal actual weight. And the next time too. And for almost a year after, Bigfoot didn't pay for fish. He never discussed it with the company – and they never said a word. They just kept sending him free fish until they figured all that retroactive skim was paid back. When Bigfoot finally stopped ordering altogether they didn't wonder why.

Bigfoot paid his purveyors on time – religiously – a very unusual thing to do in a business where a restaurateur's real partners, more often than not, are the suppliers who send him food and material on credit. Given this, pity the poor soul who sent Bigfoot a second-best piece of swordfish.

'What is it?' he'd tell them on the phone, playing the confused dumbo for a while before the metal jaws clamped shut. 'I don't pay quickly enough to get the good stuff? Is there something *wrong* with my business that you want to send me garbage? Or is it that I'm stupid? Maybe my stupidity makes you figure, well . . . that I *want* the kind of shit you send me. Or maybe . . . I *am* stupid . . . maybe I can't recognize fresh fish . . . maybe this smelly piece of *shit* is really fresh . . . and I just . . . can't recognize it. Maybe I've *encouraged* you somehow . . . to inconvenience me and my customers. May be you could explain to me . . . because I'm having a *problem* . . . you know . . .

figuring it out . . . because I'm so *stupid*. Or maybe . . . maybe you're just *really really rich guys* and you don't need my business at all. Things are going so *well* for you . . . you figure you don't need the money.' And he was always heroically willing to cut off his nose to spite his face. Who cares if he *needed* that fish delivery? If it arrived five minutes late, Bigfoot waited until the driver unloaded it – then he sent it back. I saw him do this with gigantic, multi-ton dry-goods orders that were a bit late. And let me tell you, now I often do the same thing. Make the driver unload, then reload an entire order of canned goods, 35-pound flour sacks, peanut oils, juices, tomato paste and bulk sugar, and I can assure you – your stuff will start arriving on time. Fish not what you wanted? Let the driver go, then call them up and make them send a second truck to pick it up. You say there's twenty servings of product in every box? There had better be, because Bigfoot's gonna weigh it, count it, and record it every time.

Bigfoot's entire office, the last time I worked with him, was a vault with an actual foot-thick titanium steel door, interior bars, set into brick. From there he'd pore over invoices, plan his next moves, torment his purveyors, and send and receive emanations to and from the floor and kitchen. He didn't have to be on the floor all the time. The people who worked for Bigfoot were sure that he could sense what was going on. Think an evil thought, and he'd suddenly be there. Drop a tray and Bigfoot appears. Running low on soup? Bigfoot somehow feels it, as if the entire restaurant were simply an extension of his central nervous system.

A lot of his time was spent figuring out ways to make the restaurant run more efficiently, more smoothly, faster and cheaper. And one of the earmarks of a Bigfoot operation is the tiny design features: the conveniently located hot-water hose for bartenders to melt down their ice easily at the end of the night (into convenient drains, of course), the cute little plastic handles on any electrical plug near any station where the workers' hands might be wet. And everything is always easy to clean and easy to store. Pots hang from overhead racks, always in the same place.

Bottles at the bar are arranged in mirror image, radiating out from a central cash register. Careful consideration is taken with every tiny detail, from where employees store their shoes to custom-cut inserts for the steam table.

I can still walk into a West Village bar and tell immediately if the bar manager is a graduate of Bigfoot University. The bottles are arranged in the classic pattern, free (but spicy/salty) bar snacks are laid out, equidistant from one another, along a flawlessly clean, wiped and polished bar. Ashtrays are always empty. And more than likely, the juices are freshly squeezed. Bigfoot's Presidential Guard – in addition to their cleaning and tunneling duties – also squeezed cases of grapefruit, orange and lemon juice every night, keeping them in appropriate storage containers (glass *only*), as approved by Bigfoot.

Bigfoot's bar customers had every reason to love him. There was a house-approved buy-back policy. Bartenders were chosen for their personalities as well as their ability. A television was always readily at hand, football pool a must, and Bigfoot made regular visits to the bar, handing out box seats to Knicks, Yankees, Giants, Jets, Mets and Rangers to favored customers. On Super Bowl Sunday, if you'd plunked down a C-note for the Super Bowl pool, drinks were free, and food was brought in from the Second Avenue deli – a kosher smorgasbord replenished throughout the game.

As one might imagine, living under the thumb of such a micromanaging control freak could be tough. Most downtime among employees was spent talking about – you guessed it – Bigfoot. Stories swapped, theories floated, gripes exchanged. But Bigfoot knew. He had a near-supernatural sense of exactly when, at what precise moment, one of his employees had had enough. He could tell when the bullying, the relentless sarcasm, the constant, all-encompassing vigilance had become too exhausting. When one of his people was fed up with staying awake at night anticipating his likes and dislikes, was sick of charting his mood swings, was tired of feeling demeaned and beaten down after being asked, for instance, to clean out the grease trap, was ready to burst into tears and quit, then suddenly Bigfoot would appear with courtside seats for a play-off game, a restaurant warm-up jacket (given out only to Most Honored Veterans), or a present for the wife or girlfriend – something thoughtful like a Movado watch. He always waited until the last possible second, when you were ready to shave your head, climb a tower and start gunning down strangers, when you were ready to strip off your clothes and run barking into the street, to scream to the world that you'd *never never never* again work for that manipulative, Machiavellian psychopath. And he'd get you back on the team, often with a gesture as simple and inexpensive as a baseball cap or a T-shirt. The timing was what did it, that he *knew*. He *knew* just when to apply that well-timed pat on the back, the strangled and difficult-for-him 'Thank you for your good work' appreciation of your labors.

And there was also the knowledge that Bigfoot could help you if you asked. Need an apartment? He could help. A dental emergency? No problem. Lawyer? He could hook you up with the best. Need a nice ride to the beach? Maybe Bigfoot could lend you his Corvette, which he never drove. Or his vintage Caddy ragtop, which he never drove either.

But his greatest gift was the Bigfoot System, which I use still. *My* inventory sheets, for example, are set up like the master's: in clockwise, geographical order. Instead of hopping back and forth, counting and weighing vegetables alphabetically – or by type, like most sheets – I have my sheets laid out the way the food is laid out, allowing me to pass through my inventory in a comfortable, one-directional order, ticking off items. I *know* if an order has been called in, and if a particular item was, in fact, ordered – the telltale Bigfoot-Style notations appear. Nothing is left to chance. I can tell a Bigfoot restaurant from the street: the waiters are in comfortable clothes – 100 percent cotton oxfords or same-colored T-shirts, blue jeans or khakis, road-tested aprons for their order books, and multiple pens (God help you if you don't have a pen in Bigfootland); the cooks are in restaurant-owned and washed whites, the porters in telltale blue coveralls. The phone is always answered in the same way, whoever picks up. All pots and pans are scrubbed down to bare metal; I remember some in my time exploding in the dishwasher from metal fatigue, having been scraped down one time too many. (No problem, Bigfoot will call the company and demand a free replacement! *He* remembers that lifetime guarantee.)

The most important and lasting lessons I learned from Bigfoot were about personnel and personnel management – that I have to know *everything*, that I should *never* be surprised. He taught me the value of a good, solid and independently reporting intelligence network, providing regular and confirmable reports that can be verified and cross-checked with other sources. I need to know, you see. Not just what's happening in *my* kitchen, but across the street as well. Is my saucier unhappy? Is the chef across the street ready to make a pass, maybe take him away from me at an inopportune moment? *I need to know!* Is the saucier across the street unhappy? Maybe *he*'s available. I need to know that, too. Is the cute waitress who works Saturday nights screwing my broiler man? Maybe they've got a scam running: food going out without dupes! I have to know everything, you see. What might happen, what could happen, what will happen. And I have to be prepared for it, whatever it is. Staff problems, delivery problems, technical difficulties with equipment, I have to anticipate and be ready, always with something up my sleeve, somebody in the pipeline. My penetration agent in the competition's kitchen is getting hinkey about ratting out his chef? I need another agent in development. Just in case.

Prior Preparation Prevents Poor Performance, as they say in the army – and I always, always want to be ready. Just like Bigfoot.

THIRD COURSE

I MAKE MY BONES

FRESH OUT OF CIA, I returned to the city for good.

I actually knew a few things by now. During the two-year culinary program, I'd been commuting to a weekend job at a busy West Village saloon where I'd toiled away in a smoky, cockpit-sized kitchen, knocking out brunches and dinners. There had been two summers in Provincetown, which meant I was no longer completely useless on the line. In fact, when the chips were down, and the window was filling up with dupes, I could actually keep my mouth shut and sling food. I had moves. My hands were getting nice and ugly, just like I'd wanted, and I was eager to rise in the world.

On the strength of my diploma – and my willingness to work for peanuts – I landed a job almost right away at the venerable New York institution, the Rainbow Room, high atop Rockefeller Center. It was my first experience of the real Big Time, one of the biggest, busiest and best-known restaurants in the country. I was willing to do anything to prove myself, and when I got in that elevator to the sixty-fourth floor kitchen for the first time I felt as if I was blasting off to the moon.

The Rainbow Room at that time sat a little over 200. The Rainbow Grill sat about another 150. Add to that two lounges where food was available, *and* an entire floor of banquet rooms – all of it serviced simultaneously by a single, central à la carte kitchen – and you had some major league volume, as well as some major league cooks to go along with it.

The crew at the Room was a rough bunch, a motley assortment of Puerto Ricans, Italians, Dominicans, Swiss, Americans and a Basque or two. They were mostly older guys who'd worked in the hangar-sized kitchen forever, their jobs secured by a union whose only discernible benefits were guaranteed job security and an assured mediocrity of cuisine. These were some hard-case, full-grown, eight-cylinder bastards, none of whom cared about anything outside of their station; the Room management worked them like rented mules.

A long hot line of glowing flat-tops ran along one wall, flames actually roaring back up into a fire wall behind them. A few feet across, separated by a narrow, trench-like work space, ran an equally long stainless-steel counter, much of which was taken up by a vast, open steam table which was kept at a constant, rolling boil. What the cooks had to contend with, then, was a long, uninterrupted slot, with no air circulation, with nearly unbearable dry, radiant heat on one side and clouds of wet steam heat on the other. When I say unbearable, I mean they couldn't bear it; cooks would regularly pass out on the line and have to be dragged off to recuperate, a commis taking over the station until the stricken chef de partie recovered. There was so much heat coming off those ranges – especially when the center rings were popped for direct fire – that the filters in the overhead hoods would often burst into flames, inspiring a somewhat comical scene as the overweight Italian chef would hurl himself down the narrow line with a fire extinguisher, bowling over the cooks and tripping as he hurried to put out the flames before the central Ansel System went off and filled the entire kitchen with fire-suppressant foam.

It was a madhouse. The cooks worked without dupes. The expediter, a just-off-the-boat Italian with an indecipherably thick accent droned away constantly in an uninflected monotone through a microphone, calling out – presumably – orders and pick-ups. I can still hear him: 'Pickinguppa, one-ah vealuh Orloffah . . . and three sole Balmoralla. Orderingah, twenty-three beef Wellingtonna and seventeena chicka for the Belvedera

Suite . . . orderinga three crespelle toscana seg way . . . two a
steaka one a mediuma rare one-a mediuma.'

In the middle of 300 à la carte dinners, the cooks were
required to crank out enormous sit-down banquets of fully
plated appetizers and entrees for the private catering rooms.
'Pickinguppa five hunnerta beef Wellingtonna!' and the whole
line would break formation, drag long work tables to the center
of the kitchen and re-form as a production line like you'd expect
to see in an automobile assembly plant. Two cooks at one end of
the table would slice and slap, others would pour sauce from
giant, long-spouted coffeepots, and two more would drop
vegetables and garnish. At the other end of the table, a long
line of bolero-jacketed waiters would then clap down silver plate
covers, stack the entrees ten or more at a clip onto serving trays,
and ferry them like worker ants to the distant banquet rooms –
only to return a few moments later.

It was, as I've said, hot. Ten minutes into the shift, the cheap
polyester whites we all wore would be soaked through with
sweat, clinging to chest and back. All the cooks' necks and wrists
were pink and inflamed with awful heat rashes; the end-of-shift
clothing change in the Room's fetid, septic locker-rooms was a
gruesome panorama of dermatological curiosities. One saw
boils, pimples, ingrown hair, rashes, buboes, lesions, and skin
rot of a severity and variety you'd expect to see in some jungle
backwater. And the smell of thirty not very fastidious cooks –
their sodden work boots and sneakers, armpits, cologne, fungal
feet, rotten breath – and the ambient odor of moldering three-
day-old uniforms, long-forgotten pilfered food stashes hidden in
lockers to which the combination was unknown, all combined to
form a noxious, penetrating cloud that followed you home, and
made you smell as if you'd been rolling around in sheep guts.

The atmosphere was not unlike a Pinero play, very jailhouse,
with a lot of grab-ass, heated argument, hypermacho posturing
and drunken ranting. Two burly men who'd just as soon kill you
as look at you, when talking to each other, would often nestle a
hand tenderly next to the testicles of the other, as if to say, 'I am

so *not* gay – I can even do *this*!' The common language was a mix of Nueva Yorkeno Spanish, Italian and pidgin English. The Spanish and Italians, as is often the case, had no problem understanding each other, but when speaking 'English', one had to conform to the style book: one didn't say, 'That's my knife.' One said instead, 'Is for me, the knife.'

My own personal tormentor for the first few weeks was the chef de garde-manger and shop steward, a big, ugly Puerto Rican with a ruined face named Luis. Luis considered frequent explorations of my young ass with his dirty paws to be a perk of his exalted position; at every opportunity, he'd take a running swat between my cheeks, driving his fingers as far up my ass as my checked pants would allow. I endured this in the spirit of good fun for a while – until I'd had enough. There *was* a lot of ass-grabbing and ball-fondling going on, after all, and I *did* want desperately to be one of the guys. But Luis had generally knocked off a half a fifth of cooking brandy by ten each morning, and as his drunken advances threatened to become actual penetration, I was moved to take drastic action.

I was making filling for crespelle toscana in the huge, tilting brazier one morning, stirring mushrooms, diced tongue, ham, turkey, spinach and béchamel with a big, heavyweight, curved Dexter meat fork, a nice patina of rust on its blunt and twisted tines. Out of the corner of my eye, I could see Luis coming, his right hand swinging back for a deep wallop between my cheeks. I decided right then I'd had enough; I was gonna straighten this drunken pig out. I quickly, but subtly, turned the big meat fork around and down, so the business end was pointing backwards. I timed my move for maximum impact. When Luis came in with his hand, I came down with the fork as hard as I could, sinking both tines deep into his knuckles with a satisfying crunch. Luis screamed like a burning wolverine and fell to his knees, two wide holes – one on each side of his middle knuckle – already welling up with blood. He managed to get up, the whole kitchen crew screaming and hooting with laughter, his hand blowing up to the size of a catcher's mitt and taking on an interesting black-and-blue and red color. After a visit to one of the fine, union-sponsored medical clinics, the hand was even larger, looking like a gauze-wrapped football and leaking yellow antiseptic.

My life improved immediately. The other cooks began addressing me as an equal. Nobody grabbed my ass anymore. People smiled and patted me on the back when I came to work in the morning. I had made my bones.

My job at the Room, initially, was to prepare and serve a lunch buffet for about a hundred or so regular members of the Rockefeller Center Luncheon Club – mostly geriatric business types from the building who assembled in the Rainbow Grill every day. I had to prepare a cold buffet and two hot entrees, which I'd then serve and maintain from noon to three. This was no easy feat, as the buffet was comprised solely of leftovers from the previous night's service. I'd begin each morning at seven-thirty pushing a little cart with wobbly casters down the line, where the cooks would hurl hunks of roast pork, end cuts, crocks of cooked beans, overcooked pasta, blanched vegetables and remnants of sauces at me. My job was to find a way to make all this look edible.

I have to say, I did pretty well, using every dirty trick I'd learned at CIA. I turned leftover steaks into say, Salade de Bœuf en Vinaigrette, transformed dead pasta and veggies into festive pasta salads, made elaborately aspic'd and decorated trays out of sliced leftover roast. I made mousses, pâtés, galantines, and every other thing I could think of to turn the scrapings into something our aged but wealthy clientele would gum down without complaint. And then, of course, I'd don a clean jacket and apron, cram one of those silly coffee filter-like chef's hats on my head, and stand by a voiture, slicing and serving the hot entrees.

'Would you care for some Tongue en Madère?' I'd ask through clenched teeth, my face a rictus of faux cheer as I'd have to repeat and repeat for the hard-of-hearing captains of industry who ate the same spread of sauce-disguised leftovers every lunch and for whom the hot entree was clearly the high-

light of their day. 'Boiled beef with horseradish sauce, sir?' I'd
chirp. 'And would you care for a steamed potato with that?'

The Irish waitresses who worked the Luncheon Club with me
were more like nurses after years of this. They had nicknames for
our regulars: 'Dribbling Dick' for one ninety-year-old who had a
hard time keeping his food in his mouth, 'Stinky' for an apparently incontinent banker, 'Shakey Pete' for the guy who needed
his food cut for him, and so on. There were famous names in
banking and industry with us every day, all New York laid out
below us beyond the floor-to-ceiling picture windows – eating
garbage at the top of the world.

Since shanking Luis, I'd been increasingly considered to be a
person of substance. The chef, an affable, blue-eyed Italian
named Quinto, now felt free to take full advantage of my youth,
my resilience and my willingness to work for minimum wage.
After coming in at seven, taking care of my retirement village
upstairs in the Club, breaking down the buffet (and saving what
I could for re-use tomorrow), I was now regularly called on to
stick around and help prep for the massive night-time banquets
and cocktail parties. Absenteeism being rampant in our little
corner of the Worker's Paradise, Local 6, I was taken aside more
and more at the last minute and asked to remain until midnight,
filling in on the hot line. I worked grill station, sauté, fish station
– at first only as a commis, hunting and fetching, covering the
cooks on breaks, reloading reach-ins, straining sauces, mopping
brows, running numbers to the house bookie, collecting bets,
and so on. But in no time I was working stations alone, and
keeping up my end nicely.

I made thousands and thousands of baby quiches for parties,
and gristly little kebabs from the tough, nearly inedible chain
that runs along the side of the beef tenderloin. I peeled 75 pounds
of shrimp at a clip, seared Wellingtons, made chicken liver
mousse (our version of foie gras), and in the course of my labors
as general dogsbody, got to know the far recesses and dark
corners of the vast Room facilities.

I also got to know the heavy hitters: the silent butcher and his assistant, the mercurial baby-faced chef pâtissier, the doomed-looking night saucier. And most memorably, Juan, the sixtyish day broiler man, a fierce, trash-talking Basque who, I swear, I saw one time sewing up a very bad knife wound on his hand – right on the line – with a sewing needle and thread, muttering all the while, as he pushed through the flaps of skin with the point, 'I am a *tough* (skronk!) . . . mother *fucker* (skronk!). I am a *tough* son of *beetch*! (skronk!). I am *tough* . . . mother (skronk!) . . . *fucker*!' Juan was also famous for allegedly following up a bad finger wound with a self-inflicted amputation. After catching a finger in an oven door, he had consulted the union benefit list for amount given for victims of 'partial amputation', and decided to cash in by lopping off the dangling portion. Whether this story was true or not mattered little to me; it was entirely believable after getting to know Juan. He may have been over sixty, but he lifted stockpots without help, wielded the largest knife I'd ever seen, and generally kicked more ass more quickly than any of the younger cooks.

There was a procession of Swiss, Austrian and American sous-chefs, none of whom lasted for more than a few weeks. They were quickly discouraged by our veteran crew from even attempting to impose order or quality control or change of any kind. The lifers like Juan and Luis would tell these eager young neophytes to go fuck themselves right to their faces; the intractable underlings who looked to them as role models would simply feign agreement and then do what they'd always done anyway. Short of murder, you really couldn't be fired. One beefy German sous-chef, after taking more than his share of lip from a lowly commis named Mosquito, had the poor judgment to grab him by the throat, lift him off the floor and shake him. The ensuing storm brought in the moustache Petes from the local, two sinister-looking guys in long coats who'd show up to settle disputes. Sous-chef, commis, chef and all holed up in a room for half an hour, after which the sous emerged, tail between his legs and suitably apologetic, having found out who the bosses really were. Like all his predecessors, he disappeared soon after.

I began to move more freely through the halls, back stairways, offices, dining and storage areas of the Rainbow Room. I made an interesting discovery. There was, in an unused area, a narrow passage through stacked tables, where employees could actually crawl out an open window. On my union-mandated fifteen-minute breaks, I would sit out on a narrow precipice, sixty-four flights up, my legs dangling over the edge, one arm wrapped around a sash, smoking weed with the dishwashers, Central Park and upper Manhattan splayed out before me. The observation deck on the roof was open as well, for a little mid-shift sunbathing.

If you looked carefully, there were other perks. There was a healthy sports book up and running – and side bets aplenty. When a Panamanian and a Dominican were duking it out for the world middleweight title, there was always an employee willing to bet big bucks along national pride lines – whatever the Vegas odds were. A Puerto Rican has a hard time betting on a boxer from Ecuador, even if he's heavily favored. Sensibly, however, I'd buy a case of beer for the whole crew with a portion of my winnings, so there was never any ill will. Many of the Spanish-speaking members of the crew took part in an unusual 'banking' scheme where each week all the members of a large group would sign over all their paychecks to one guy. The recipient was selected on a rotating basis, and the way it worked, I gathered, was that for about two months or so everybody squeaked by, doing their best to make do without a check, spending little . . . until the day it was their turn, at which point they came into thousands of dollars and could spend like drunken sailors. This practice made no sense to me. It also required an extraordinary amount of trust in one's fellow cooks. I did not share my comrades' confidence that Luis, for instance, wouldn't skip town on a drunk after getting his big payday, and leave the others in the lurch. I held on to my meager paycheck. I had no time to spend it anyway.

One foggy night around ten, with only a few customers left in the main dining room, an electric current seemed to run through the floor staff. There was a sudden gang-rush to the upstairs bus station, where one could just barely see and hear what was going on in the Room. 'Frank is here! *Frank* is here!' was the battle cry. Even the cooks abandoned their stations to see what the commotion was about. Sure enough, the Man Himself had come to dinner: Frank Sinatra was in the house – and *he was singing!* Sinatra had swung by with a posse of thick-necked pals, ordered up some bottles and snacks, and now, backed by the house orchestra, was belting out tunes to an awe-struck audience of about twenty customers who had been lucky enough to linger over dessert. These few tourists who, up to now, must have been bemoaning the bad weather, the lack of visibility ruining the famous view, the empty dining room and the miserable food, were suddenly the luckiest bastards in New York. Sinatra, having a good time apparently, sang for quite a while. He was still there when I knocked off work.

Other celebrity sightings included a well-known member of a Sicilian fraternal organization – in the 'entertainment and financial services sector' – who made an impromptu visit to the kitchen for a few words with our kindly Neapolitan chef. I saw a fifty go into poor Quinto's chest pocket, with an affectionate slap on the cheek. Now the hapless bastard was committed to making 'Gnocchi genovese . . . like I used to get'. Gnocchi genovese was *not* on our regular menu, and I doubt that the chef had actually cooked *anything* – much less gnocchi and meat sauce – from scratch in years. Quinto was more like an air-traffic controller than a cook, but he'd taken the man's money (not that he'd had a choice) and he spent the next hour, in the middle of a busy dinner service, spooning batch after batch of gnocchi into simmering water, his hands shaking with fear and tears streaming down his face, as one batch after another failed to meet his expectations. I don't remember the finished product going out, but the chef showed up to work the next day, so I imagine the customer was happy.

Another memorable evening was the RFK charity tennis tournament. The whole place was taken over by actors, politicians, famous faces, and long-haired Kennedy kids in tuxes and basketball sneakers. Secret Service agents and sniffer dogs combed the kitchen for fissionable material and hidden weapons. I was surprised when they didn't find any. The highlight of the event was a mishap involving honored guest Dina Merrill, sitting near the head of the banquet table with hubby Cliff Robertson. One of our veteran waiters lost control of an entire tray of bubbling tortellini alfredo, depositing an upended pile of Parmesan-laced heavy cream and pasta directly on Ms Merrill's coif. There was weeping and rending of garments in the kitchen that night, I can tell you, the offending waiter nearly suicidal with fear, shame and grief. He was part of a father–son waiting team, Dad having been relegated to running coffee orders for his golden years, and son was despondent. I don't know what he was crying about; it *was* a union house, after all.

As in any large restaurant operation, there were tiny centers of power, fiefdoms, little empires that seemed to exist outside of the normal hierarchy. Gianni was the pastry chef, and his shop, set apart from the main kitchen, was a relative fortress of solitude and civility in a sea of chaos. I worked with Gianni every once in a while – just to escape the heat and frenzied pace of the main kitchen, and because the quality of life was significantly better in Gianni's tiny kingdom. I could, thanks to Chef Bernard at CIA, throw together a decent soufflé when called upon to do so, and I was good at decorating and inscribing cakes, for which there was a lot of call. The Gianni crew consisted of a taciturn Swiss who worked three other jobs and always looked ready to die from fatigue, and an aged ex-Wehrmacht corporal with dyed red hair and moustache who loved to regale me with stories of Weimar era perversions: 'Zey vould feed ze girls bananas,' he said once, leering and winking as he described a purported club for coprophiles. 'Hitler and Goering . . . yah, Goering, zey would go these places.' Daytime with Gianni involved a lot of very fast, very hard work, mostly production–cake assembly, wrapping of the ever-present Wellingtons in pastry dough, rolls, pastries, stacks of crêpes for crespelle, cookies, the sectioning of fruit for later dipping in caramelized sugar. All the while, Gianni urged us on with cries of '*Cha! Cha! Via!* Let's go!'

But the atmosphere in Gianniland was remarkably happy-go-lucky. At the beginning of the workday a waiter would appear with an urn of steaming hot espresso, and we would actually sit down for a nice demi-tasse, accompanied by homemade sticky buns. Even in the middle of full-bore production, Gianni found time to hurl profiteroles at the skaters sixty-four flights down in the Rock Center rink, all of us having a good laugh when he scored a direct hit. And Gianni was a skilled raconteur. His romantic adventures and misadventures made for much enter-tainment. Though married, he was relentless in his pursuit of every woman in the restaurant – most of them looked like whichever was the uglier of Cagney and Lacey (the later episodes when they bulked up to cruiserweights). He was always be-fuddled when one of them would resist his affections: 'So I saya to thees girl, "I bring you out to nice dinner which I *pay* . . . and I drive you in nice car – a *Buick* . . . and you no wanna fuck me?" I don't unnerstan!' He was kind of charming, totally untrust-worthy, conspiratorial, possessing mysterious juice with the ownership, able to operate completely outside the normal chain of command. What I loved about Gianni, though, was that at the stroke of four, when the day-shift ended, we all sat down and had a lovely meal of prosciutto, arugula, sliced tomato and mozzarella on fresh-baked Italian bread, often accompanied by a nice bottle of red wine and more espresso.

Where Gianni got this stuff, I have no idea, particularly since edible food was decidedly *not* a perk enjoyed by the rest of the staff and kitchen crew. In the main kitchen, and for the floor staff, the 'family meal' was uniformly awful. Hunks of silver-skin-covered breast flaps of veal – not even braised until tender, just poached grey with a few slices of onion – accompanied by leftover pellets of gluey steam-table rice or two-day-old pasta. There might be some inattentively chopped fried peppers and onions if you were lucky. The Big Event was when one of the cooks was allowed to thaw out a few boxes of freezer-burned sweet sausages, lovingly referred to by the cooks as pingas. This was everybody's favorite meal, and the excitement and enthusiasm with which my comrades-in-arms scarfed these things down was truly tragic to watch. Compared to Raft Day, however, the pingas were indeed a luxury. The Room prep area always had three gigantic steam kettles filled with a dark, all-purpose stock, simmering endlessly under a 'raft' of ground beef, meat scraps, chicken bones, turkey carcasses, the trimmings of vegetables, carrot peelings and egg shells. When stuck for gruel, the cooks would actually skim this floating compost off the surface, toss it with a little tomato sauce and dead pasta and serve it to the inexplicably grateful staff.

It was but one of many food crimes I witnessed and took part in during my time at the Rainbow Room. During service, châteaubriands – big hunks of beef tenderloin for two – if ordered well done, were routinely thrown into the deep-fryer until crispy, then tossed into an oven to incinerate further until pick up. Everything was seared off in advance. When the expeditor called for the order, one simply heated the plate – vegetable, garnish and all – under a salamander, drizzled a little sauce over the item and sent it out to the unsuspecting rubes. Any magic I'd imagined about a big-time fancy New York kitchen was replaced by a grim pride in creative expediency and the technical satisfaction of being fast enough to keep up, getting away with trickery, deception and disguise. 'An ounce of sauce covers a multitude of sins,' as we used to say.

I didn't care what atrocities we were inflicting on a credulous public, lulled into docility by our spectacular view, our swank appointments, big band and high prices. I was putting up serious numbers, and holding my own with the best of the lifers. I could destroy and serve a nice piece of veal or a Dover sole as fast as, if not faster than any of them. I was working every station in the kitchen, keeping up with the ugliest, meanest twenty-year veterans anyone back in Provincetown had even dreamed of. I was a line stud, an all-around guy, a man's man. I was on top of the world.

On the other hand, I was tired. By now, I was going in to work at 7:30 A.M. and working straight through until midnight almost every day. As soon as I'd finish up in the Luncheon Club or the pastry shop, the chef seemed always to be wanting to take me aside and squeeze me for another night on the hot-line. After weeks of this, and still not taking home over 200 dollars on payday, I finally balked. Unable to convince me, the chef summoned me for a private chat with the boss, a sinister Italian with yet another thick accent. The boss looked up at me from his desk, fixing me in a shark like gaze and said, 'I understand you don't want to help us tonight by staying late?'

I was tired, I explained, and in love, I added, hoping to appeal to that romantic Mediterranean nature I'd read and heard about. 'My girlfriend,' I said, 'I don't see her anymore . . . and I miss her . . . I have,' I added, 'a life . . . outside of this place.' I went on to describe going home each night to a sleeping girl, rolling exhausted into the sheets, still stinking from work, and how I arose at six with the girl still asleep, never exchanging so much as a word before leaving for work again, for yet another double. This was no good for a relationship, I said.

'Look at me,' said my boss, as if the nice suit and the haircut and the desk explained everything. 'I am married ten years to my wife.' He smiled. 'I work all the time. I never see her . . . she never sees me.' He paused now to show me some teeth, his eyes growing more penetrating and a little scary. 'We are very happy.'

What my boss meant by this little glimpse into his soul, I have no idea. But he impressed me. I worked the double, figuring maybe this was what was required: total dedication. Forget the loved ones. Forget the outside world. There *is* no life other than this life. I didn't spend much time trying to figure it out. The man scared me. Years later, I got another perspective on things. I opened the *Post* to see a photo of my old boss's wife, draped over the awning of a Chinese restaurant on the Upper East Side. She'd apparently performed a double-gainer from the window of her high-rise apartment and not quite made it to the pavement. So I guess she wasn't that happy after all.

All in all, I was at the Rainbow Room for about a year and a half before elections for shop steward came around. When one of the garde-manger guys suggested I run for the position, I was only too happy to give it a shot. Luis, after all, was a disgrace. I was, by now, an accepted, even popular, member of the Rainbow Room crew, a dues-paying, card-carrying union member, and as a young, semi-educated firebrand with a couple of years of college under my belt, a fine private school vocabulary, a culinary degree and a predilection for left-wing politics, I assumed I'd be a welcome addition to the restaurant workers' union – a young man with the workers' interests at heart, a fighter for the downtrodden, an activist who could get things done, someone who could lead and inspire, help to achieve better working conditions and benefits for one of the largest union shops in the country. Certainly the union biggies would be pleased to see the dipsomaniacal Luis replaced by a young go-getter like me! And I wanted to see the mysterious 'contract', the Rosetta Stone of our union benefits. According to our little union books, any union member could inspect this important document at any time – yet none of us had ever seen it. Our rights as employees of the Rainbow Room, as negotiated by our duly elected representatives and officers of the union, remained a matter of rumor and conjecture. I wanted to clap eyes on this thing. So I ran.

I won handily. Luis, strangely, didn't even put up a fight. I figured that my shanking him with the meat fork had something to do with his reluctance to mount a campaign, but I was wrong about that. After a quick vote, I was the shop steward.

You'd think the union would be happy about this development, or at least curious, with an energetic young organizer in their midst. I scheduled a meeting with the union president, looking forward to commiserating about the Imperialist Jackboot on the Necks of the Workers, and the Struggle Against the Controllers of the Means of Production. When finally I sat down with the president of Local 6 (yet another Italian with a thick accent), he was oddly unenthusiastic. He looked up sleepily at me from behind the desk of his dark office, as if I were a delivery boy bringing him a sandwich. When I asked him if I could, as shop steward, familiarize myself with The Contract, so that I might better serve our members, the president fiddled with his cufflinks and said, 'I seem to have . . . temporarily . . . misplaced it.' It was clear from his inflection and posture that he didn't give a fuck whether I believed him or not. After a few more minutes of near total silence and zero enthusiasm on the president's part, I got the hint and skulked back to work empty-handed.

The next day, someone from management came by and made an unusually frank suggestion: if I wanted a long, successful and, most important, healthy career in the restaurant business, perhaps I should step down and let that nice Luis continue his good works as shop steward. It would, I was assured, 'be in everybody's best interest.' He didn't have to tell me twice. I made a few discreet inquiries of a few trusted veterans and quickly resigned from my newly elected position. Luis once again picked up the reins of power, as if he'd known all along what would happen. I didn't raise a stink and a few weeks later left the Rainbow Room entirely.

I'd seen *On The Waterfront*. And I learned fast.

THE HAPPY TIME

IN 1981, MY GOOD friend from high school, and later Provincetown, Sam G., became the chef de cuisine of Work Progress. A
once trendy restaurant on Spring Street in SoHo, the place had
fallen on hard times. It was now under new ownership and
Sammy – one of *us*! – was in charge of putting the kitchen
together. It was what a lot of us had been waiting for, our own
thing, and the call went out to all our old cronies. From
Provincetown came Dimitri, finally enticed from off-season exile
at the tip of the Cape by excited promises of culinary history in
the making. I would share sous-chef responsibilities with my
mentor. From West Village saloons, we recruited every young,
pot-smoking, head-banging hooligan we'd ever worked with,
filling their heads with dreams of glory. 'We're forming . . . like
. . . a rock and roll band, man, an all-star group of culinary
superstars . . . kinda like Blind Faith. We're going to tear a new
asshole into the New York restaurant scene.'

We fancied ourselves the most knowledgeable and experienced young Turks in town, and our hearts were filled with hope
and the promise of enviable futures. We thought we were the
only cooks in New York who could quote from the *Larousse
Gastronomique* and *Répertoire de la Cuisine*, who knew who
Vatel, Carême and Escoffier were, what Bocuse, Vergé and
Guérard were doing across the water, and we were determined
to replicate their successes and their fame. There was no one on
the horizon we could see who could touch us.

Okay – there was one guy. Patrick Clark. Patrick was the chef of the red-hot Odeon in nascent Tribeca, a neighborhood that seemed not to have existed until Patrick started cooking there. We followed his exploits with no small amount of envy.

'Born under a broiler,' people said.

'He's screwing Gael Greene,' claimed others.

There were a lot of stories, most of them, like most chefs' gossip, apocryphal. But what we did know about Patrick for sure impressed the hell out of us. He was kind of famous; he was big and black; most important, he was an *American*, one of us, not some cheese-eating, surrender specialist Froggie. Patrick Clark, whether he would have appreciated it or not, was our hometown hero, our Joe Di Maggio – a shining example that *it could be done*.

As we assembled for menu-planning sessions, the process of getting our kitchen up and running began. We formed in our already dope-fogged brains a plan, a notional *movement* even, that would sweep away all the moribund old European chefs and dazzle the world with our New American act . . . as soon as we figured out what that was.

We even planned a hit, a sort of Night of the Sicilian Vespers thing, where we'd straighten them all out in one fell swoop. Back in those days, the older European chefs – Soltner and his generation – would attend an annual Chefs' Race, a downhill ski event at Hunter Mountain where contestants would bomb the slopes in full kitchen whites, toques strapped to their chins. Our plan was to lurk in the woods at the side of the trail, also dressed in whites, but luridly adorned with skull-and-crossbones painted in chicken blood. We'd intercept the geezer contingent as they waddled down the slope and whack them rudely with our ski poles, maybe bombard them with foie gras. We were younger and (we assumed) better skiers, so we would have no problem fending off any counterattack. We believed this would be a bold and memorable way to announce ourselves to the world – until the coke ran out and our enthusiasm with it.

I still laugh out loud when I remember our earnest strategy

sessions. However cruel and pointless and stupid the idea might have been, it was a measure of our faith in ourselves. Soltner, of course, was a god to us; the idea of whacking him upside the head with my ski poles, or running over his Rossignols with my rented skis was always unthinkable when lucid.

The new owners of Work Progress, our putative masters, were a textbook example of People Who Should Never Own A Restaurant. There were two brothers – one half-smart, the other genuinely dumb – who'd gotten a few bucks from Mommy and Daddy, along with their partner, a slightly more cognizant college friend who could actually read a P and L sheet and crunch a few numbers. Their principal business was investing in off-Broadway shows. As this, apparently, wasn't unprofitable enough, they'd chosen the restaurant business as a way to lose their money more quickly and assuredly.

From the get-go, Sammy, Dimitri and I managed to intimidate the partners right out of their own restaurant. At every suggestion from this novice triumvirate, we'd snort with contempt, roll our eyes with world-weary derision and shoot down whatever outrage – be it tablecloths, flatware or menu items – they'd come up with. We were merciless in our naked contempt for every idea they came in with, and we out-snobbed, out-maneuvered and out-bullied them at every turn.

As the three principal masterminds of this culinary utopia were all P-Town veterans, we constructed our downstairs kitchen along familiar lines – as a faithful re-creation of the kitchens we'd grown up in: insular, chaotic, drenched in drugs and alcohol, and accompanied constantly by loud rock and roll music. When the restaurant opened, we'd begin every shift with a solemn invocation of the first moments of *Apocalypse Now*, our favorite movie. Emulating the title sequence, we'd play the soundtrack album, choppers coming in low and fast, the whirr of the blades getting louder and more unearthly, and just before Jim Morrison kicked in with the first few words, 'This is the end, my brand-new friend . . . the end . . .' we'd soak the entire range-top with brandy and ignite it, causing a huge, napalm-like fireball to rush up into the hoods – just like in the movie when the tree-line goes up. If our boobish owners and newly hired floor staff weren't already thoroughly spooked by our antics, then they were by this act.

We fought all the time, Sam, Dimitri and I. Waving our cookbooks at each other, we'd squabble endlessly over the 'correct' way to prepare certain dishes. We teased, poked, prodded, sulked, conspired and competed. We *wanted* to be the best, we wanted to be different, but at the same time, correct. We yearned to bring honor to our clan, and in that vein, we came up with the looniest, most ambitious menu our super-heated, endorphin-overloaded brains could agree on, a sort of *Greatest Hits of Our Checkered Careers So Far* collection. French classics sat side-by-side with Portuguese squid stew, my Tante Jeanne's humble salade de tomates, dishes we'd lifted out of cookbooks, stolen from other chefs, remembered seeing on TV. There were Wellfleet oysters on the halfshell, oysters Mitcham (in honor of Howard), there was a pasta dish from Mario's – a sort of taglierini with trail-mix and anchovies as I recall – scallops in sorrel sauce (from Bocuse maybe?), calves' liver with raspberry vinegar sauce, swordfish with black beans and white rice, pompano en papillotte, my mom's crème renversée . . .

We were high all the time, sneaking off to the walk-in at every opportunity to 'conceptualize'. Hardly a decision was made without drugs. Pot, quaaludes, cocaine, LSD, psilocybin mushrooms soaked in honey and used to sweeten tea, Seconal, Tuinal, speed, codeine and, increasingly, heroin, which we'd send a Spanish-speaking busboy over to Alphabet City to get. We worked long hours and took considerable pride in our efforts – the drugs, we thought, having little effect on the end-product. That was what the whole life we were in was about, we believed: to work *through* the drugs, the fatigue, the lack of sleep, the pain, to show no visible effects. We might be tripping out on blotter acid, sleepless for three days and halfway through a bottle of Stoli, but we were *professionals*, goddammit! We didn't let it affect our line work. And we were happy, truly happy, like

Henry V's lucky few, a band of brothers, ragged, slightly debauched warriors, who anticipated nothing less than total victory – an Agincourt of the mind and stomach.

We were pretty busy initially, and along with the young protégés who held us in something like awe, Sam, Dimitri and I would work all day and late into the night. When the restaurant closed, we'd take over the bar, drinking Cristal – which we'd buy at cost – and running fat rails of coke from one end of the bar to the other, then crawling along on all-fours to snort them. The cuter and more degenerate members of the floor staff would hang with us, so there was a lot of humping in the dry-goods area and on the banquettes, 50-pound flour sacks being popular staging areas for after-work copulation. We'd bribed the doormen and security people of all the local night-clubs and rock and roll venues with steak sandwiches and free snacks, so that after we'd finished with our pleasures at the Work Progress bar, we'd bounce around from club to club without waiting on line or paying admission. A squadron of punk rocker junkie guitar heroes ate for free at Work Progress – so we got free tickets and backstage passes to the Mudd Club, CBGB, Tier Three, Hurrah, Club 57 and so on. And when the clubs closed it was off to after-hours where we'd drink and do more drugs until, weather permitting, we'd hit the seven o'clock train to Long Beach. We'd finish the last of our smack on the train, then pass out on the beach. Whichever one of us woke from the nod would roll the others over to avoid an uneven burn. When we finally arrived back at work, sand in our hair, we looked tanned, rested and ready.

We considered ourselves a tribe. As such, we had a number of unusual customs, rituals and practices all our own. If you cut yourself in the Work Progress kitchen, tradition called for maximum spillage and dispersion of blood. One squeezed the wound till it ran freely, then hurled great gouts of red spray on the jackets and aprons of comrades. We *loved* blood in our kitchen. If you dinged yourself badly, it was no disgrace; we'd stencil a little cut-out shape of a chef knife under your station to commemorate the event. After a while, you'd have a little row of these things, like a fighter pilot. The house cat – a mouse-killer – got her own stencil (a tiny mouse shape) sprayed on the wall by her water bowl, signifying confirmed kills.

Departing cooks and favored waiters, on their last day of employment, were invited to nail their grotty work shoes to a Wall of Fame by Sammy's cellar office. As time went on, row after row of moldering work boots, shoes and sneakers were pounded into the wall, a somewhat grim reminder of departed friends. On slow nights – and there were, disconcertingly, a growing number of these – we'd have fun with food color and sweet dough. Dimitri, it turned out, was remarkably adept at crafting life-like fingers, toes and sexual organs from basic ingredients. He'd fashion frighteningly realistic severed thumbs – skin rudely shredded at one end, bone fragments made from leek white projecting from the wound – and we'd leave these things around for unsuspecting waiters and managers to find. A waiter would open a reach-in in the morning to find a leaking, torn fingertip, Band-Aid still attached, pinioned to a slice of Wonderbread with a frilled toothpick. A floor manager would be called down to the kitchen in the middle of a dinner shift to find one of us standing by a bloody cutting board, red-smeared side-towel wrapped around a hand, and as they approached, one of Dimitri's grisly fingers would drop onto his foot. We experimented constantly, finding to our delight that not only did the sweet dough *look* like flesh when shaped and colored correctly, but it *drew flies* like the real thing! Left overnight at room temperature, Dimitri's fake digits could develop into a truly horrifying spectacle.

Eventually, when every member of the staff was thoroughly inured to the sight of a severed, fly-covered penis in the urinal, or finding a bloody finger in his apron pocket, we moved on to even greater atrocities. One night, with his full cooperation, we stripped Dimitri naked, spattered and filled his ears, nose and mouth with stage blood, and wrapped him in Saran Wrap before helping him into a chest freezer in the dark, rear storage area of the restaurant, his limbs arranged in an unnaturally contorted pose – as if he'd been rudely dumped there post-mortem. We then called the manager on the intercom, asking first if he'd seen Dimitri. We hadn't seen him in hours, we explained, and we were worried. Then we asked the poor bastard if he'd be kind enough to grab a box of shrimp out of the freezer for us, as we were short-handed, Dimitri being missing and all, and four tables going out at once. I think you can imagine what the manager experienced: hurrying back to the dank corner of the cellar, a single, bare light-bulb illuminating the chest freezer; he lifts the lid, only to find the nude, fishbelly-white, blood-splattered corpse of our missing comrade staring up at him with dead eyes through a thin layer of plastic wrap, the beginnings of a light frost under the film making the already gruesome scene even more terrifyingly real.

We ended up having to give the guy a shot of ammonia inhaler; his knees buckled and he was unable to return to work for over an hour. Dimitri, of course, caught a terrible cold for his efforts, but it was worth it: the manager left shortly after – and he didn't bother to nail up his work boots on our Wall of Fame. But we cared little for managers or owners – or customers for that matter.

By now, unsurprisingly, our restaurant was rapidly failing. I began to see, for the first time, what I would later recognize as 'Failing Restaurant Syndrome', an affliction that causes owners to flail about looking for a quick fix, a fast masterstroke that will 'turn things around', cure all their ills, reverse the already irreversible trend toward insolvency. We tried New Orleans Brunch – complete with Dixieland band. We tried a prix fixe menu, a Sunday night buffet, we advertised, we hired a publicist. Each successive brainstorm was more counterproductive than the one before. All of this floundering about and concept-tinkering only further demoralized an already demoralized staff.

When the paychecks started bouncing, and the vendors started to put us on COD, the owners called in the restaurant consultants. Even then, we knew what that meant: the consultants usually arrive just ahead of the repo men and the marshals. It was the death knell. We had tried. We had failed. Naturally, we held the owners responsible. It was a tough spot, the ambiance was no good, the music in the dining room sucked, the waiters weren't well trained . . . we tried to console ourselves with the usual excuses. But the truth was, we just weren't good enough. Our food, while charming to some, was unappealing to most. We did not commit seppuku. Sam and Dimitri stayed on, determined to go down with the ship.

But my cousin had hooked me up with my very first chef job, at a spanking-new but already troubled boîte in the theater district and I jumped at the offer. I felt bad about leaving my friends behind. And I had the beginnings of a very nasty little heroin habit from all the dope I'd been sniffing – but hey! I was about to become a chef!

CHEF OF THE FUTURE!

I WAS TWENTY-TWO YEARS old and the chef of a new theater district restaurant on West 46th Street (Restaurant Row). As would become something of a recurring theme in my career, I was following close on the heels of the departed opening chef – who'd turned out, it was said, to be an alcoholic psychopath, a compulsive liar and a thief. I, it was hoped, was the solution to the problem: a fresh-faced, eager kid just out of culinary school, who would respond to my novice owners' wishes, and was willing and capable of turning an already bad situation around.

Tom H., as the place was called, was a classic vanity/boutique-type operation. Named for one of its owners, it was a small, glass and crushed velvet jewelbox of a place on the ground floor of a three-story brownstone. Tom, the principal owner, had been a clothing designer, and with Fred, his longtime lover, had been a popular host to his many famous friends in the theater, fashion, music and film industries. Tom and Fred were the beloved hosts of hundreds of well-remembered dinner parties. They were genuinely lovely, intelligent, warm-hearted and funny older guys who cooked well, had impeccable taste and were considered (rightly) to be wonderful, charming and entertaining hosts – naturals, it had been said, for the restaurant business, especially a restaurant in the heart of the theater district where they knew and were liked by so many.

Tom was famous among his wide circle for his meat loaf, his jalapeño corn pudding, and Fred for his dill bread and jalapeño jelly, and in spite of the fact that meat loaf was a tad lower in the hierarchy of menu items than I would have liked – I was still the *chef*, and nominally in charge of *my own* kitchen – I was not unhappy about continuing with these cherished signature dishes. The meat loaf got a lot of press from friendly gossip columnists, and in the first months at Tom's, limos full of famous people lined up outside to try the stuff: John and Angelica Huston, Liv Ullmann, José Quintero, Glenda Jackson, Chita Rivera, Lauren Bacall come to mind.

The entire staff outside of the kitchen was gay, a situation I was entirely comfortable with after Vassar, Provincetown, the West Village and SoHo. The gossipy, self-effacing, overtly queer atmosphere was not only fun but, in many ways, completely in line with the gossipy, self-effacing, overtly depraved world of chefs and cooks. The waiters and bartenders could always be counted on for funny personal anecdotes of sexual misadventures – particularly as this was the early '80s – and they were always willing to share, in hilarious and clinical detail, their excesses of the previous night.

Our bar crowd, however, the guys you saw when you first walked in the door at Tom's, were almost uniformly like their hosts, older gay men. The floor staff and bartenders, far younger and hunkier, uncharitably referred to the restaurant as a 'wrinkle room' and made much fun of the somewhat sad, even desperate longings of some of our clientele. We may have been in the gossip columns a lot, and dinners, when I arrived, were still fairly busy for pre- and post-theater, but Tom's was decidedly *not* hot – not with an average age of sixty staking out the bar making goo-goo eyes at the bartender.

We were busy for pre-theater, a mad rush to get them in and get them out in time to make curtain, followed by nearly three hours of complete inactivity. The far end of West 46th Street in 1982 was nowheresville. Only predators, Guardian Angels and junkies seemed to walk by; the whole crew, kitchen, floor and even Tom and Fred would hang out and gossip to stay amused, hoping for a second pop when the shows let out near eleven.

Work Progress was by now only a few weeks from complete ruin, so I began peeling away a few key men; Dimitri became my sous-chef, and a couple of other cooks and dishwashers followed me uptown as well. I did my best to punch up the menu, putting on some beloved American regional/comfort dishes I thought in keeping with the meat loaf and jalapeño corn pudding theme. We fooled around with a lot of retro classics like chicken pot pie, fried chicken steak with cream gravy, black-eyed peas and collards, ham steak with red-eye gravy, New England clam chowder, San Francisco cioppino, and the like. I did my best to work the line responsibly, spend Tom and Fred's money wisely, and generally behave in such a way as not to offend the delicate sensibilities of my very kindly new masters.

But things were already not going as planned. Tom and Fred had taken over the entire building, and dropped big money making it over into the bistro of their dreams. They'd purchased a lovely serpentine zinc bar at an auction in France, put in all-new equipment, built living quarters, office space and a small prep kitchen upstairs. It had, I'm sure, cost them a lot of money. But I don't think they were prepared for a sudden requirement that they extend the range-hood exhaust vent another 200 feet and three floors to project beyond the roof – requiring a new motor the size of a small economy car to provide suction. And there were the bafflers and filters to muffle the damn thing to meet city sound-level requirements. Lunch was quiet, and a decent pre-theater followed by a so-so post-theater rush was not enough to pay for rent, food, liquor, labor, power and all the other hidden and unglamorous expenses of a midtown restaurant. Tom didn't help matters by hovering at the door, peering out into the street in search of a walk-in trade that would never come. The closest we got to that was when one of our aged bar customers got lucky over at the Haymarket, a particularly nasty, mob-run hustler bar over on Eighth, and would treat one of their under-age, dirty and potentially vicious pick-ups to a nice meal.

Tom and Fred had taken a lifetime lease on the building. They lived on the top floor, fully intending, I believe, to spend the rest of their lives there. So it pained me to see their dream die in increments, to see the realization dawn – with each expensive repair, each slow night, each unforeseen expense – that things were not turning out as hoped. The waiters, not uncharacteristically, joked bitterly about the situation. Where were all of Tom and Fred's friends now, they asked knowingly, now that they were no longer getting comped free meals?

'But Betty Bacall *loves* that dish!' Tom would protest when I suggested removing a particularly moribund item from the menu. He'd keep certain things on, favorites of celebrity pals, day in and day out, waiting for them to return. But Betty Bacall was not coming to dinner every day, I could have pointed out, nor every *week* – in fact, she probably wasn't ever coming back. The place was dying. The smell of desperation was in the air. You could detect it halfway down the block – as we were surrounded by equally customer-hungry places – you could see it in Tom's face, and when a few straggling celebrities would on occasion wander through the door, he'd pounce on them like a starved remora.

I soldiered on. I didn't know what else to do. Restrained from putting much of my own imprint on the place – and unprepared, in any case, to offer a viable alternative – I occupied myself with scoring drugs on Ninth Avenue, maintaining a nice buzz at the bar, and keeping a stiff upper lip about our declining fortunes. I may have been the chef but I had in no way learned the chefly arts; there was really no need to at Tom's. I was working with friends, so there was no call for the manipulation, intelligence gathering and detective work of later posts. The place was slow, so the air-traffic controller aspects of chef work had yet to come into play. And the food wasn't mine. I came quickly to hate (unjustifiably) Tom's now-not-so-famous meat loaf as an immovable object, and I settled not very happily into a position that was more overpaid line cook than chef. What I learned at Tom's was a sad lesson that has served me well in decades since: I learned to recognize failure. I saw, for the first time, how two beloved, funny and popular guys can end up less beloved, not so funny and much less popular after trying to do nothing more than what their friends told them they were good at. Friendships, I'm sure, were destroyed. Loyal pals stopped coming, causing real feelings of betrayal and embitterment. In the end, I guess, we all let them down. I found a job in the *Post* and jumped ship at the first opportunity.

Rick's Café was an even more boneheaded venture: an absolutely idiotic, Bogart-themed restaurant on a deserted street in Tribeca, run as a caprice by the near-brainless wife of a successful Greek deli owner. One look at this sinkhole – the faux-taverna decor left over from a previous establishment, the framed photos of Bogie and Ingrid Bergman, the (always fatal) absence of a liquor license – and I should have run for the hills. I could recognize failure when I saw it, but I was desperate to get away from Tom's. And the deli owner paid me cash money from a fat roll in his pocket. It seemed like an okay place to lie low while I looked for a real chef's job.

It was a horror. Our purveyors were all sinister Greek jobbers who bought cheap and sold cheap. Our floor staff were the lame, the halt and the ugly, and our only business was a lunch crowd from nearby city agency offices: cheapskates and well-done eaters all. Dinner? We might as well have been stationed on an ice floe in Antarctica; the whole neighborhood closed down at six, and as we were the antithesis of hip, and as yet without booze, no sane person would travel out of their way to visit our little Bogie Brattle Museum. I tried, to go along with the witless *Casablanca* concept, a sort of French/North African theme, making a (I thought) very nice tagine with couscous like I'd enjoyed in France, merguez, and some Southern French Mediterranean dishes. It was clearly hopeless. Even my boss, the deli-master, knew. I think he was stoically flushing money down the tubes to keep his wife out of his hair.

Things had apparently gotten so grim at Tom's after my departure that Dimitri joined me in my Bogie-themed hell. I was now within walking distance of readily available heroin, so I was reasonably satisfied, and Dimitri, while not exactly enjoying the fame and fortune I'd promised him in P-town, was soon getting regular blowjobs from one of the Rick's Café waitresses. Life was not all bad.

I was three for three for my last three restaurants. Fortunately, I was still young, so I could comfortably blame other factors on my unhappy success rate: bad owners, bad location, ugly clientele, crappy decor . . . I could live with that. I still had hope.

My problem was the money. I was making too much of it. Instead of doing the smart thing, taking a massive pay cut to go work for one of the now numerous emerging stars of American cooking, I continued my trajectory of working for a series of knuckleheaded, wacko, one-lung operations, usually already hemorrhaging when I arrived. Instead of running off to France, or California, or even uptown to work in one of the three-star Frog ponds as commis – the kind of Euro-style stage that helps build résumés and character – I chased the money. I was hooked on a chef-sized paycheck – and increasing dosages of heroin. I was condemned to become Mr Travelling Fixit, always arriving after a first chef had screwed things up horribly, the wolves already at the door. I was more of an undertaker than a doctor; I don't think I ever saved a single patient. They were terminal when I arrived; I might, at best, have only prolonged their death throes.

Having only recently achieved my dream of becoming a chef, I disappeared into the wilderness, feeding on the expiring dreams of a succession of misguided souls – a hungry ghost, yearning for money, and drugs.

APOCALYPSE NOW

THEY WERE ASSEMBLING MACHINE-GUNS for sale in the employee bathroom when I arrived. All the line cooks were hunched over Armalites and M-16s, while outside, in the nearly unmanned kitchen, orders spewed out of the chattering printer and were ignored.

Let's-Call-It-Gino's was a gigantic, two-story Northern Italian place on the waterfront, and the latest, most foolish venture from a guy everyone called the Silver Shadow, named for his Rolls-Royce and the fact that he never spent more than three or four minutes in any one of his restaurants.

When I first walked in the door, it was like the Do Luong bridge scene in *Apocalypse Now*, where Martin Sheen shows up in the middle of a firefight, Hendrix blaring in the background, and inquires of a soldier, 'Where's your CO?' To which the soldier replies, 'Ain't you?' Nobody knew who was in charge, what was going on, who was ordering the food, or what was going to happen next. It was a big, expensive and crowded asylum, run almost entirely by the inmates. Money flowed in – God knows it was busy enough – and money flowed out, but where? No one seemed to have any idea, least of all the Silver Shadow.

Gino's, and its sister restaurant in Baltimore, were classic Don't Let This Happen To You examples of over-reaching by a successful restaurateur. The Silver Shadow had expanded a profitable family provision business into a smoking-hot restaurant catering to the Upper East Side Mortimer's, Elaine's, Coco Pazzo crowd, spun that restaurant off into another restaurant next door with a well-liked Italian race-car driver freeloader as front man, and followed those successes with a string of high-quality places in the Village and elsewhere. It had seemed, for a while, as if he could do no wrong. He was hiring chefs by the bunch; my old friend Sammy already worked for him, and he'd apparently asked Sammy, 'Do you know any more like you?' and Sammy had said, 'Sure!' which is how I (and eventually Dimitri) got involved in one of the biggest, ugliest train wrecks of an organization in the history of New York.

The Silver Shadow couldn't keep track. Gino's New York – two kitchens, two dining rooms, outdoor café and 300 seats – opened on the waterfront nearly simultaneously with its slightly smaller sister in Baltimore's Harborplace. Plans were under way for more of them in Boston, New Orleans and elsewhere. It was Big '80 s time, with all that implied: too much money, too much coke, both in the hands of hyperactive, overconfident yuppie businessmen and investors – and at Gino's, it reached critical mass. The Shadow seemed to start up a new enterprise every other day. In the food court across the way from Gino's, he opened a gelato shop and a thin-crust pizzeria, then zipped off to Italy to buy warehouses full of plates, flatware, gelato bases, furnishings – and then forgot where he put them. Chefs, managers, sous-chefs, partners rotated in and out with no rhyme or reason to their comings and goings; there were always a few chefs in the pipeline, shacked up in hotels, on full salary, waiting for the call telling them where to go. The Silver Shadow bought chefs the way most people buy *TV Guide* at the supermarket – an impulse buy at the register, after they do their real shopping.

I had been hired, typically of the Silver Shadow, on impulse, and immediately tasked to take over Let's-Call-It-Dexter's, his relatively small American bistro on the Upper East Side.

'They really need you over there!' crowed the Shadow enthusiastically. 'They're really looking forward to meeting you!'

So, I quit the Columbus Avenue pick-up joint I'd been working, and hustled over to Dexter's. They had, it turned out, no idea I was coming. Worse, Dexter's and the Shadow's *other* restaurant – a Northern Italian place next door – shared the same kitchen *and* the same chef and crew; there were simply two different kitchen doors leading to two different dining rooms. The chef, a mincing, freakish-looking albino, was apparently quite capably taking care of business without me – and he let me know so immediately. After grudgingly introducing me to the kitchen crew who, it was immediately clear, held him in high regard, he took me aside and said, 'I don't care what the Shadow fucking told you, this is *my* kitchen . . . and you ain't doing nothing more than picking spinach as long as I'm here – which is forever!'

No way was I going to be stuck in a corner, in a hostile kitchen, working under this geek. I'd been promised a chef's job – my own kitchen, with all that implied – and the idea of *two* chefs sharing responsibility for *one* crew was ridiculous, even if the albino had been willing. And I didn't care to pick spinach, even for a thousand dollars a week.

I left immediately, calling the Shadow from a pay-phone.

'What have you *done* to me?' I inquired, pissed off. 'They'd rather rub shit in their hair over there than let me in! You *have* a chef already!'

'No problem,' replied the Shadow, as if he'd just now re-membered that the two restaurants shared a kitchen. 'They really need you in Baltimore. Go down to Gino's on the water-front, see the GM; he'll fill you in and give you some expense money.'

Which is how I found myself on the TurboLiner to Baltimore, junk-sick, confused, with an overnight bag and no idea of my mission.

Baltimore sucks.

If you haven't been there, it's a fairly quaint excuse for a city. (At the time I was there it was undergoing massive rehabilitation; an entire neighborhood by the waterfront was being 'restored' into a sort of red-brick and cobblestone theme park.) Bars close at 1 A.M. they start flashing the lights for last call at twelve-thirty. The permanent residents speak of New York and DC with strangely wistful expressions on their faces, as if they can't understand how they ended up here, rather than a few miles north or south, where there's a *real* city. There's an element of the South, an almost rural quality to Baltimore, an Ozark fatalism that's amusing in John Waters' films but not so much fun to live with. Worst of all, I had no idea where to score drugs.

Gino's Baltimore occupied the second floor of a large new structure on the water in Baltimore's Harborplace. The kitchen was bigger than the dining room – which I liked – but the dining room was pretty empty most times, which I didn't like so much. The crew, not uncommonly for most far-flung outposts in a restaurant empire, were already used to being the neglected bastard offspring, largely ignored by their leader. Supplies, which were supposed to arrive from New York, were sporadic. Guidance, such as it was, was erratic in the extreme. I was told immediately that another chef had just preceded me. He had set up a menu, showed the recent culinary graduate cooks how to dunk pasta, and then quit.

My first night, I slept in a vacationing waiter's apartment. It was a strange bed, with a strange cat, in a shabby, two-family Victorian. I lay awake, kicking and scratching, swatting the cat at my feet. The next day, I was brought over to the official residence of visiting dignitaries from New York: a three-story townhouse, brand-new but built to look old, in the center of the fake historical district. It was pretty swank: wall-to-wall carpeting, four bathrooms, vast dining room, living room and top-floor studio. The only problem was, there was no furniture. A bare futon lay in the middle of the floor on the third story, a pathetic black and white TV with coat-hanger antenna the only offered amusement. The spacious kitchen contained only some calcified rice cakes. The only other sign that anyone had ever lived there was a lone chef's jacket on a hanger in one of the closets – like an artifact, evidence of an ancient astronaut who'd been here before me.

It was make-work, and I knew it. The Shadow called to let me know that he wanted me to create a brunch menu and a happy-hour buffet. This was an easy enough assignment, as there were only about three bar customers who spent their evening chatting with the manager; and brunch, such as it was, consisted of about five tables of Sunday tourists who'd wandered into the empty dining room by mistake while window shopping and been too embarrassed to leave after realizing their mistake. The place had been open only a few months and already gave off the distinct odor of doom. Large-scale doom. There were twelve cooks, all new equipment, a bake shop, a pasta-making department. The Silver Shadow had spent millions on this colossal monument to hubris and cocaine. And you could see, in the cooks' faces, that they *knew* – as sure as they knew that they lived in a second-class city – that they'd be out of work soon. The body was dying; only the brain had yet to receive the message.

I worked fast, spending a lot of time shuttling back and forth to New York to score in bombed-out shooting galleries on the Lower East Side. My pay had never been arranged properly; when I needed money, I simply asked the GM to give me a few hundred, which he seemed happy to do, as money bled quickly out of Gino's every orifice. There was no business at the restaurant, so there was soon nothing to do. When I couldn't make it back to the real city, I'd drink at the Club Charles, an atmospherically crappy dive with a vaguely punk-rock clientele, or watch TV in my lonely room with a view.

I passed the Baltimore job to Dimitri as soon as I could. Maybe it wasn't the nicest thing I ever did, but it *was* a chef's job, and the money was good – and hey, room and board was free! Once again, I called the Shadow, told him there was nothing for me to do, and was told in response, 'They need you in New York! Get right back! They're really looking forward to meeting you!'

Which is how I found myself in a bathroom full of machine-guns.

Gino's New York, unlike its little brother in Baltimore, was still busy – crazy busy – and in every way, an out-of-control madhouse. If I wasn't already a burnt-out case from four years of drug abuse and two years in a Columbus Avenue pick-up joint and the cumulative effects of my whole checkered career to this point, I was after Gino's. Gino's finished me.

Brought in as the chef to replace the man whose jacket I'd discovered in Baltimore, I was shocked – even *I* was shocked – at the level of debauchery and open criminality. On my first day in Gino's New York, I found that the extremely well-paid head of prep could not so much as peel an onion – when he deigned to show up at work at all. When I inquired, I was matter-of-factly informed by the New York GM that he was the boss's coke dealer, kept around so that the boss and upper management could conveniently re-up if their little screwtop bottles ran empty.

The GM, a jangly, untrustworthy character, who seemed to be high on quaaludes most of the time, would disappear on benders for days at a time. This was problematic, as he had the only keys to the office. When the local wise guys showed up – as they did every Tuesday – looking for protection money (this kept our delivery trucks from having their tires slashed), we had to jimmy the office door to get at the safe. When no one with the combination was around, the assistant manager would simply ask the service bartender for a loan of a few thousand; he was always good for a few grand, as he did a bang-up business dealing coke to the employees.

A quick review of the schedule and time cards for my mammoth kitchen staff revealed more than a few irregularities. Juan Rodriguez, sauté man, for instance, had been punching in as Juan Martinez, Juan García, and Juan Pérez – all of whom were imaginary creations the front office had been kind enough to keep paying, in spite of the fact that they clearly did not exist. If half the cooks were on the line when they were supposed to be – as opposed to selling guns, or hiding in a stairwell smoking weed, or cooking up freebase in a bathroom, it was a good thing. Expediting was done by whoever happened to be in the kitchen at the time. Food for Baltimore was trucked into our walk-ins, rotated into our stocks, and then shipped out – such as it was – the next day. We made our own pasta . . . sometimes. We also bought pasta from our other stores, we bought pasta from outside, often all three at once. Gigantic steam kettles simmered with Gorgonzola and garlic cream for our very popular garlic bread. (Eight bucks for a baguette and some goo.) And herds of sightseers, tourists, businessmen, gawkers, rubes and hungry fanny-packers poured through the doors.

The food was not bad. God knows we had enough cooks, plenty of equipment, and room to put it. Somehow, things got done, though I have no idea how; the place had its own momentum, like some rudderless ocean liner, captain and crew long gone – it just kept going, plowing through ice fields. Someone with a brain had designed the line: a sensible trough of water for pasta, with cute fitted baskets, ran the length of the range-tops, for easy dunking. Nice refrigerated bains held garnishes and mise-en-place, so that each cook had an artist's palette of easy-access ingredients at hand. Downstairs, a long bar curled around the dining room, serving a lighter menu of trattoria items, sandwiches, quick-grilled foods, cheese, shellfish. Outside, when it was warm, a long barbecue grill serviced the café.

I fine-tuned the menu, meeting with the Shadow for a few minutes a day, satisfying him by simply responding to his culinary whims. 'Bagna cauda? I can do that. No problem! Clams oreganata? Why not?' I had no delusions of chefly integrity or personal agenda where Italian menu items were concerned, so I was relatively responsive compared to my mysterious predecessor – and the Shadow seemed happy with me. In fact, after people started asking me, in hushed voices, what the Shadow thinks of this, and what the Shadow thinks of that, I realized that the three or four minutes a day I spent talking to him made me, in the eyes of everyone else in the organization, his closest associate – though I couldn't have told them, if asked, what shade his eyes were, or anything else. With six different things going on, the man was a blur – like Patty Hearst in those security camera photos from the bank job – perpetually in motion, always on the way out the door.

I wasn't really very good at Italian food. I relied on Dimitri for most of my recipes, though his experience at Mario's was almost entirely Southern Italian red sauce and the like. But I got by nodding at whatever high concept the Shadow had a hot nut for that week, my real value to the organization becoming apparent after I had finally had enough and cut loose the coke-dealing head of prep.

The Shadow and upper management were impressed by this. It showed frugality: the man was deadwood after all; he had been absent from work without explanation two Saturdays in a row, and truth be told, he couldn't cook at all. I'd shown balls, too, firing *their* coke dealer, and they kinda liked that. *They* couldn't have done it, as the bastard knew too much – and I'd shown real talent and diplomatic skill in the way I'd done the deed: the already financially comfortable prep chief was easily convinced that this showing up at the restaurant thing was an inconvenience, and a distraction from his real calling, and that he'd be happier reverting to his former lifestyle, scooting around New York's bars and nightclubs in expensive Italian automobiles selling drugs. When I sorted out the Rodriguez, García, Pérez problem, unloaded a couple of wise-ass slacker waitrons, and replaced some no-show cooks with loyalists from Tom's and Work Progress, the Shadow saw in me *my* real calling – which was hatchet man.

Not that I was happy with this mantle.

But I was off dope now . . . and comfortably sedated by methadone, I felt free to visit the service bar numerous times a night, so that I could pack my nose with cocaine. This gave me that lovably psychotic edge so useful for mood swings, erratic bursts of rage, and the serious business of canning people, thus saving my master money. Every day I'd wake up, lounge around in bed for a while, come in to work – where service was already on automatic full swing – and look around for someone to fire. I had, really, no other responsibility. Supplies were ordered by a steward. The cooks served the food, the same way they'd always done. Expediting was done by committee (although I did it now and then). I scheduled, hired and fired, and as we were greatly overstaffed, it was mostly the latter.

But I was not happy in my work.

Every day, having to look in some desperate cookie's eyes and tell him 'No *más trabajo aquí . . .*' was taking a toll. Especially when they'd ask why. White boys were no problem; I could bang those goofballs out all day. They *knew* anyway, they'd been expecting it, amazed that they hadn't been canned earlier. But the Mexicans and Ecuadorians and Salvadorians and Latinos, who'd look at me with moist eyes as they realized that there'd be no check next week or the week after – when they asked that terrible question, '*Porqué?* Why, Chef? No work for me?' as if maybe they'd heard wrong – this was really grinding me down, tearing at what was left of my conscience. Every day, I'd stay in bed later and later, paralyzed with guilt and self-loathing, hoping that if I stayed in bed a little later, showed up a little later, maybe, just maybe, it would be me that got fired this time – that I wouldn't have to do this anymore, that this whole terrible business would end.

It didn't. Things only got worse. Pleased by my cost-cutting, the Shadow and his minions urged me on to even greater efforts. When I finally had to start messing around with some loyalists' schedules, giving them split shifts for no additional money, and I saw the terrible look of betrayal in *their* eyes – guys who'd come up with me, some Egyptian cooks I'd trained from dishwasher – I could take no more. One day I simply turned to the GM and said, 'I quit,' and it was over.

I slept for three weeks. When I woke up, I was determined never again to be a chef.

I'd cook. I had to make money. But I would never again be a leader of men. I would never again carry a clipboard, betray an old comrade, fire another living soul.

I left none too soon. Gino's, in the end, dragged down the

entire Silver Shadow empire, bankrupting even the family provisions business. Last I heard of the Shadow, he was doing time in federal lock-up, for tax evasion.

I was about to enter the wilderness.

THE WILDERNESS YEARS

IT IS ONE OF the central ironies of my career that as soon as I got off heroin, things started getting really bad. High on dope, I was – prior to Gino's – at least a chef, well paid, much liked by crew and floor and owners alike. Stabilized on methadone, I became nearly unemployable by polite society: a shiftless, untrustworthy coke-sniffer, sneak thief and corner-cutting hack, toiling in obscurity in the culinary backwaters. I worked mostly as a cook, moving from place to place, often working under an alias.

I worked a seedy hotel on upper Madison, a place so slow that the one waiter would have to come downstairs and wake me when customers came in. I was the lone cook, my only companions the hotel super and a gimpy dishwasher. I worked a lunch counter on Amsterdam, flipping pancakes and doing short-order eggs for democratic politicos and their bagmen. I worked a bizarre combination art gallery/bistro on Columbus, just me and a coke-dealing bartender – a typically convenient and destructive symbiotic arrangement. I was a sous-chef at a very fine two-star place on 39th, where I dimly recall preparing a four-course meal for Paul Bocuse; he thanked me in French, I think. My brain, at this point, was shriveled by cocaine, and I made the mistake of telling a garde-manger man that if he didn't hurry up with an order I'd tear his eyes out and skull-fuck him, which did not endear me to the fussy owner manager. I worked a deserted crab house on Second Avenue, steaming blue crabs and frying crab cakes. I cooked brunches in SoHo, I slopped out steam-table chow at a bar on 8th Street to a bunch of drunks.

For a time, I took another chef's job – of sorts – at a moment of need at Billy's, a combo sit-down/take-out upscale chicken joint on Bleecker Street. It was an operation that was to be the flagship of another planned empire, a chain of chicken joints that would stretch across the globe.

At this low point in my career, I didn't care if the place succeeded or not. I needed the money.

My boss was an older Jewish guy, fresh out of prison, who'd named the place after his youngest son, Billy, a feckless ne'er-do-well. He had been, in an earlier life, the head of the counting room at a Las Vegas casino, and after being caught skimming off millions for the 'boys back in New York and Cincinnati', had been offered a friendly deal should he cooperate with the prosecutors. He had, admirably, declined, and as a result spent the last five years eating prison chow. When he got out, a near-broken man, his old buddies in New York, being Men of Honor, set him up with this restaurant – with promises of more to come – as a sign of gratitude for services rendered.

Unfortunately, while in prison, the old man had completely lost his mind. He may have been a stand-up guy, but he was absolutely barking mad.

This was not a classic bust-out operation, where the mob deliberately runs a place into the ground, using a front man/ straw owner to run up bills, then pillage the place for merchandise and credit. I think that the wise guys, who from the early days of start-up were always around, really wanted the poor slob to make money and be a success. They made earnest efforts to help at every turn, enduring much nonsense from their visibly deranged partner.

It was, in retrospect, a useful experience for me, one I relied on for later works of fiction. I'd seen mobsters around before, of course, but I'd never worked in a place that was out-and-out mobbed up, where I came to know on a personal basis *real* wise guys, whose names I recognized from the papers. Everyone was astonishingly up front about their connections. My boss was fond of yelling into the phone when discussing prices with a purveyor: 'You know who I am? You know who I'm *with*?!'

We did things differently at Billy's.

My cooks, for one: every one of them came from the Fortune Society, guys who spent their off-hours in halfway houses, allowed out only to work. I was used to working with a fairly rough bunch, a lot of whom, at one time or another, had had problems with the law – but at Billy's, every single one of my cooks was *still* basically a convict. I can't say that it was an unhappy arrangement, either; for once I *knew* my cooks were going to show up at work every day, if they didn't, they went back to prison.

And credit was easily obtained. I knew, from previous experience, how difficult it is to set up terms for a new restaurant; even getting a week's credit with some of these companies was usually a lengthy process, involving credit applications, a long wait, initial periods of cash on delivery. At Billy's, no sooner was I off the phone than stuff was arriving, often on *sixty-day* terms. Produce and dry-goods people who'd been loath to offer even two weeks at other places I'd worked were suddenly all too happy to give me all the time I wanted.

My boss spent a lot of time on the phone, investigating the serious business of horses and their bloodlines, and how well they ran in mud or on grass. Billy himself, at eighteen, was happy to drive his sports car around and chase girls. So my day-to-day was spent mostly with some genial gentlemen from an Italian Fraternal Organization. They helpfully told me where to buy my meat and poultry and how to meet the folks who would be supplying my linen, bread, paper goods and so on. I had a lot of meetings in cars.

'The bread guy is here,' I'd be told, and a late-model Buick would pull up out front. An old guy in a mashed-down golf cap would beckon me from the driver's seat and then get out of the car. The older guy in the passenger seat would slide over, indicating he wanted me to get in, sit next to him and talk.

We'd sit there in the idling car, talking cryptically about bread, before he brought me around to the trunk to examine some product. It was a strange business.

Yet some things were off-limits. Trash removal, I found, was a mysteriously pre-arranged division of labor. When I called around for price quotes, told them who I was calling for, I was repeatedly quoted prices far exceeding the national debt – until I called the company I'd obviously been intended to do business with. 'Oh yeah, Billy's!' said the voice on the phone, 'I was waiting for youse to call!' and quoted me a very reasonable price. I rang up a meat company, inquiring if they'd care to sell me tens of thousands of dollars of burger patties a year, and they gave me a flat 'No!' They wouldn't even quote me prices. I was confused by this until years later, when I read a Paul Castellano biography called *Boss of Bosses*, and recognized the name of the meat company as a business operated by another family.

And there was the Chicken Guy, who also met me in a car, and showed me samples in a trunk. When I introduced him to my boss, the old man bitched about the price, telling the Chicken Guy, in his blood-smeared white butcher's coat, that the price was too high, that he could 'just fly to fucking Virginia, buy the stuff direct,' and 'Do you know *who I'm with anyway*?!'

The Chicken Guy was not impressed. He spat on the floor, looked my boss in the eye and said, 'Fuck *you*, asshole! You know who *I'm with*?! You can fly to fuckin' Virginia and buy direct all you want – you *still* gonna pay me! Frank Fuckin' Perdue pays me, asshole! *And you're gonna pay me too*!'

My boss was suitably chastened – for a time.

But he got wackier and wackier. When we finally opened, we were packed from the first minute. Orders flooded in over the phone and at the counter and at the tables. We were unprepared and understaffed, so the Italian contingent – including various visiting dignitaries, all with oddly anglicized names ('This is Mr Dee, Tony, and meet a friend, Mr Brown . . . This is Mr Lang'), all of them overweight, cigar-chomping middle-aged guys with bodyguards and 10,000-dollar watches – pitched in to help out with deliveries and at the counter. Guys I'd read about later in the papers as running construction in the outer boroughs, purported killers, made men, who lived in concrete piles on Staten Island and Long Beach and security-fenced estates in Jersey, carried brown paper bags of chicken sandwiches up three flights of stairs to Greenwich Village walk-up apartments to make deliveries; they slathered mayo and avocado slices on pita bread behind the counter, and bussed tables in the dining room. I have to say I liked them for that.

But when my boss, inexplicably, showed up one day and told me to fire everyone with a tattoo on my staff, I was faced with a dilemma. Every one of my cooks was festooned with prison tats: screaming skulls, Jesus on hypodermic crosses, bound in barbed wire, gang tats, flaming dice, swastikas, SS flashes, *Born to Lose*, *Born Dead*, *Born to Raise Hell*, *Love*, *Hate*, *Mom*, portraits of the Madonna, wives, girlfriends, Ozzy Osbourne. I tried to put him off, explaining that we couldn't do without these guys, that the hardest-working, most indispensable guy we had – the guy who right now was loading trash cans with hundreds of marinating chicken parts in the cramped, stifling unrefrigerated cellar on his twenty-second consecutive double shift – he was a goddamn Sistine Chapel of skin art. And where am I going to find a convict without a tattoo? The Watergate burglars weren't, to my knowledge, available.

Things only got worse. He came in the next day, obsessing about gold chains and jewelry. My grill man had the usual ghetto adornments of the day. 'Where do you think that eggplant *got* all that gold?!' he raved, spraying food and saliva as he talked. 'Selling *drugs*. That shit is *poison*! Mugging old ladies! I don't want that in my restaurant! Get him out!'

This was clearly impossible, and I sought counsel with one of the silent partners who, as my boss had become increasingly distracted and unpredictable, had grown noticeably less silent. He and his associates had started to attend management meetings. 'You hear what he wants me to do?' I asked. The man just nodded and rolled his eyes, sympathetically, I thought.

'Do nothing', he said, and then, with truly dangerous intonation, added, '*Aspeta*,' meaning 'Wait' in Italian.

I didn't like the sound of that at all. He smiled at me, and I couldn't help picturing my boss, slumped over a dashboard after one of those meetings in a car they were all so fond of. When things came to a head a few days later, my boss openly screaming in the middle of a crowded dining room that he wanted all the tattooed guys and gold chain-wearers 'Out! Now!' I told him to pay me what he owed – I was leaving for good. He refused. The silent partner came over, peeled off my pay and an extra hundred from a fat roll in his suit pocket, and gave me a warm smile as he bade me goodbye.

I don't know what happened to Billy's. It certainly never developed into a worldwide chain as my crazed boss had envisioned – or even a second store. The next time I was in the neighborhood, a picture framer occupied the space where the restaurant had been. What happened to the old man and his dreams of a poultry empire for his son? I can only guess.

I worked at a Mexican restaurant on upper Second Avenue for a while, one of those places on the frat-boy strip with the obligatory margarita sno-cone machine grinding away all night and vomit running ankle-deep in the gutters outside. The place was owned by a very aggressive rat population, fattened up and emboldened by the easily obtained stacks of avocados left to ripen outside the walk-in each night. They ran over our feet in the kitchen, hopped out of the garbage when you approached and, worst of all, stashed their leavings in the walls and ceilings. Every once in a while, the soggy, acoustic tile ceilings would crumble, and moist avalanches of avocado pits, chewed chicken bones and half-eaten potatoes would come tumbling out on our heads.

I was reaching rock-bottom, both personally and professionally. I got canned from the Mexican place, for which particular reason I don't know; there were plenty of good ones – alcoholism, drug abuse, pilferage, laziness – I don't know which of these unlovely traits actually did me in. But I didn't mind; the rats were really bugging me, especially when I was high on coke, which was most of the time.

I worked in an all-Chinese kitchen for a time, squatting on the floor with my fellow cooks, sharing their simple staff meals of rice gruel, pork broth and fish bones each day, shoveling in my food with chop sticks and betting on how many plum tomatoes would be in a case in the day's delivery. I cracked oysters at a shellfish bar, watching as drunken customers gobbled jumbo shrimps without bothering to remove the shells – so pickled from booze they were beyond caring. I came to know actors, loan sharks, enforcers, car thieves, guys who sold false ID, phone scammers, porno stars, and a dope-fiend hostess who attended mortician school during the day. She came up to me one night at the shellfish bar, a blissed-out look on her face, and said, 'We did a baby today in school . . . and it . . . like . . . aspirated in my arms, man. You could hear it sigh when I picked it up!' She looked happy about this. She had a fetish for Con Ed workers – something about the uniforms, I guess. And whenever they were doing electrical work or repairing a gas line in her neighbor-hood, she'd come in the next day singing the praises of the fine folks who kept our utilities running.

I got to know a steely-eyed Irish hood in his fifties who worked 'with' the pressmen's union, sometimes. When he had a big tune-up scheduled, he'd recruit other regulars from the bar to go down to some warehouse or printing plant and smack some heads together. One night he came in with his right hand busted up terribly, the knuckles pushed back nearly to his wrist, and a bone jutting horribly through the skin.

'Dude!' I said, 'You should go to the hospital for that!'

He just smiled and ordered a round for the house, then a dozen oysters and some shrimp with that – and ended up drinking and dancing and partying until closing time, waving his bloody hand around like a merit badge. His pal James, who wore the same fatigue jacket he'd worn in Vietnam fifteen years earlier, liked to hang out by my shellfish bar, telling stories. James was a West Village celebrity, never, to anyone's knowledge, having paid for a drink. He lived off the generosity of others, throwing a well-attended rent party once a month so he could pay for the curtained-off illegal cellar cubicle he called home. James carried a mysterious stainless-steel attaché case with him wherever he went, hinting that it contained the Great American Novel, the Nuclear Codes, Unlimited Firepower. I suspected it was a few tattered copies of *Penthouse* and maybe a change of socks – but smelling James, I was less sure about the socks. He was a bright, sweet, apparently educated guy from a military family. He'd been 86'd from half the bars in the Village, but the place I worked put up with him as long as the customers were willing to endure him. I admired his survival skills, his longevity, his staying power. He certainly didn't get by on his looks. He'd just learned how to hustle, instinctively – he didn't do it in a calculating way – he just did what was necessary to stay alive.

I saw myself becoming like him, and I didn't like it. Okay, I wasn't cadging drinks for a living, listening to a bunch of drunks in return for the occasional freebie, or throwing rent parties. I did have a job, and an apartment and a girlfriend who still, it appeared, loved me. But there was little good happening in my life. I was living paycheck to paycheck. My apartment was a dark, dusty cavern with paint peeling off the ceilings. Though I was no longer getting high at work, my off-hours were still revolving around the acquiring and doing of controlled substances – even if they weren't heroin. I was barely a cook. My culinary education, my early food epiphanies, the tastes and textures and experiences of my childhood in France and my rather privileged high school and college years were of little use to me behind a shellfish bar.

Something had to change. I had to get it together. I'd been the culinary equivalent of the Flying Dutchman too long, living a half-life with no future in mind, just oozing from sensation to sensation. I was a disgrace, a disappointment to friends and family and myself – and the drugs and the booze no longer chased that disappointment away. I could no longer bear even to pick up the phone; I'd just listen to the answering machine, afraid or unwilling to pick up, the plaintive entreaties of the caller an annoyance. If they had good news, it would simply make me envious and unhappy; if they had bad news, I was the last guy in the world who could help. Whatever I had to say to anybody would have been inappropriate. I was in hiding, in a deep, dark hole, and it was dawning on me – as I cracked my oysters, and opened clams, and spooned cocktail sauce into ramekins – that it was time, *really* time, to try to climb out.

WHAT I KNOW ABOUT MEAT

AN EPISODE FROM THE Wilderness Years.

Things were not going well. It was August, and my tree from the previous year's Christmas still lay in a heap of brown, dead pine needles in my dark, unused dining room. I was ashamed to take it out to the trash, not wanting my neighbors to see how far I'd fallen, how utterly paralyzed I'd become by my years of excess. Eventually, my wife and I would make a heroic effort to dispose of the incriminating object – chopping it up like a dead body and stuffing it in plastic bags before lugging it in the dead of night a few floors down and leaving it near a known coke dealer's doorway. Let him take the rap, we figured.

My unemployment was running out, and the responses to the résumés I'd sent out inevitably invited me to meet with such a transparently doomed bunch of chuckleheads that even I, the seasoned carrion feeder, couldn't stomach the prospect of working for them. There was a guy planning a Marla Maples restaurant; Marla would sing in the upstairs cocktail lounge, he confided, ensuring hordes of high-spending gourmets. The feng shui advisor was riding a cosmic groove around the half-completed restaurant when I arrived for the interview, boding poorly for the man's prospects. I deliberately tanked the interview.

Another well-known New York restaurateur summoned me to a series of highly secret meetings to discuss the changeover of his current operation – an unbelievably loud, grotesque, television-themed monstrosity – into a fine French bistro. I took the job, sight unseen, on the strength of his reputation, a generous money offer and the prospect of serving fine French food, which he knew quite a bit about. But one night in that place was more than I could take. Squealing children shoved up against the expeditor as they lined up to buy lunch-boxes, gummy bears, T-shirts and bomber jackets from the merchandising concession. Waiters with microphones urged customers to Name That TV Show as the theme music from *Green Acres* and *Petticoat Junction* blared over Volkswagen-sized speakers. The food was what you might expect to find on Air Uganda tourist class: boil-in-the-bag veggie burgers, pre-cooked bacon slices, greasy meat patties which were pre-seared and left to marinate in grease in the steam cabinet. It was soul destroying, and at the end of the night, I scrawled a quick note to the owner, something along the lines of: 'I could never last even another ten minutes in this shithole. I don't care if you're turning the joint into Lutèce – it's too horrible NOW.'

A couple of '70s survivors wanted me for a new seafood restaurant on the Upper East Side, but when I called my connection at a reputable fish wholesaler to tell him I was thinking of taking the job, he groaned out loud.

'Those guys are deadbeats of the month every fucking month. Their other place is on COD – and I hear the paychecks are bouncing like Schwarzenegger's tits . . .'

I thanked him for the information and politely declined further discussions.

I was utterly depressed. I lay in bed all day, immobilized by guilt, fear, shame and regret, my ashtrays overflowing with butts, unpaid bills stacked everywhere, dirty clothes heaped in the corners. At night, I lay awake with heart palpitations, terrors, bouts of self-loathing so powerful that only the thought of diving through my sixth-floor window onto Riverside Drive gave me any comfort and allowed me to lull myself into a resigned sleep.

Finally, I landed an interview that sounded promising. It was a steakhouse on Park Avenue with a large business clientele, a respectable 24 from the Zagat Guide, and a well-thought-of outpost in the Hamptons. They served top-quality dry-aged steaks, manly portions of seafood, oversized martinis and single malt scotches and had the inevitable cigar room. As I cabbed downtown, I was confident that a) this place would *not* be an embarrassment to work at, and b) I could run a steakhouse kitchen standing on my head. In fifteen years, I had learned everything there was to know about beef, pork, veal, about grilling, roasting – it was easy, the kind of simple, honest food I could put my mark on without working up too much of a sweat. The specials, for one, could be easily upgraded; steakhouses were notoriously lax in their specials and seafood offerings. There was plenty about this place I could improve, I was sure of it.

Typically, I arrived about a half-hour early for the interview. Nervous and thirsty, I decided to take the edge off with a pint. I tend to overanalyze questions during the interview process, to answer too wise-ass, and these were not qualities one seeks in a chef. So, I figured, a pint would dumb me down a little, relax me.

I ducked into an inviting-looking workingman's pub – Irish bartender, bowls of stale pretzels on the bar, Van Morrison on the jukebox. After a couple of sips I felt perfectly at home with the daytime drinker crowd and the stale beer stink. I sipped and smoked, looked longingly at a plate of chicken wings a couple of stools down. I couldn't eat before the interview, I reminded myself, I didn't want a big hunk of chicken in my teeth while a potential new boss grilled me about my less than brilliant career. As the hour approached, I yearned just to blow off the interview, stay here all day, drop a few quarters in the jukebox, play Steppenwolf's 'Magic Carpet Ride' and have a few more Bass ales. It would be so nice, I mused, to get paid for this – twelve hundred a week to hang out in the fading daylight of Irish bars, instead of having to go through the full mind-body press of taking on a new kitchen. But I needed the money. I needed the work. I needed to get back in the game.

When I walked out into the sweltering, mid-August afternoon, I was about as loose and ready as I was ever going to be.

The place was done up with the usual dark-wood walls and historical prints of horses, old New York, handlebar-mustached ball players and clubby accouterments. It was between lunch and dinner service, and the dining room was empty except for a frosty-haired man with a well-trimmed beard in the casual clothes that say 'owner' and a younger man in a business suit. They were interviewing another candidate, a stack of résumés in front of them.

A bushy-browed maître d' ushered me to a bar, where I recognized immediately that this was a cattle call. A full bar of serious-looking chef candidates, in civilian mufti, sat drinking club sodas while they waited. Most were as badly dressed as I was, looking broken and defeated as they stared into space, sallow-skinned from years under fluorescent kitchen lighting. We ignored each other and tried to look as if we didn't need this job. My fellow chefs looked like sub commanders on shore leave, I thought, nervously fiddling with swizzle sticks and tearing at their bar napkins, unwilling to smoke at interviews. I gave my name to an indifferent bartender who assured me that the boss would be with me 'soon', and waited and waited and waited. It was quite a while and I was pissed that I, an executive (if recently disgraced) chef, was being made to wait like this, herded into a holding pen like . . . like . . . a waiter.

A Frenchman with dark circles under his eyes and bad burns on his hands read soccer scores next to me. Down the bar, the other chefs pretended they were customers, pretended they weren't the type to wait compliantly on line for an interview at a steakhouse. I drew strength from their misery.

A lone civilian stopped in for a quick, midday maintenance cocktail, answering the bartender's 'Howaya?' with an entirely-too-chipper-for-my-taste account of a vacation in Aruba, a golfing trip to New Mexico, a mention of the comparative merits of the Beemer versus the Mercedes coupé. Then he answered his ringing cellphone with a dirty joke. I couldn't help eavesdropping and then – in an awful epiphany – saw that all the other chefs were listening in too, wistful expressions on their faces as they perhaps imagined, like me, what it was like to take vacations, own a car, combine a little golf with business. I felt myself sinking into a dark funk.

Finally, my name was called. I straightened my ten-year-old jacket, ran a hand through mousse-stiffened hair and strode confidently to the interview table. Firm handshakes all around, and I sat down, looking as crisp and cool as an ex-junkie skell with a culinary degree could look.

Initially, the interview went well. The owner, an affable Scot with a thick brogue, handed my résumé to his aide-de-camp, an American, who immediately smiled with recognition at some of the places I'd worked.

'So . . . Supper Club . . . How they doing now? You worked for Marvin and Elliot?' he asked, all smiles now. 'Those were crazy times,' he reflected, a dreamy look on his face. The guy was letting me know that he too had gotten laid a lot back in the '70s and '80s and done a lot of cocaine.

We moved on, the American casually inquiring about various periods of my employment history, thankfully missing the fudged parts, the missing months, the long-dead restaurants that I'd helped to bury.

'You worked with Jimmy S.?' he inquired, chuckling and shaking his head. 'He still wear roller blades in the kitchen?'

I nodded, laughed, greatly relieved at this trip down memory lane. Clearly the man had also suffered under Jimmy at one point in his career. We were bonding!

'Haven't seen him in *years*,' I replied, separating myself deftly from my one-time mentor as fast as I could. 'Ha ha . . .'

I continued to smile warmly at both owner and the American manager, listened carefully, with a serious, yet calculatedly pleasant expression on my face as the owner began to fill me in on the history, philosophy and long-term aspirations for his steakhouse. There were a few questions from each of them, which I knocked down easily. I could see from their expressions that things were going well. I was acing every question. I had all the answers. No matter what they threw at me, I was ready.

'What kind of hours would you expect to put in?'

I knew that one. 'Whatever it takes. I'll put up a pup tent in the kitchen for the first few months . . . After that? I usually work ten to ten . . . *at least*. Six, seven days, whatever's needed.'

'What would you say your strengths and weaknesses are?'

I'd fielded this one before, neatly handling it with a wry but self-deprecating assessment of my finer qualities.

'Why are you leaving your current position?'

Snore. I knocked that out of the park, knowing full well that to slag on my most recent employer would not speak well of me. I embarked on an articulate dissertation on 'honest, straightforward American food'.

'What kind of positive changes could you bring to the table?'

I was doing fine. Every answer brought smiles and nods, the rote answers falling trippingly and amusingly off my tongue. Soon they were all laughing. I larded my account of my hopes for the future with casual references to owner-friendly buzzwords like 'point-of-sale', 'food cost percent', 'labor-intensive' and 'more bang for the buck', careful to slowly, almost accidentally reveal that I was a serious, experienced chef, a reasonable man – good-tempered, reliable – the sort of guy a fifty-five-year-old Scottish steakhouse owner could talk to, spend time with – a realist, a journeyman professional – without airs, illusion or pretense.

I finished a sentence and smiled at the two men, pleased with myself at how things had gone so far. When bossman asked how much money I was looking for, I took a chance, said 85,000 dollars plus family health plan – I was a happily married man after all – and the guy didn't blink, he just jotted the number down on the corner of my résumé with a sharpened pencil and said, 'That's do able.' I kept the conversation moving, more than anything else trying to avoid the obvious – that sure, goddamn right I could do the job! I could train a schnauzer to knock out a few hundred broiled steaks a day, wrap a few spuds in foil and make floury clam chowder for customers who smoked cigars while they ate. This gig would be ridiculously *easy* for me – practically free money. I didn't say this, of course. That wouldn't be good.

I was closing in on the position. I could feel it. I cleverly volunteered that my personal approach to cuisine was apprecia-tion of fine ingredients, that too much frou-frou on the plates, food too sculpted, excessively garnished like that of many of my peers, was a distraction. Owners usually like this rap. And by saying it, I had inoculated myself against the 'I'm too good for this place' issue. Oh yeah, I assured them, all those squeeze-bottle Jackson Pollock designs on plates, the carved veggies and the frizzled this-and-thats, they detracted from the natural beauty of fine ingredients – a time-consuming and costly indul-gence that satisfied only the chef's ego. 'Good food, honestly prepared,' I repeated, 'doesn't need that silliness. If the ingre-dients are the best, and they're prepared conscientiously, you don't need it,' my tone implying that there was something less than masculine – even gay – about dressing a hunk of meat up like a goddamn birthday cake.

This was going down very well – until suddenly, things took a strange and confusing turn. The owner leaned in close, and with unexpected gravity, lowered his voice and asked what was clearly the Big Question. His blue eyes searched the inner recesses of my skull as he asked it, his thick brogue and a passing delivery truck obscuring the words. I didn't hear. I asked the man to repeat the question, suddenly thrown com-pletely off my game. I listened intently this time, feeling suddenly at a disadvantage, not wanting this guy to think I was hard of hearing – or worse, having trouble with his accent.

'I'm sorry,' I said, 'What was that?'

'I asked,' said the owner, slightly irritated, 'What do you know about me?'

This was a tough one. The man had seemed strictly business the whole time so far. What kind of an answer was he looking for? How did he expect his future chef to answer such a question: 'What do you know about me?'

Did he want his ass kissed, I wondered. Was he looking for something along the lines of: 'Oh, yes! Of *course* I've heard about you! How could I *not*? Why, every schoolboy in America is aware of your heroic trip from Scotland in steerage, your resolute climb up the ladder, how you worked your way up from piss-boy to magnate and created this fine, fine steakhouse, where the food is *legendarily* good. Why . . . why . . . I've got your bio tattooed on my chest as a matter of fact! You . . . you're an *inspiration*, I tell ya! A childhood fucking *role model*!' Was this what he was looking for?

I thought not. It couldn't be that. I had to think fast. What could this guy want? Maybe it was just the seriousness of the enterprise he wanted acknowledged, something like: 'Sure! I've heard of you – that you're a no-nonsense, stand-up guy, a man who works his people hard, expects a lot from them . . . that you've been fucked over before by bullshit artist chefs, early in your career, and you're unlikely to allow that to happen again . . . that you clawed your way to the top over the broken skulls and shattered limbs of your competitors . . .' Was that what he wanted?

Or, I wondered shrewdly. Did he want to see if the applicant had any balls on him. 'Oh yeah' the right answer there might be, 'everybody says you're a miserable, Machiavellian, cold-blooded rat bastard with a million enemies and balls the size of casaba melons – but I *also* hear you're *fair*.'

Maybe that was it!

The fact was, though, I'd never heard of this guy before

walking in the door. Not a thing. Sure, he got a 24 in Zagat's, but that was about it. It was all I knew of the man! To lie . . . to flatter now . . . when everything was going so *well* – it could be a fatal mistake.

So I decided to take a shot at the truth,

Proudly, with what I later realized must have seemed to be nearly idiotic pride, I answered the 'What do you know about me' question with complete honesty. I stared back into the owner's eyes, smiled, and with forceful determination and complete candor, answered as breezily as I could, considering my heart was pounding in my chest:

'Next to nothing!' I said.

It was not the answer he was looking for.

Both owner and manager gave me tight, shocked smiles. They might have been impressed with my balls, but this was clearly outweighed by an instant appreciation that I was *not* going to be the next chef – nor would I ever be. I'd got it wrong somehow.

Oh, they laughed. They were even amused. A little too amused, I thought, as they tidied up the stack of résumés, signaling the interview was over. In what seemed like seconds, I was being politely if quickly escorted to the door, being handed the pro forma kiss-off of 'We have other candidates to interview before we make a decision.'

I was halfway down the block, already in a full flop-sweat from the August heat and the wringer these guys had put me through, when I realized my mistake. I groaned out loud, practically bursting into tears at the foolishness of it all, as I realized, exasperated, what this proud Scot had *actually* asked me. This steakhouse owner – whose end-of-week sales reports probably constituted at least 90 percent meat sales – hadn't been asking me what 'I knew about *me* . . .' He'd asked a more reasonable question for the owner of a very successful steak-house.

He'd asked me '*WHAT DO YOU KNOW ABOUT MEAT?*'

And I, like some half-crazed, suicidal idiot-savant kamikaze pilot, had asked him to repeat the question, pondered it thoughtfully, then proudly replied, '*Next to nothing!*'

It was not my finest hour.

PINO NOIR: TUSCAN INTERLUDE

OF ALL THE HIGH-PRESSURE, full mind-body crunches, strange interludes, unexpected twists and 'learning experiences' in my long and largely undistinguished career, my brief Tuscan interlude with New York's Prince of Restaurant Darkness, Pino Luongo, was perhaps the most illuminating, if exhausting. The owner of Coco Pazzo, Le Madri, Sapporo di Mare, Il Toscanaccio and other businesses, Pino was, and remains, one of the most controversial figures in the business, a man envied, feared, despised, emulated and admired by many who have worked for and with him.

I'll flash forward a few weeks into my account to give you a general idea of what the perception of life under Pino was. I was the newest executive chef in Toscorp, Pino's umbrella company, looking as chefly as possible in my brand-new Bragard jacket with my name stitched in appropriate Tuscan blue, standing in the front cocktail area of Pino's newest: Coco Pazzo Teatro on the ground floor of the swank and stylish Paramount Hotel on West 46th Street. A journalist acquaintance, whom I knew from Vassar, came in with a large party of high-cheekboned models and sensitive-looking young men in designer clothes. Startled to see me, he shook my hand and said, 'Tony! I didn't know you were working for Pino now!' Then he lowered his voice and only half-jokingly added, 'I guess this means that in a few months you'll either own your own restaurant . . . or be *ground to dust*.'

How did *I*, a chef with limited Italian experience in my

background, a guy who up to now had sneered at Italian food, had even written a book about a young Italian American chef who'd wanted nothing more than to get away from the red sauce and garlic and Parmesan cheese of his childhood and cook *French*, and was willing, ultimately, to *betray his own family* rather than cook fried calamari – how did *I* end up as the opening chef of Pino Luongo's newest, high-profile Tuscan venture?

I don't really know.

I was enjoying a period of unemployment after the moribund One Fifth had finally succumbed – lying around my dusty apartment, watching daytime TV, interrupting my pleasurable torpor occasionally to fax out the occasional résumé or two – when my old crony, Rob Ruiz, another Bigfoot protégé, called me.

'Tony! It's Elvis! [Bigfoot always called him Elvis] What are you *doing*? I'm at Le Madri . . . They need a sous-chef! You should get down here right away!'

'It's *Italian*,' I said.

'Doesn't matter. Just get down here. Meet the chef! He wants to meet you. Believe me – you'll *like* it!'

Now, I like Rob. He's a dyed-in-the-wool, bone-deep, old-school sonofabitch – a guy who knows what's going on in every restaurant in New York, who can call up just about any purveyor in the city and get them to supply his restaurant with free stuff, cheaper stuff, better stuff, and fast. He's a prodigious drinker, a funny guy, and generally he knows a good thing when he sees it. We have a lot of history between us, all of it good. I said, 'Why not?' My schedule, after all, was pretty loose – if you didn't count *Rockford Files* reruns at five and *Simpsons* at seven. I managed to find some clean clothes, make myself look presentable, and hurried down to Chelsea.

Le Madri was, and remains, in my opinion, the very best of Pino's many restaurants, a place designed around Pino's love for 'Mama cooking', meaning the Tuscan home cooking of his youth, as prepared at home by mothers and grandmothers –

coupled with the sort of cold-blooded professional efficiency for which he is justifiably notorious. The chef, Gianni Scappin, was a likeable, light-complected Italian who wore his jacket buttoned all the way up, with a bone or ivory clasp around a very proper little kerchief. He met with me in his downstairs office, predisposed to like me, I think, by the excellent job that Rob was still doing as his steward and purchaser. What Gianni wanted sounded reasonable: show up six shifts a week, create some lunch specials, make soup, do a little prep, keep an eye on the Ecuadorians, help out on the line as needed – maybe expedite a bit – and one night a week, work the sauté station. The money was good, and Gianni impressed me. The kicker was his casual question, near the end of our interview, if I was interested in becoming the executive chef at Coco Pazzo Teatro, scheduled to open in a few weeks. 'I don't want it,' he said. 'I'm too busy.'

Thus began my crash course in all things Tuscan.

A few hours earlier, I'd been lying dazed and hopeless in my unmade bed, wondering whether to take another nap or call out for pizza. Now I was the sous-chef at one of the best Italian restaurants in New York, with an inside track – I was assured – to become the executive chef at Pino Luongo's latest celeb-friendly restaurant in the ultra-cool, Philippe Starck-designed, Schrager-owned hotel. It was a dazzling development.

And I *was* dazzled. Remember, I was not a fan of Italian food. But when I arrived that first day at Le Madri, saw that the walk-ins were absolutely *empty*, saw how tomato sauce, chicken stock, pasta, bread – in short, *everything* – was made fresh (the tomato sauce from fresh, seeded, peeled tomatoes), I was stunned. Meat, fish and produce deliveries arrived and the cooks would fall on them like marauders, yanking out what they needed – frequently right off the truck – so it would be ready for lunch. The quality of food was magnificent. Orders started coming in and I'd have to run down to the butcher who was cutting meat *to order*. A short, Ecuadorian pasta maker with nubs where two fingers had been rolled garganelli, cut spaghetti alla chitarra, laid out sheet pasta for ravioli and punched out fresh gnocchi which were immediately sent upstairs to be served. On the line, a truly awe-inspiring crew of talented Ecuadorians made focaccia and white truffle oil-filled pizzas, rubbed fresh striped bass with sea salt, filled them with herbs and roasted them until crispy, sliced translucently thin sheets of Parma ham and speck, and prepared an amazing array of pasta dishes, yanking the fresh-cooked stuff to order out of two simmering pasta cookers and finishing them in pans from a mise-en-place of ingredients so vast and well prepared that I had no idea how they kept them all straight.

I never really *knew* how to cook pasta before. Here, dried pasta was blanched in small, undercooked batches and laid out *unrinsed* and still warm on lightly oiled sheet pans before being finished in sauce a few minutes later. Fresh pasta and thin-cut pasta was cooked to order.

Pasta was cooked the right way. Meaning, the penne, for instance, after saucing, stood *up* on the plate in a mound, rather than sliding around on the plate or being left to drown in a bowl.

'You want to taste *the pasta*,' explained Gianni, 'not just the sauce.' It was, I must admit, a revelation. A simple pasta pomodoro – just about the simplest thing I could think of, pasta in red sauce – suddenly became a thing of real beauty and excitement.

All the food was simple. And I don't mean easy, or dumb. I mean that for the first time, I saw how three or four ingredients, as long as they are of the highest and freshest quality, can be combined in a straightforward way to make a truly excellent and occasionally wondrous product. Homey, peasant dishes like Tuscan bread soup, white bean salad, grilled calamari, baby octopus, tender baby artichokes in olive oil and garlic, a simple sautéed calf's liver with caramelized onions, immediately became inspiring and new. The clean, simple, unassuming integrity of it all was a whole new approach, very different from the sauces and squeeze bottles and exotic ingredients of my recent past.

The fear level was not too bad, possibly because Rob was

there. He'd call up on speaker phone at odd times and make hideous groaning and slurping and choking sounds over the PA system. And Gianni seemed comfortably expert in navigating the canals and vias of Pino's empire; he was apparently a centurion in good standing, so I felt comfortably under his protection.

I was set to meet the man himself in a few days, so he could take a sniff of the new chef candidate with the French-sounding name. Wisely, I decided to do my homework. I read Pino's two excellent books: *A Tuscan in the Kitchen* – much of which was about the opening of Le Madri – and *Fish Talking*, an ode to the tiny, oily little fishes and now neglected seafood items of his childhood in Italy. I read them with real interest, particularly *Fish Talking*, which shared in its appreciation of 'garbage fish' an attitude with my earlier mentor, Howard Mitcham. Pino, whatever you might say about the man, clearly *adored* food, and it came through in his books as well as in his restaurants. At one point in one of his books, Pino discusses his near heartbreak when standing by the antipasti bar at Coco Pazzo, when he used to ask some of his regular guests to sample some fresh anchovies or sardines only to have them decline. His frustration with the difficulty of trying to get his guests to even *try* something he found so wonderful made an endearing impression on me.

I knew, when given an opportunity to cook for the man, what I was going to do.

We met at Le Madri and went over my résumé – thankfully without too much scrutiny. Pino is one of those guys who puts a lot of stock, I think, in his first-hand impressions of character when interviewing a candidate. The meeting went well. I was invited to a taste-off at Mad 61, another Pino operation in the cellar of the uptown Barney's department store where, presumably, I would lead with my best shot: do everything I could to show the man I could cook.

My fellow chef candidates, and some others already employed by Toscorp who were aiding and abetting the company-wide drive to come up with a menu for the new store, arrived with the usual, 'Look how pretty I can cook' stuff: swordfish tartare with avocado (!), California-inspired faux Tuscan updates, various ring-molded and squeeze-bottled presentations using expensive ingredients. I picked the cheapest, oiliest, and most unpopular fish I knew, one which I'd always liked, and suspected that Pino would like, too: the humble bluefish. I grilled it and added a warm potato and chorizo salad, topped with a little shaved fennel and red onion with mint and basil. Then a braised shoulder of lamb with Sicilian olives, rosemary and garlic – on basil-mashed potatoes – as well as a giant raviolone of codfish brandade with crabmeat and lobster . . . just to play it safe. Pino smiled when he saw the bluefish, figuring that if nothing else, I had some balls on me.

I got the job.

Salary negotiations were brief. Pino asked me how much I wanted. I asked for a lot more than I thought I deserved. He suggested 5,000 less. That was still a number far, far higher than I had *ever* – or still, for that matter have – been paid. After leaving Pino's 59th Street offices, I walked on air over to the Oak Room and treated myself to a martini, my voice still too shaky to speak. When I finally managed to call my wife on the phone, I must have sounded like a breathless young girl: 'Dad! You'll never *guess*! He asked me to *marry him*!'

An announcement was made in the *New York Times*. I was introduced to the company publicist, asked to provide a bio, and my short but memorable adventure on Planet Pino had begun.

In a subsequent meeting – and there would be many, as designing the new menu was a painstaking and tortuous affair – was informed that though I would be executive chef, my chef de cuisine (a ferret-like Italian) would fill in the obvious gaps in my knowledge of Tuscan cuisine and provide the sort of street-level, line-cooking, risotto-stirring experience I was lacking. It seemed like a reasonable idea. I *could* choose my own team of sous-chefs (two would be required) and cooks, but I had better do it *fast*, because Coco Pazzo Teatro was set to open in *ten days*. In that time, we would need a menu, equipment, and somewhere between twenty-five and thirty cooks – all of it ready for a celebrity-studded and media-scrutinized soft opening.

It was my greatest, most frantic, madcap and mad-dash recruiting drive ever.

First things first: I called Steven (my perennial sous-chef, but I'll get to him later) and excitedly told him to drop *everything*, because this was the Big One: the biggest break in our careers! Get over here fast, we need some bodies quickly! Look at this place, I told him, walking him through the rubble of the unfinished restaurant, showing him where the deck ovens and ranges would go, pointing out the tilting brazier, the steam kettle, the pasta machines, the ice-cream makers, the butcher station, the store rooms and offices – everything new and of the finest quality. We were given sixty grand to spend in the next few days, on pots, pans, blenders, beurre mixers, utensils and *toys*! And that wasn't counting the heavy equipment, which was already in the pipeline.

Steven responded with his usual speed and skill, and became my sous-chef. Alfredo, let's call him, a nice, talented Colombian American from the Supper Club, came aboard as second sous. It was a race now. Gianni, at Le Madri, had taken one look at my chef de cuisine, shaken his head and warned, 'Watch out for dees guy. He'll stobb you inna back,' making a stabbing gesture as he said it.

'What? What's his problem? He's Sicilian?' I asked jokingly, knowing Gianni's preference for all things Northern.

'Worse,' said Gianni. 'He's from *Naples*'.

I had yet to understand that I was surrounded by blue-eyed Northerners, people who felt that even I – though not Italian – was still preferable to someone from the South. Shrewd, conspiratorial, absolutely obsessed with which way the tide was going, by who was in and who was out, and by the daily mood of our leader, some of these characters lived and breathed the kind of existence you'd expect of a Medici. These guys were good! Good at the politics and shifting alliances of a big, essentially Italian business, good at the kind of stuff I thought I'd always been good at. They were expert at keeping the boss as happy as he needed to be, while at the same time deftly neutralizing potential competitors and detractors. I was in way over my head – and we're not even talking about my relative ignorance of the cuisine. This was a jungle that, however beautiful and exotic, was decidedly *not* my jungle.

Gianni was right about everything, and perhaps I should have listened more carefully. But Pino – and I'm sorry to disappoint his enemies here – was *always* perfectly correct with me: charming, straightforward, generous and truthful. He never said he'd do a thing for me and then failed to do it. I *liked* the guy, and if I bumped into him today, I'd say so. I liked that he could tell you all about exhaust fans, electrical outlets, point of sale and the history of pasta, that he knew everybody by name in all of his many restaurants, that he knew about the faulty compressor in the number two freezer in one of them, and that he could list every ingredient of every dish in every restaurant. He was on top of things – if relentlessly so. I had to respect that after working for so many knuckleheads over the years. Here was a guy who only a few years earlier had been a busboy, speaking only a few words of English, and now he ran an empire. Not too shabby. Admittedly, the atmosphere around his many functionaries and underlings was paranoid and conspiratorial. Fear, treachery, speculation, supposition and anticipation permeated the air. The pressure to perform at a high level was enormous. Everyone was very eager to please, the rewards being so potentially enormous, and the punishment for failure so sudden and final.

My first mission was not only to hire twenty-five to thirty talented cooks, but to hire *more* of them than my chef de cuisine did. The idea was to pack my crew with as many loyalists – guys and girls who were answerable personally to me and who could be trusted to watch my back – as I could, before my chef de cuisine overloaded me with *his* people, folks who wouldn't tell me if my hair was on fire, much less that somebody was waiting in the wings with their knife out.

Steven and I *raped* every kitchen we could think of. We stripped the Boathouse clean, lifting practically their whole line in one week, convincing many to leave without even giving notice. We pillaged other chefs' kitchens, sniffing around for the disgruntled, the underpaid, the unhappy, the susceptible and the ambitious. We conducted vast cattle calls, relay interviews, three or four of us at a time, simultaneously interviewing herds of applicants who'd answered our newspaper ads. The quality of applicant from these mass gatherings was discouraging; we managed to cull maybe two or three cooks from literally hundreds of illiterate loners, glue-sniffing fry cooks, and wack-jobs who'd never cooked professionally before. My chef de cuisine, on the other hand, was engaged in a similar recruiting drive, and to much better result. From Paglio and Torre de Pisa, both excellent Italian restaurants, he was peeling off some really superb Ecuadorian pasta, grill and sauté cooks, largely people he'd worked with before. All of us were making enemies of many a restaurateur as we bribed, begged, cajoled and induced people to drop everything and come immediately to work for us. We knew, of course, that many of these cooks wouldn't work out, that we'd actually need more like forty cooks, figuring that in the first few weeks we'd have to winnow out the losers and still have some extra good ones in holding pattern. It was crazy and exciting and not good for any of our karmic account balances – but this *was* the big one, after all.

When I wasn't conducting clandestine meetings in the parking lots of restaurants and smoky Irish bars with potential job applicants, or helping out Gianni at Le Madri, or sorting through truckloads of incoming equipment, I was meeting with Pino and his executive chef of Toscorp: the warm and wise Marta Pulini, a tiny, talented, fiftyish one-time contessa. We would meet in the kitchen of Mad 61 or in the offices of Toscorp on 59th Street, fine-tuning the menu, taste-testing, poring over menu copy and haggling over prices. Originally, the idea was that the Coco Pazzo Teatro menu would be 'fun' and 'theatrical', and described in defiant English on the menu, regardless of its country of origin. Center stations had been constructed in the dining room at Teatro where food from the kitchen would be 'finished' on futuristic induction burners, carved or taken off the bone if necessary, and presented tableside by rigorously trained and designer-outfitted waitrons.

Every week, before and after Coco finally opened, there would be a regular chefs' meeting in a conference room at the Toscorp offices. If I was the last to arrive at a meeting, the conversation would frequently change suddenly from Italian to English. The Coco opening was still a few days away when, in the middle of a chefs' meeting – probably a conversation about whose dry aged #109 rib was better, De Bragga or Master Purveyors, or whether we could all agree on a single olive oil so we could get a better price (we couldn't) – Pino suddenly stuck his head round the door and said ominously, 'Anthony, could I see you a minute?'

The mood in the room was one of tangible relief. Beads of sweat had sprouted on many a forehead as the other chefs realized what a close call it had been, that it might have been *them* summoned without warning to the inner sanctum, for a private and serious discussion with the ultimate leader. I stood up, puzzled, and left the room to meet in camera with Pino.

He led me to his office, closed the door, sat back on his comfortable-looking couch and threw one leg over the other.

'Anthony, do you have any . . . *enemies?*' he asked.

'Huh?' I stammered unintelligibly, not having any idea what he could be talking about.

'I received a call,' he began slowly. 'Someone . . . someone who . . . doesn't like you, who saw the *Times* notice . . . Have you been *stealing* sous-chefs?'

'I . . . I . . . no! . . . I don't know.' I managed to squeak, my voice constricting with terror.

'They say . . . this person says you are stealing sous-chefs. That you are . . . a pothead. Who,' he mused, inquisitively, '*who* could hate you that much?'

I was completely thrown. I denied, flat out, stealing any sous-chefs – though, of course I'd been stealing every goddamn cook and dishwasher I could lay my hands on. Later, much later, I recalled, during one of the cattle calls, hearing an applicant for a floor job mention her boyfriend was a sous-chef, and at a restaurant I knew. The chef there was someone I thought to be an utter prick, and I might have said something about why don't you have him give me a call. There might have been some inappropriate ex parte communications between my represen-tative (Steven) and this person. And I later found out that the sous-chef in question had simply used our presumed interest in his services to jack up his current chef for a fat and not easily afforded raise. But at the time, all I was thinking in Pino's dimly lit private office was that my Great Opportunity was slipping away fast – and before I'd even gotten started.

I was completely flummoxed, but I did manage to assure Pino, truthfully, that as far as pot or drugs were concerned, that would never be an issue, we would never have to have *that* conversa-tion. He waved the matter off, boring in more on *who* could hate me so much as to find out his private number, take the time and energy to call him up and badmouth me, hoping to torpedo my Great Opportunity. I couldn't think of anyone.

Pino suddenly smiled warmly. He looked . . . well . . . *pleased.*

'You know, Anthony,' he said, 'I have many, many enemies. It's *good*, sometimes, to have enemies – even if you don't know who they are. It means you are . . . *important.* You must be important . . . important enough to have an enemy.' He clapped me on the back on the way out the door. I was thoroughly charmed – if damn near shattered by the experience.

In the opening weeks at Coco Pazzo Teatro, I lost 11 pounds. These were not pounds I had to spare. I'm a bony, whippet-thin, gristly, tendony strip of humanity, and after two weeks running up and down the steps at Teatro from prep kitchen to à la carte kitchen – like some hyperactive forest ranger, always trying to put out brush fires in order to avoid actual conflagrations – I looked as if I'd been breathing pure crack in some VC tiger cage for the last ten years. I had twenty-five cooks, plus dishwashers, porters, visiting specialists, moonlighting pasta makers, man-agers, assistant managers, waiters, runners and other entities to contend with, deal with, schedule and replace. The *New York*

Times reviewer had *already* been in; we had someone who knew her by appearance staked out at the door full-time, just to be ready. Celebrities, friends of the house and Pino himself were all dropping in at all hours. The cooks worked entirely on a call system – no printed-out dupes – and managing the crew alone was a full-time job. My second sous, Alfredo, was already on the verge of cracking under the pressure.

'They don't *respect* me,' he complained of the Ecuadorian line cooks. 'Tell them! Tell them I can *fire them* if I want to.' This was *not* what I was looking for in a sous-chef. If the cooks were giving him attitude, my telling them that the guy could fire them was not going to make them respect him. The fact that Alfredo, alone among all of us, wore a big, floppy chef's hat on his head (made all the more ridiculous by his limited height) didn't help, nor did the fact that he was a rather proud Colombian. The Ecuadorians hated him and razzed him at every opportunity. When he began mulling aloud the possibility that maybe I should just put him back on the line and forget about all this sous-chef stuff, I promptly rescheduled him. He ended up bursting into tears and going over my head to the oily general manager, begging for his job back. I was appalled at this ultimate betrayal and reluctantly reinstated him, swallowing a poison pill I knew in the end would help kill me. This was a good friend and a good cook, whom I've never hired again. It's a measure of what pressure can do – and did – to both of us.

The restaurant itself was beautiful. Randy Gerber's Whiskey Bar was right next door, the outer space-style lobby of the Paramount could be reached through a side door in the dining room, and the walls were done in Morandi-inspired murals, warm Tuscan colors against blond, unfinished wood. The waiters dressed like Vatican Guards. But the most truly amazing feature of my temporary kingdom was to be found deep in the bowels of the Paramount Hotel, through twisting catacomb-like service passageways adjoining our downstairs prep kitchen. If one squeezed past the linen carts and discarded mattresses and bus trays from the hotel, and followed the waft of cold, dank air to its source, one came upon a truly awe-inspiring sight: the long-forgotten Diamond Horseshoe, Billy Rose's legendary New York nightclub, closed for generations. The space was gigantic, an underground Temple of Luxor, one huge, uninterrupted space. The vaulted ceiling was still decorated with Renaissance-style chandeliers and elaborate plasterwork. The original rhinestone-aproned stage, where Billy Rose's famously zaftig chorus line once kicked, was still there, and the giant space where the horseshoe-shaped bar once stood was empty, the floorboards torn up. Around the edges of the cavernous chamber were the remnants of private booths and banquettes where Legs Diamond and Damon Runyon and Arnold Rothstein and gangsters, showgirls, floozies and celebrities – the whole Old Broadway demi-monde of the Winchell era – used to meet and greet and make deals, place bets, listen to the great singers of the time and get up to all sorts of glamorous debauchery. The sheer size, and the fact that you had to slip through a roughly smashed-in wall to enter the chamber, made the visitor feel he was gazing upon ancient Troy for the first time.

Upstairs, in the real world, however, things were going quickly sour.

I *was*, I'm telling you for the record, unqualified for the job. I was in deep waters and fast-flowing ones at that. The currents could change at any time, without warning. One day, I attended a chefs' committee meeting on the East Side and returned to find that the whole menu had been changed back into Italian! This included the listings on the computer, so that when I expedited that evening, I found myself in the unenviable position of having to read off items in Italian, translate them into English in my head, and call them out to my Ecuadorian crew in Spanish. I had to learn some fast mnemonic tricks to keep up, like: 'I want to Lambada – just for the Halibut,' so that I would remember that *lambatini* was Italian for halibut, or 'I fucka you in the liver' to recall that *'fegato'* meant liver.

I worked seventeen hours a day, seven days a week, surrounded by a front-of-the-house crew who'd been, for the most part, with the company a long time, and were fiercely dedicated to all things Pino. They were so gung-ho in their ambitions, or so frightened of failing, that they'd cheerfully drag a knife across your throat if you so much as dropped a fork. The GM was an overgroomed tall blond northern Italian, an unctuous and transparently duplicitous cheerleader who was always urging his terrorized waiters to 'smile' and 'have fun' – while he calmly planned their imminent termination. This was a guy who would daily invite me over to the Whiskey Bar, supposedly to discuss strategy, buy me a drink, and then make repeated overtures about how we were a great 'team' and how 'we' were going to 'work together' against 'the others' – while all along he was doubtless dishing me as an alcoholic rube. I suspect that I was providing a valuable service to him on these trips – by providing official cover for his own need of a strong drink.

I soon found myself paralyzed by it all. I was just too tired and too confused and too spiritually empty to move this way or that. There was always something that needed doing, and none of it pleasant. Then sudden austerity measures required that I begin laying off crew and working line shifts in addition to my other duties (which I was having a hard time with already). Poor Steven and I were firing people whom, only a few weeks earlier, we had lured away from good-paying jobs – so many of them that often Steven would be letting somebody go in one room while I demolished someone's life in another. Each firing, each incident, each accident then had to be recorded on an appropriate form for the truly vapid director of human re-sources, who rambled on earnestly in New Agey patter about self-actualization and job satisfaction and fairness in hiring and appropriate down time – when she *knew* that the whole business rested firmly on the backs of a mob of underpaid, overworked and underfed (ten minutes for chicken leg, penne and salad, every single day, lunch and dinner) Ecuadorians of dubious legal status. Listening to this witless, hypocrite ramble on as if we all worked for Ben and Jerry rather than the realpolitik Kissingeresque Pino was to dream of smacking her stupid face with a pepper-mill, give her something to write about.

At one point, near the end, Steven and Alfredo, both reaching the end of their ropes as well, summoned me for a quiet word at a nearby bar, Scruffy Duffy's.

'They're gonna screw you, man,' they said. 'You gotta *do something*. You're fucking up! They're gonna get you!'

By this time I was thoroughly wiped out.

'Guys, I *know*, believe me . . . I *know*. But I'm not prepared to do any better than I'm doing now. I'm going on all eight cylinders, I'm doing the best I can, and *I know* I'm gonna get fucked sooner or later. When it happens it happens. I'm not prepared to do anything I'm not doing already. Sorry.'

When Mad 61 suddenly and unexpectedly closed, supposedly the result of a pissing contest between Pino and the Barney's owners, the Pressmans, I knew my goose was cooked. More as an academic exercise than out of real interest, I inquired of the reptilian GM and my chef de cuisine what they thought would happen here, now that there were fifty or so longtime loyalists footloose and fancy free and looking for work elsewhere in the company. I *knew* the answer, of course; I just wanted to see if they'd lie to my face. They didn't disappoint me.

A bunch of us went out for drinks one night and I found myself among a party of eight, all of whom knew that of which I had yet to be informed: namely that I would be asked to step down, to work with the nauseating and sadistic little creep who was my chef de cuisine. (I caught him constantly *hitting* the Ecuadorians on the shoulder, them not knowing whether to take it as a joke or not, and immediately I offered a bounty of five dollars for every time one of them hit him back.)

The next night, at the end of the shift, the GM had a martini waiting for me at the bar. I knew it was over. He began, elegantly couching his words in all sorts of qualifiers, yammering on about redeployment, unfelt and insincere praise for my work etcetera. I quickly cut him off. I'd injured my thumb earlier, and in spite of a butterfly closure and three layers of bandage, it just wouldn't stop bleeding; blood drained onto my pants leg as he talked, fell on the floor in big noisy droplets.

'Just cut the shit and tell me what you have to,' I said. 'Am I canned or what?'

'No, no . . . of course not,' he said, flashing a mouthful of pearly-white teeth at me, 'We'd like you to stay on – as chef de cuisine.' I declined his offer, packed up my stuff and went immediately home where I slept, nearly without interruption, for three and a half straight days and nights.

There is little I miss about the experience at Coco Pazzo Teatro. I do miss the food: strawberries macerated with balsamic vinegar, sugar and a little mint, Patti Jackson's wonderful watermelon parfait, the incredible focaccia, robiola and white truffle pizza, the carta di musica flatbread, served with sea salt and olive oil, the homemade pasta and freshly made tomato sauces.

And I think fondly of Pino, the times I sat at the table with him and some of his other chefs, sampling food, each taking a bite and passing to the left. I miss hearing him regale us with stories of his first few years in America, his difficulties and pleasures, and I think fondly of his enthusiasm for food, the food he ate as a little boy in Italy – the squid and octopus and mackerel and sardines – a time and place far from the life he lives now: the sharp-cut suits, cellphones and fancy chauffeur-driven cars, the attendants and supplicants. Despite all the things that some chefs who've been through Pino's wringer have to say about him – much of it undoubtedly true – I owe him a big one. He taught me to love Italian food. To know it a little. He taught me, by extension, how to cook pasta, really cook pasta, and how to manage three or four ingredients in a noble, pure and unaffected way. He also taught me to watch my back better, and to make the most of my opportunities. I picked up a slew of recipes and techniques that I use to this day.

And I owe him something else, for which I am grateful, as I am to my old chef de cuisine, too. I amassed a lot of phone numbers in my brief time at Coco Pazzo Teatro and at Le Madri: some very fine Ecuadorian talent.

The next job I landed, I peeled off some of the best cooks in his organization. They are close pals and valued associates to this day.

DESSERT

A DAY IN THE LIFE

THANKS TO MY BIGFOOT training I wake up automatically at five minutes before six. It's still dark, and I lie in bed in the pitch-black for a while, smoking, the day's specials and prep lists already coming together in my head. It's Friday, so the weekend orders will be coming in: twenty-five cases of mesclun, eighteen cases of GPOD 70-count potatoes, four whole forequarters of lamb, two cases of beef tenderloins, hundreds and hundreds of pounds of meat, bones, produce, seafood, dry goods and dairy. I know what's coming, and the general order in which it will probably arrive, so I'm thinking triage – sorting out in my head what gets done first, and by whom, and what gets left until later.

As I brush my teeth, turn on the shower, swallow my first couple of aspirin of the day, I'm reviewing what's still kicking around in my walk-in from previous days, what I have to unload, use in specials, merchandize. I hear the coffee grinder going, so Nancy is awake, which leaves me only a few more minutes of undisturbed reflection on food deployment before I have to behave like a civilian for a few minutes.

I watch the local news and weather with my wife, noting, for professional reasons, any major sporting events, commuter traffic and, most important, the weekend weather forecast. Nice crisp weather and no big games? That means we're going to get slammed tonight. That means I won't come crawling home until close to midnight. By now, half-watching the tube, and half-listening to Nancy, I'm fine-tuning the specials in my head: grill station will be too busy for any elaborate presentations or a special with too many pans involved, so I need something quick, simple and easily plated – and something that will be popular with the weekend rubes. The people coming to dinner tonight and Saturday night are different from the ones who eat at my restaurant during the week, and I have to take this into account. Saddle of wild hare stuffed with foie gras is *not* a good weekend special, for instance. Fish with names unrecognizable to the greater part of the general public won't sell. The weekend is a time for buzzwords: items like shrimp, lobster, T-bone, crab-meat, tuna and swordfish. Fortunately, I've got some hamachi tuna coming in, always a crowd-pleaser.

As I walk up to Broadway and climb into a taxi, I'm thinking grilled tuna livornaise with roasted potatoes and grilled asparagus for fish special. My overworked grill man can heat the already cooked-off spuds and the pre-blanched asparagus on a sizzle-platter during service, the tuna will get a quick walk across the grill, so all he has to do is heat the sauce to order. That takes care of fish special. Appetizer special will be cockles steamed with chorizo, leek, tomato and white wine – a one-pan wonder; my garde-manger man can plate salads, rillettes, ravioli, confits de canard while the cockle special steams happily away on a back burner. Meat special is problematic. I ran the ever-popular T-bone last week – two weeks in a row would threaten the French theme, and I run about a 50 percent food cost on the massive hunks of expensive beef. Tuna is already coming off the grill, so the meat special has got to go to the sauté station. My sous-chef, who's working sauté tonight, will already have an enormous amount of mise-en-place to contend with, struggling to retrieve all the garnishes and prep from an already crowded low-boy reach-in – just to keep up with the requirements of the regular menu. At any one time, he has to expect and be ready for orders for moules marinières, boudin noir with caramelized apples, navarin of lamb (with an appalling array of garnishes: baby carrots, pearled onions, niçoise olives, garlic confit, tomato concassée, fava beans and chopped fresh herbs), filet au poivre, steak au poivre, steak tartare, calf's liver persillé, cassoulet toulousaine, magret de moulard with quince and sauce miel, the ridiculously popular mignon de porc, pieds du cochon – and tonight's special, whatever that's going to be.

I've got some play here: both leg of venison and some whole pheasants are coming in, so I opt for the pheasant. It's a roasted dish, meaning I can par-roast it ahead of time, requiring my sous-chef simply to take it off the bone and sling it into the oven to finish, then heat the garnishes and sauce before serving. Easy special. A lay-up. That should help matters somewhat.

By the time I arrive at Les Halles, I have my ducks pretty much in a row.

I'm the first to arrive, as usual – though sometimes my pastry chef surprises me with an early appearance – and the restaurant is dark. Salsa music is playing loudly over the stereo behind the bar, for the night porter. I check the reservation book for tonight, see that we already have eighty or so res on the book, then check the previous night's numbers (the maître d' has already totaled up reservations and walk-ins) and see that we did a very respectable 280 meals – a good portent for my food cost. The more steak-frites I sell, the better the numbers will be. I flip through the manager's log, the notebook where the night manager communicates with the day management, noting customer complaints, repair requirements, employee misbehavior, important phone calls. I see from the log that my grill man called one of the waiters a 'cocksucker' and pounded his fist on his cutting board in a 'menacing way' when five diners waddled into the restaurant at three minutes of midnight closing and ordered five côtes du boeuf, medium-well (cooking time forty-five minutes). I sip my cardboard-tasting take-out coffee from the deli next door and walk through the kitchen, taking notice of the clean-up job the night porter has done. It looks good. Jaime grins at me from the stairwell. He's dragging down a bag full of sodden linen, says, 'Hola, chef.' He's covered with grime, his whites almost black from handling dirty, food-smeared kitchen floor mats, and hauling hundreds of pounds of garbage out to the street. I follow him down, walk through the still wet cellar to the office, plop down at my desk and light my tenth cigarette of the day while I rummage around in my drawer for a meat inventory sheet/order form. First thing to do is find out exactly how much cut, fabricated meat I have on hand. If I'm low, I'll need to get the butcher on it early. If I have enough stuff on hand to make it through tonight, I'll still have to get tomorrow's order in soon. The boucherie is very busy at Les Halles, cutting meat not just for the Park Avenue store, but for our outposts in DC, Miami and Tokyo.

I kick off my shoes and change into checks, chef's jacket, clogs and apron. I find my knife kit, jam a thick stack of side-towels into it, clip a pen into my jacket sideways (so it doesn't fall out when I bend over) and, taking a ring of keys from my desk, pop the locks on the dry-goods room, walk-in, reach-ins, pastry box and freezers. I push back the plastic curtains to the refrigerated boucherie, a cool room where the butchers do their cutting, and grab the assistant butcher's boom-box from the work-table. Knives, towels, radio, clipboards and keys in hand, I climb the Stairmaster back up to the kitchen.

I've assembled a pretty good collection of mid-'70s New York punk classics on tape: Dead Boys, Richard Hell and the Voidoids, Heartbreakers, Ramones, Television and so on, which my Mexican grill man enjoys as well (he's a young headbanger fond of Rob Zombie, Marilyn Manson, Rage Against the Machine, so my musical selections don't offend him). I'm emptying the sauté station reach-in when he arrives. Carlos has got a pierced eyebrow, a body by Michelangelo, and considers himself a master soup-maker. The first thing he asks me is if I've got snapper bones coming in. I nod. Carlos dearly loves any soup he can jack with Ricard or Pernod, so today's soupe de poisson with rouille is a favorite of his. Omar, the garde-manger man, who sports a thick, barbed-wire tattoo around his upper arm, arrives next, followed quickly by the rest of the Queens residents; Segundo the *vato loco* prep centurion, Ramón the dishwasher, and Janine the pastry chef. Camelia, the general manager, is last – she walks to work – and we exchange '*Bonjour!*' and '*Comment ça va?*'

Soon everyone is working: Carlos roasting bones for stock, me heating sauces and portioning pavées, filet mignons, porc mignons, duck breasts and liver. Before twelve, I've got to cut and pepper pavées and filets, skin and slice the calf's liver, lug up cassoulet, caramelize apples, blanch baby carrots, make garlic confit, reload grated cheese, onion soup, sea salt, crushed pepper, breadcrumbs, oils. I've got to come up with a pasta special using what's on hand, make livornaise sauce for Carlos, make a sauce for the pheasant and, most annoying, make a new batch of navarin, which will monopolize most of my range-top for much of the morning. Somewhere in the middle of this, I have to write up the specials for Camelia to input into the computer and set the prices (at nine-thirty sharp, she's going to start buzzing me on the intercom, asking me in her thick French accent if I have 'le muh-NEW').

Delivery guys keep interrupting me for signatures, and I don't have nearly as much time as I'd like to check over the stuff. As much as I'd like to push my snout into every fish gill and fondle every vegetable that comes in the door, I can't – there's just not enough time. Fortunately, my purveyors know me as a dangerously unstable and profane rat-bastard, so if I don't like what I receive, they know I'll be on the phone later, screaming at them to come and 'pick this shit up!' Generally, I get very good product. It's in my purveyors' interests to make me happy. Produce, however, is unusually late. I look at the kitchen clock nervously – not much time left. I have a tasting to conduct at eleven-thirty, a sampler of the day's specials for the floor staff, accompanied by detailed explanation, so they won't describe the pheasant as 'kinda like chicken'.

The butcher arrives, looking like he slept in his clothes. I rush downstairs, hot on his heels, to pick up my meat order: a towering stack of milk crates, loaded with plastic-wrapped côtes du boeuf, entrecôtes, rumpsteaks, racks of lamb, lamb stew-meat, merguez, saucisson de Toulouse, rosette, pork belly, onglets, scraps, meat for tartare, pork tenderloins larded with bacon and garlic, pâtés, rillettes, galantines and chickens. I sign for it and push the stack around the corner for Segundo to rotate into my stock. Still downstairs, I start loading up milk crates of my own. I try to get everything I need for the day into as few loads as possible, limiting my trips up and down the Stairmaster as much as I can. I have a feeling I'm going to get hit on lunch today and I'll be up and down those stairs like a jack-in-the-box tonight, so those extra trips make a difference. Into my crates go the pork, the liver, the pavées, filets, some duck breasts, a bag of fava beans, herbs and vinegar for sauce. I give Ramón, the dishwasher, a list of additional supplies for him to haul up – the sauces to be reduced, the grated cheese – easily recognizable stuff he won't need a translator or a search party to locate.

On my station (sauté), I've got only a six-burner Garland to work with. There's another range next to it which is taken up with a bain-marie for sauces and onion soup, the rest of it with stocks – veal, chicken, lamb; and pork – which will be reducing at a slow simmer all day and into the night. One of my burners during service will be occupied permanently by a pot of water for Omar to dunk ravioli in, leaving me five with which to work. Another burner, my front right, will be used mostly by him as well, to sauté lardons for frisée salads, to sear tidbits of hanger steak for onglet salad, for sautéing diced potatoes in duck fat for the confit de canard, and the cockles – which will leave me, most likely, with four full-time burners with which to prepare a wide range of dishes, any one of which alone could require two burners for a single plate. Soon, there'll be a choo-choo train of sauté pans lined up waiting for heat, requiring constant prioritizing. If I get a six-top, for instance, with an order for, say, two orders of magret de moulard, a porc mignon, a cassoulet, a boudin noir and a pasta, that's *nine* sauté pans needed for that table alone.

Reducing gastrite (sugar and vinegar) for duck sauce while

the Dead Boys play 'Sonic Reducer' on the boom-box, I have to squeeze over for Janine, who melts chocolate over the simmering pasta water. I'm not annoyed much, as she's pretty good about staying out of my way, and I like her. She's an ex-waitress from Queens, and though right out of school, she's hung tough. Already she's endured a leering, pricky French sous-chef before my arrival, the usual women-friendly Mexicans, and a manager who seems to take personal delight in making her life miserable. She's never called in sick, never been late, and is learning on the job very nicely. She inventories her own supplies on Saturdays, and as I hate sticky, goopy, sweet-tasting, fruity stuff, this is a great help to me. As I've said before, I greatly admire tough women in busy kitchens. They have, as you might imagine from accounts in this book, a lot to put up with in our deliberately dumb little corner of Hell's Locker-room, and women who can survive and prosper in such a high-testosterone universe are all too rare. Janine has dug in well. She's already managed to infuriate the whole floor staff by claiming she inventories the free madeleines we give away with coffee. I'm pleased with her work, making an exception in my usual dim view of pâtissiers.

Next to me, Omar, my garde-manger man, is on automatic. I don't even have to look over at his station because I know exactly what he's doing: loading crocks, making dressing, rubbing down duck legs with sea salt for confit, slowly braising pork bellies for cassoulet, whipping mushroom sabayon for the ravioli de Royan. I rarely have any worries about his end. I smell Pernod, so I know without looking what Carlos is up to: soupe de poisson.

Segundo is downstairs receiving orders from the front delivery ramp. I hear the bell every few minutes, as a few more tons of stuff arrive. He'll have my walk-in opened up like a cardiac patient by now, rotating in the new, winnowing out the old, the ugly and the 'science experiments' that sometimes lurk, forgotten and fuzzy, in dark corners, tucked behind the sauces and stocks. He's a mean-looking bastard. The other Mexicans claim he carries a gun, insist that he sniffs 'thinner' and 'pintura', that he's done a lot of prison time. I don't care if he killed Kennedy, the man is the greatest prep cook I've ever had. How he finds the time and the strength to keep up with deliveries, the nuts and bolts of deep prep, like cleaning squid, washing mussels and spinach, dicing tomato, julienning leek, filleting fish, wrapping and deboning pigs' feet, crushing peppercorns and so on, and yet still finds time to make me beautiful, filament-thin chiffonaded parsley (which he cuts with a full-sized butcher's scimitar) is beyond me.

The last cook to arrive is our French fry guy. This is a full-time job at Les Halles, where we are justifiably famous for our frites. Miguel, who looks like a direct descendant of some Aztec king, spends his entire day doing nothing but peeling potatoes, cutting potatoes, blanching potatoes, and then, during service, dropping them into 375-degree peanut oil, tossing them with salt, and stacking the sizzling hot spuds onto plates with his bare hands. I've had to do this a few times, and it requires *serious* calluses.

I hold the waiters' meeting and tasting at eleven-thirty. The new waiter doesn't know what prosciutto is, and my heart sinks. I run down the specials, speaking slowly and enunciating each syllable as best I can for the slower, stupider ones. The soup is soupe de poisson with rouille – that's a garlic pepper mayonnaise garnish, for the newbies. Pasta is linguine with roasted vegetables, garlic, baby artichokes, basil and extra virgin olive oil. The whole roasted fish of the day is black sea bass – that's not *striped* bass, for our slower students – and crusted with sel de Bretagne. The fish of the day is grilled tuna livornaise, asparagus and roasted potatoes. Does anyone need 'livornaise' explained . . . *again*? The meat special is roast pheasant with port wine sauce and braised red cabbage. There *are* faux filets for two available (that's the big, hip-end piece off the sirloin, strip-carved tableside for fifty bucks). Dessert special is tarte Tatin. It's not *too* bad a line-up on the floor today: Doogie Howser, 'Morgan the part-time underwear model,' Ken the veteran (who has a maniacal laugh you can hear out on the street; he's everyone's first choice for Waiter Most Likely to Snap, Shave His Head, Climb a Tower and Start Shooting Strangers); and some new waiter, the one who doesn't know what prosciutto is. I haven't bothered to learn his name, as I suspect he will not remain with us for long. There are two busboys, a taciturn workaholic from Portugal and a lazy-ass Bengali; they should balance out, as usual.

My runner today is the awesome Mohammed, nicknamed Cachundo by the kitchen – the best we have. I'm lucky to have him, as it looks like it's going to be busy, and the other runner, let's call him Osman, tends to lose it when things get hectic and has an annoyingly sibilant way of pronouncing the letter 's', making his calls for 'mussselss' 'meat sspesssiall' and 'Calvesss' leever particularly painful to hear when you're under fire. Cachundo immediately begins picking chervil tops, arranging garnishes, filling small crocks with grated Parmesan, harissa sauce, rosemary and thyme, gaufrette potato chips, and picking out my favorite saucing spoons from the silver bins.

At various times during my labors, I manage to conduct two clandestine meetings out on the street: agent reports on the activities of the previous night (after my departure). I'm investigating the grill man incident from the manager's log. Nothing earth-shaking. I have another brief encounter near the liquor room with someone who gives me the latest gossip from our Miami store and a rundown of latest developments at Le Marais, our sister restaurant on 47th Street, as well as some speculation about imminent moves by upper management and ownership. Again, nothing I don't know or assume already. I like my bosses – and think they like me – so it's really only curiosity, not paranoia, that keeps me collecting and analyzing information from our distant outposts and conference rooms. Also, I like to hear different accounts of the same incident from different sources. It adds perspective and reveals, sometimes, what a particular source is *leaving out*, or skewing to leave a particular impression, making me wonder: *Why?* I like to tell selected people things in supposed confidence a few times a week, for fun. Later, when it comes back to me it provides an interesting road map of data transfer, a barium meal, revealing who squeals and to whom. There are a number of interesting variations on this practice – feeding *false* information to a known loudmouth, for instance, with a particular target in mind. A lot of what I hear is utterly useless, untrue and uninteresting. But I like to keep myself informed. You never know what might prove useful later.

Twelve noon and already customers are pouring in. I get a quick kick in the crotch right away: an order for porc mignon, two boudins, a liver and a pheasant all on one table. The boudins take the longest, so they have to go in the oven right away. First, I prick their skins with a cocktail fork so they don't explode, grab a fistful of caramelized apple sections and throw them in a sauté pan with some whole butter for finishing later. I heat a pan with butter and oil for the pork, fling a thick slab of calf's liver into a pan of flour after salting and peppering it, heat another sauté pan with butter and oil for that. While the pans are heating, I take half a pheasant off the bone and lay it on a sizzle-platter for the oven, spinning around to fill a small saucepan with the port sauce to reduce. Pans ready, I sear the pork, sauté the liver – the pork goes straight into the oven on another sizzler – the hot pan I degrease, deglaze with wine and stock, add pork sauce, a few garlic confit, then put aside to finish reducing and mounting later. The liver half-cooked, I put aside on another sizzler. I sauté some chopped shallots, deglaze the pan with red wine vinegar, give it a shot of demi-glace, season it and put that aside too. An order for mussels comes in, with a breast of duck order right after. I throw on another pan for the duck, load a cold pan with mussels, tomato coulis, garlic, shallots, white wine and seasoning. The mussels will get cooked à la minute and finished with butter and parsley.

More orders come in. It's getting to be full-tilt boogie time: another pheasant, more pork, another liver, and *ouch!* a navarin – a one-pot wonder but requiring a lot of digging around in my low-boy for all the garnishes. The key to staying ahead on a busy station is moving on a dish as soon as its name is out of Cachundo's mouth – setting up the pan, doing the pre-searing, getting it into the oven quickly, making the initial moves – so that later, when the whole board is fluttering with dupes, I can still tell what I have working and what I have waiting without having to read the actual tickets again.

'Ready on twelve!' says Carlos, who's already got a load of steaks and chops and a few tunas coming up. He wants to know if I'm close on my end. 'Let's go on twelve!' I say. Miguel starts dunking spuds. I call for mashed potatoes for the boudins from Omar, give the apples a few tosses over flame, heat and mount my liver sauce, pull the pork mignons from the oven and clip off the strings that hold them together, heat potatoes and veg for the pheasant, squeeze the sauce for the pheasant between pots on to a back burner, move the mussels off the heat and into a ready bowl, calling, '*Papas fritas para conchas negras*' to Miguel as I spin and bend to check my duck breasts. Sauce pot with duck sauce and quince, I'll heat those right in the sauce, no room now, the orders are really coming in, the printer chattering away non-stop. I'm sneaking peeks at the dupes while they're still coming off the printer, trying to pick out what I'll be needing, like a base runner stealing signals. The intercom buzzes and I pick up, annoyed.

'Line one for the chef,' says the hostess.

I push the blinking green light. It's a salesman, wanting to sell me smoked fish. I answer all sweetness and light, lulling him into the bear trap in the Bigfoot style: 'So let me get this straight,' I say, after he's jabbered away about his full line of delicacies, me trying to sound a little slow and confused, 'you want to sell me food, right?' 'Yes!' comes the reply, the salesman sounding encouraged by my interest and apparent stupidity. 'And in general, you'd say,' I continue, 'you have like, a *lot* of restaurant accounts – in fact, you'd probably say that, like, you are in the business of servicing restaurants . . . and *chefs* in particular?' 'Oh, yes! says the witless salesman, beginning a litany of the usual prestigious accounts, the names of other chefs who buy his fine smoked sturgeon, salmon, trout and fish eggs. I have had enough and cut him off cold. 'So . . . WHAT THE FUCK ARE YOU DOING CALLING ME IN THE MIDDLE OF THE FUCKING LUNCH RUSH?!' I scream into the phone, smashing it abruptly into the cradle.

I catch the duck just in time, roll it over skin-side down again and pull it out of the oven. I've got a filet au poivre on order – not on the regular lunch menu – but it's a steady customer, says Cachundo, and I'm set up for it anyway, so I start searing one off. Another pasta. I pour extra virgin into a pan and sauté some paper-thin garlic slices with some crushed red pepper, add the artichoke hearts, roasted vegetables, some olives. I don't know why, but I always start humming Tony Bennett or Dino – today it's 'Ain't That a Kick in the Head' – when I'm cooking pasta. I *like* cooking pasta. Maybe it's that I always wanted to be Italian American in some dark part of my soul; maybe I get off on that final squirt of emulsifying extra virgin, just after the basil goes in, I don't know. More porc mignons, the runner calls down to Janine, who's making clafoutis batter at her work station in the cellar, and she comes running up to plate desserts . . .

We're doing well, so far. I'm keeping up with the grill, which is a faster station (unless a table orders a côte de boeuf or a faux filet for two or a whole roasted fish, which slows the order down). Omar is up to date with the appetizers, and I'm actually feeling pretty good, right in the zone. No matter what comes in, or how much of it, my hands are landing in the right places, my moves are still sharp and my station still looks clean and organized. I'm feeling fine, putting a little English on the plates when I spin them into the window, exchanging cracks with Carlos, finding time to chide Doogie Howser for slipping that filet poivre by me without checking first.

'Doogie, you syphilitic, whitebread, mayonnaise-eating, John Tesh-ass wannabe – next time you slip a special order in without checking with me first? Me and Carlos gonna punch two holes in your neck and bump dicks in the middle!'

Doogie cringes, laughs nervously and scurries out on to the floor, trailing muttered apologies.

'Chef,' says Omar, looking guilty, 'no más tomates . . .'

My jaw drops, and I see white.

I *ordered* tomatoes. I had thought that tomatoes had arrived – then remember I broke up the order between three companies. I call Segundo on the intercom, tell him to come up *ahorita*. I'm also furious with Omar for waiting until we're out of tomatoes to tell me there are no more.

'What the fuck is going on?' I ask Segundo, who slouches in the doorway like a convict in the exercise yard. 'No Baldor,' he says, causing me to erupt in a blind, smoking rage. Baldor, though a superb produce purveyor, has been late twice in recent weeks, prompting me to make some very uncivil telephone calls to their people – and worse, forcing me to do business with another, lesser company until they got the message and began delivering earlier. Now, with no tomatoes, and no delivery, and the rush building, I'm furious. I call Baldor and start screaming right away: 'What kind of glue-sniffing, crackhead mesomorphs you got working for you? You don't *have* an order for me? *What*?! I called the shit in *myself* . . . I spoke to a *human*! I didn't even leave it on the tape! And you're telling me you *don't have my order*? I got three fucking produce companies! THREE! AND IT'S ALWAYS *YOU* THAT FUCKS ME IN THE ASS!' I hang up, pull a few pans off the flame, load up some more mussels, sauce a duck, arrange a few pheasants, and check my clipboard. I'm in the middle of telling Cachundo to run across the street to Park Bistro and ask the chef there if we can borrow some tomatoes when I see, from my neat columns of checked-off items on my clipboard, that in fact I ordered the tomatoes from another company, that I didn't order anything from Baldor. I have no time to feel bad about my mistake – that'll come later. After screaming at the blameless Baldor, my anger is gone, so when I call the guilty company, I can barely summon a serious tone. It turns out that my order has been routed to another restaurant – Layla, instead of Les Halles. I make a mental note to refer to my restaurant as 'Less Halluss' in the future. The dispatcher at the guilty company apologizes for the mix-up, promises my order within the hour and gives me a hundred dollars in credit.

More ducks, more pheasant, lots of mussels, the relentless tidal wave of pork mignons . . . finally lunch begins to wind down. I enjoy a cigarette in the stairwell while Carlos continues drilling out steaks, chops and paillards, nothing for my station. D'Artagnan arrives, my specialty purveyor, bearing foie gras, duck legs, and an unexpected treat – a 200-pound free-range pig, whole, which José, one of my masters, has ordered for use in pâtés and tête du porc by the charcutier. Now, I can lift a 200-pound, living breathing human – for a few seconds anyway – but dragging 200 pounds of ungainly dead weight by the legs through the restaurant and down the stairs to the boucherie requires four strong men. The boucher, charcutier, dishwasher and I wrestle the beast down the stairs, its head bouncing gruesomely on each step. I now know what it must be like to dispose of a body, I mutter. I do not envy the Gambino crime family – this is *work*!

The general manager sits down to lunch with the hostess. Two calamari, no oil, no garlic, a fish special no sauce, a céleri rémoulade. Frank, my new French sous-chef, arrives. I have a list for him: dinner specials, mise-en-place, things to do, things to look out for. When he takes over the sauté station later, relieving me, I am grateful . . . my knees are hurting and the familiar pain in my feet is worse than usual.

José, my boss, stops by, wanting to take me to the Greenmarket. I quickly tie up a few loose ends, make sure Frank is briefed, and walk down to the market – about eleven blocks. We fondle, sniff, squeeze and rummage through produce for a while, returning to the restaurant an hour later with pears, lemon verbena, some baby fennel, fingerling potatoes and some turnips with greens, for all of which I'll have to come up with specials. The joke around Les Halles is that every time José walks in the door, the food cost climbs 2 percent. The man would have me mount all my sauces with Normandy butter and foie gras, garnish everything with fresh truffles if I didn't squawk – but he *loves* food, a good thing in an owner. José gets a dreamy look on his face when he hears about black truffles coming into season, or the first softshell crabs of the season, even at sixty dollars (!) a dozen, or anything seasonal, high-quality, classic French, gamey, or difficult to find. He wants to be the first to sell it, whatever it costs. It's a strategy that seems to be working. The backbone of the business may be steak-frites but our regulars are often pleasantly surprised to find 15 dollars-worth of exotic food on a plate they're only paying 20 for, and little extras like that help develop a loyal clientele. Life with José means frequent surprise deliveries of very perishable and very expensive items, which I have to scramble to find outlets for, but what chef *doesn't* enjoy a load of Dover sole, still dripping with channel water and twisted with rigor, falling into his clutches? Okay, my grill man won't be too thrilled – *he*'s the guy who'll have to skin and bone and reassemble them to order – but that's just tough.

Back from the market, night crew suiting up in the locker-room, I have just enough time to assemble the orders for Saturday. This is something I *enjoy* doing. My young gangster friend Segundo and I take a full tour of my walk-in and reach-ins. I've got two clipboards under my arm: one to assemble my orders (one page for Saturday, another to begin the Monday list) and a second for prep lists – my Things To Do Tomorrow list.

I break it down by company as I go along. De Bragga gets the Monday meat order; Schaller and Webber, the bacon. Riviera and Ridge get the produce – I'm too embarrassed to talk to Baldor right now. I see I need 40 pounds of whitewater mussels, 30 pounds of squid, eight whole fish, and a new fish of the day for Saturday and Sunday. I call Wild Edibles and talk to Chris Gerage, who was also a chef for Pino at one point, and we discuss what's good for tomorrow. I go for some wild striped bass, some king salmon, and some baby octopus for appetizer special. Dry goods, I'm locked in for the weekend – no Saturday deliveries – but I start building a Monday list anyway. From

D'Artagnan, I'll need some more foie gras by Monday, some duck bones, maybe some magret, and maybe I'll splurge on some fresh black trumpets and some chanterelles for a special – José will be thrilled – and since wild boar has been a big moneymaker for me lately, maybe I'll make up on the boar what I lose on the 'shrooms. I add two boar legs to my D'Artagnan list. Segundo knows exactly what I'm going to ask him and in what order – he's ready for me.

We go through the familiar list of items, in my inept, but still useful Spanish:

'Mesclun?'

'*Veinte*,' he replies.

'*Cebolla blanca*'

'*Una*'

'Shallot?'

'*Tres.*'

And so on . . .

Dairy has to be in early or they'll call *me* which I hate. So I call the Monday dairy in right away: two poly milks, four 55-pound blocks of sweet butter, one case of heavy cream ultra, a case of large eggs. Gourmand, another specialty purveyor, needs lead time – they ship out of Washington, DC, so I get that order together as quickly as possible: haricots de Tarbe, the expensive white beans we use for cassoulet (perfect absorption), feuille de brik for pastry, Provence honey for the duck sauce, white anchovies in olive oil for niçoise salad, escargots, flageolets . . . I'm already thinking about pot-au-feu for next week and will need plenty of the expensive grey sea salt for condiment.

Ramón, the day dishwasher, tells me he'll need the day off tomorrow to visit a relative in the hospital, but he's replaced himself with Jaime II, the night dishwasher who'll double for him. I'm grateful, as nothing causes me more grief than last-minute emergency scheduling, and I'm always pleased when my crew takes care of things internally. Phoning my Mafia at home is a near impossibility. Most of them claim not to own phones.

For those who do, their phones are answered by people suspicious of strange Norteamericanos asking questions, and are not likely to acknowledge that, yes, Mr Pérez, Rodriguez, García, Sanchez, Rivera is actually in residence at said address.

Dinner-tasting for the floor staff is at five-thirty, when the heavy-hitting veteran waiters have arrived. They fall on the family gruel and the tasting plates like rabid jackals. It's never pretty watching waiters eat; you'd think they had no money the way they dive into any available trough. Dinner-tasting is conducted in the kitchen, as there are customers in the dining room straight through lunch into dinner. It looks like a crowded subway car as I describe the evening's specials and present each plate. They tear at the four plates of food, ripping apart the pheasant with their hands, nearly spearing each other with forks as they gouge at the tuna, drag cockles to their greasy maws with bare hands, and quickly turn Janine's lovely tarte Tatin into a dark smear. I swallow some more aspirins.

At five forty-five, the downstairs is clogged with the night-time lifer waiter crew, sitting on milk crates, folding napkins, smoking and talking about each other. Who got drunk last night, who got thrown out of a mob-run after-hours club then woke up in the bushes outside their house, who thinks the new maître d' is going to lose it tonight when the room fills up and the customers stacked up at the bar start screaming for their tables, who's going to win the World Cup, who thinks Heather Graham is a babe, who probably takes it in the ass *this* week, and how about the time the Bengali busboys got into a fight in the middle of the dining room and one stuck a steak knife into the other?

Dinner service. Overbooked as usual – with two whopping twelve-tops booked for prime time. I remain in the kitchen to expedite, hoping that maybe, just maybe, things'll slow down enough by ten for me to have a couple of cocktails and get home by eleven. But I know full well that the two big tables will hold up seatings by at least an hour; more than likely, I'll be here for the full tour.

By eight-thirty, the board is full. Entree tickets flutter in the pull from the exhaust fans. To my right, below the window, plated appetizers are lined up, waiting to get delivered to the tables, the window is full of sauté dishes, the work table in front of the fry station a panorama of steaks of different donenesses. It's still Cachundo – he's working a double too – and he ferries the plates out by hand, four or five at a time. Still, I have to press-gang the occasional busboy or empty-handed waiter, separating them out from the herd at the coffee and bread stations and returning dirty plates and glasses, into delivering desserts. I don't want ice cream melting over the clafoutis, or the whipped cream on the chocolate mousse to start falling. Food's getting cold, and my voice is already blown out from calling out orders over the noise from the dishwasher, the hum of the exhaust, the whine of the Paco-Jet machine and the growing roar from the dining room. I make a hand gesture to a friendly waiter, who knows what I want, and he soon arrives with an 'Industrial', a beer stein filled with margarita, for me. The drink manages to take the edge off my raging adrenaline buzz and goes down nicely after the three double espressos, two beers, three cranberry juices, eight aspirins, two ephedrine drinks, and a hastily gobbled hunk of merguez, which I managed to squeeze into a heel of bread before swallowing in two bites. By now, my stomach is a roiling hell broth of suppressed frustration, nervous energy, caffeine and alcohol. The night garde-manger man, Angel, who looks like he's twelve but sports a tattoo of a skull impaled with a dagger on his chest (future wife-beater, I think) is falling behind; he's got three raviolis, two duck confits, five green salads, two escargots, two Belgian endive and Stilton salads, two cockles, a smoked salmon and blini, two foie gras and a pâté working – *and* the sauté and grill stations are calling for urgent vegetable sides and mashed potatoes. I swing the pastry commis over to Angel's station to help out, but there's so little room, they just bump into each other.

Tim, a veteran waiter, is dry-humping Cachundo – to Cachundo's apparent displeasure. He's blocking the lane and impeding traffic in the narrow kitchen with his thrusting. I have to ask Tim nicely not to sexually harass my runners *during* service . . . after work, please. An order comes back for refire and Isidoro is *not* happy about it; it's cooked perfectly. I peer out into the dark dining room and see nothing except the dark silhouettes of customers waiting for tables at the bar, hear, even over the noise in the kitchen, the ambient chatter, the constant roar of diners as they shout over the music, the waiters describing specials over that noise, then fighting each other to get at the limited number of computer terminals to place orders, print out checks. 'Fire table *fourteen*! Catorsayy! . . . That's *six*, *seven*, *fourteen* and *one* on *fire*!' I shout 'Isidoro! You time it!' 'I ready fourteen,' says Isidoro, the grill man, as he slaps the refire back on a plate. Cachundo reaches around me and loads up with food, picking out plates seemingly at random, as if he's plucking daisies. I dry-swallow some more aspirins, and duck back into the stairwell for a few puffs of a cigarette.

A whole roasted fish comes back. 'The customer wants it deboned,' says an apologetic waiter. 'I told them it comes on the bone,' he whines, anticipating decapitation himself. Isidoro growls and works on the returned fish, slipping off the fillets by hand and then replating it. The printer is going non-stop now. My left hand grabs tickets, separates out white copy for grill, yellow copy for sauté, pink copy for me, coffee orders for the busboys. My right hand wipes plates, jams gaufrette potatoes and rosemary sprigs into mashed potatoes, moves tickets from the order to the fire positions, appetizers on order to appetizers out, I'm yelling full-time now, trying to hold it together, keep an even pace. My radar screen is filled with incoming bogeys and I'm shooting them down as fast as I can. One mistake, where a whole table comes back because of a prematurely fired dupe, or a bad combination of special requests ties up a station for a few critical seconds, or a whole roasted fish or a côte du boeuf has been forgotten? The whole line could come grinding to a dead stop, like someone dropping a wrench into a GM assembly line – utter meltdown, what every chef fears most. If something like that happens it could blow the whole pace of the evening, screw up everybody's heads, and create a deep, dark hole that could be very hard to climb out of.

'I gotta hot nut for table *six*!' I yell. There's a rapidly cooling boudin in the window, waiting for a tuna special to join it.

'Two minutes,' says Isidoro.

'Where's that fucking *confit*?' I hiss at poor Angel, who's struggling valiantly to make blini for smoked salmon, brown ravioli under the salamander, lay out pâtés and do five endive salads at once. A hot escargot explodes in the window, spattering me with boiling garlic butter and snail guts. 'Shit!' I say, dabbing my eye with a side-towel. '*Peenchayy* escargots!'

Frank's doing well, very well, keeping up. He did his apprenticeship with Robuchon, making food somewhat more elegant and delicately arranged than our Les Halles' humble workingman's fare, so it's a nice surprise that he's turned out to be such a line stud, cheerfully cranking out simple brasserie chow with speed and efficiency. He doesn't over-rely on the salamander, which I like (a lot of his French predecessors insist on cooking everything stone-rare, slicing and then coloring the slices under the salamander – something I hate to see); he makes minimal use of the microwave, which the cholo contingent has come to refer to contemptuously as 'cooking French-style', and I've only seen him throw one steak in the fry-o-lator. All-in-all, he's worked out well so far.

'*Platos*!' screams Isidoro. The dishwasher is buried up to his shoulders in the pot sink, his pre-wash area stacked with plates of unscraped leftovers and haphazardly dumped silver. I snarl and grab a Bengali busboy, shove his snout into a plate heaped with gnawed bones and half-eaten vegetables. 'Scrape!' I hiss menacingly, referring to the mess of unscraped plates. 'Busy, chef,' complains the busboy who, from what I've seen, has been wandering around with his thumb up his ass, taking out the occasional coffee, for hours. 'I don't give a fuck if you're saving the world,' I say. 'Scrape the plates *now*, or I'll tear your booga off and hurl it across the street at Park Bistro!'

David the Portuguese busboy is making espressos and cappuccinos behind me, but he moves pretty gracefully back there, not bumping me or spilling. We're used to each other's movements in the narrow space we share, knowing when to move laterally, when to make way for incoming dishes, outgoing food, the fry guy returning from downstairs with another 100-pound load of freshly cut spuds. I feel only the occasional light tap on the shoulder as he squeezes through with another tray of coffee and petit-fours, maybe a whispered, 'Behind you' or '*Bajando.*' Fred and Ginger time.

Finally the printer starts slowing down, and I can see by the thinning crowd at the bar that the last seating is under way: white spaces opening up in the dining room, stripped tables waiting for customers. We've got 280 dinners under our belts already. I turn the expediting over to Cachundo, drag my ass down the Stairmaster for a final walk-through. I check the stocks cooling in plastic buckets outside the walk-in, the gauze-wrapped pigs' feet which will have to be painstakingly deboned tomorrow, the soaking tarbais beans which have to be blanched, the salt-rubbed duck legs which will have to be confited in duck fat and herbs, and I notice the produce that José and I bought earlier at the market.

I make a final swing through the dry-goods room, note that I'll be needing more peanut oil soon, more peppercorns, more sherry wine vinegar. I'm already working on an early draft of tomorrow's Things To Do list, tomorrow's order list. I've got striped bass already ordered, and baby octopus, I remind myself. José's got a hard-on for black mission figs – he saw some at the market – so I'll have to tell Janine to start thinking about figs for a special. I have weekly inventory tomorrow morning, which means I'll have to weigh every scrap of meat and fish and cheese in the store and record it, count every can, bottle, case and box. There will be payroll tomorrow, making sense of the punch-ins and punch-outs of my not very computer-wise cooks and porters and dishwashers, all fourteen of them – and there's that extra shift for Carlos who worked extra for me last week, and the extra half for Isidoro the night he covered Omar and Omar doubled twice to cover the vacationing Angel – and shit! – there's the, overtime for that event at Beard House, and a promo party for what was it? A Taste of NoHo? Burgundy Night? A benefit for prickly heat? I have to record all the transfers of food from my stores to our outposts: the smoked salmon I shipped off to Washington, the flageolets I sent to Miami, the rosette and jambon de Paris I sent to Tokyo. I have to record all the stuff I gave to the butcher counter up front, and Philippe, my other boss, wants a list of suggestions for specials for the Tokyo chef. I peel off my fetid whites, groaning like a 2,000-year-old man as I struggle into my jeans and pullover.

I'm on the way out the door but Isidoro wants to talk to me. My blood runs cold. When a cook wants to talk to you, it's seldom good news: problem with another cook, minor feud, paycheck problem, request for time off. In Isidoro's case, he wants a raise. I gave Carlos a raise last week so I'll have a rash of greedy line cooks jumping me for money for the next few weeks. Another note to self: Frank needs the 16th off so I have to call Steven. I'm still buzzed with adrenaline when I finally push through the last waiting customers by the hostess stand and out the door, and wave for a taxi.

I'm thinking about going home but I know I'll just lie there, grinding my teeth and smoking. I tell the cabbie to take me to the corner of 50th and Broadway, where I walk downstairs to the subway arcade and the Siberia Bar, a grungy little underground rumpus room where the drinks are served in plastic cups and the jukebox suits my taste. There are a few cookies from the Hilton at the bar, as well as a couple of saggy, bruised-looking strippers from a club up the street. Tracy, the owner of the joint, is there, which means I won't be paying for drinks tonight. It's 1 A.M., and I have to be in at seven-thirty mañana, but the Cramps are playing on the jukebox, Tracy immediately fiddles with the machine so there's twenty free credits – and that first beer tastes mighty good. The Hilton cookies are arguing about mise-en-place. One of them is bitching about another cook nicking salt off his station, and the other cook doesn't see why that's such a big deal – so I'm gonna be involved in *this* conversation. The Cramps tune is followed by the Velvets singing 'Pale Blue Eyes', and Tracy suggests a shot of Georgian vodka he's got stashed in the freezer . . .

SOUS-CHEF

MY SOUS-CHEF, IN AN ideal situation, is like my wife.

I'll go further: my sous-chef, in an ideal situation, is *closer* to me than my wife. I mean no disrespect to my wife, Nancy, whom I adore, and with whom I've been stealing horses since high school. It's just that I spend a lot more time with my sous-chef. The judge, as Nancy likes to remind me, will never believe it.

Steven, my sous-chef from 1993 until recently – when he finally took on a kitchen of his own – was my evil twin, my doppelgänger, my director of clandestine services, a Bilko-esque character who, in addition to the usual sous-chef responsibilities such as running the kitchen in my absence, line cooking at a high level and watching my back, was invaluable to me for his remarkable ability to *get things done.*

Key to the walk-in lost? Just ask Steven. He'll have that door off its hinges in minutes. Robot-Coupe need a replacement part in the middle of a busy holiday rush? Steven will slip out the door and be back in minutes with the part – slightly used – and with another restaurant's shallots still in it. Want to know what they're thinking in the office? Ask Steven. He's suborned the secretaries and is reading the interoffice e-mail on a regular basis. Need bail money? A codeine pill for that knife wound? A new offset serrated knife real cheap? He's your boy. When I wonder what's in the heart and mind of someone I work with? I ask Steven. He'll take them out, get them liquored up so they blab their guts out, and I'll have a full report by noon next.

All the things I couldn't do – or couldn't be *seen* to do – he did. And he did them well. In fact, though a highly paid executive chef now for a major corporate outfit, he *still* works for me one night a week on my grill station, to keep his hand in, I guess. So there is still an action arm to my administration, a covert-action arm.

Having a sous-chef with excellent cooking skills *and* a criminal mind is one of God's great gifts. In our glory days together, like the capo of a crime family, or the director of the CIA, I could look across the room at Steven, raise an eyebrow, maybe make an imperceptible movement with my chin, and the *thing* – whatever the *thing* was at the time – would be done. Espionage, Impromptu Collection of Matériel, Revenge, Disinformation and Interrogation . . . our specialties.

I met Steven at the Supper Club. It was 1993, my return to the 'bigs'. I'd been working for Bigfoot at his West Village saloon, comfortable but in career limbo. I took a few weeks off to kick back in the Caribbean, and when I returned, I found a down-on-his luck Jimmy Sears in Bigfoot's kitchen. Bigfoot had been eating dinner at the Gotham recently, and had experienced some kind of culinary epiphany. Suddenly, he wanted a real chef, and Sears, whose restaurant in the Hamptons had just gone under, was sleeping on floors around Manhattan, dodging creditors and ex-girlfriends, and in general, going through a rough patch – prime time for a Bigfoot recruiting effort.

Jimmy was a brilliant cook. He'd come up with Brendan Walsh at Arizona 206, and the food he turned out in his brief time working the Bigfoot mines was so good, I'd stay after my shift was over, sit at the bar and order dinner and *pay for it*. Seeing what Jimmy could do in the kitchen really inspired me; I'd been slinging hash for way too long, and tasting a *real* demi-glace again, eating new, exciting food, seeing new presentations, made me remember what I'd enjoyed about food in the first place. I worked hard for Jimmy, and after knocking out a few thousand meals, going skiing together a few times, we'd become pals, and we determined that when Jimmy and Bigfoot's relationship came to an end, as it inevitably would, I'd keep an eye on the talented Mr Sears, maybe come along for the ride when he made his next move.

That clash of wills was not long in coming. A few months later, Jimmy's period of saloon exile was over; he landed the exec chef gig at the Supper Club, a huge restaurant/nightclub/disco on West 47th Street, and began hiring cooks. I was one of the first to get the call.

It was a plum job to be executive chef at the Supper Club. Hell, it was a plum job doing *anything* at the Supper Club. Perk-o-delic. The main dining room sat about 200, with private banquettes and booths along the walls, a dance floor, and a stage from which a twelve-piece orchestra played '40s swing music. There was an upstairs mezzanine – a holdover from the Club's previous incarnation as a Broadway theater – which sat another 150 or so, with a second bar, and off to the side, also on the second floor, was a smaller venue, a cabaret-cum-VIP lounge called the Blue Room, which sat another eighty. It was a pretty swank place, what they used to call a 'rug-joint' back in the '30s and '40s – a big, glitzy operation with plenty of cracks to fall through, a place where you could easily picture a young Burt Lancaster (just out of the joint), returning to find a young Kirk Douglas (the club owner) counting the night's take in one of the private banquettes. Dinner and dancing to swing music went on from five to eleven, after which the smoke machines would start belching chocolate-smelling fumes, the laser intellabeams would kick into action, the mirror ball would begin turning, a DJ would take over, and the Supper Club would become (for a while) the hottest dance club in town.

Every night there was a different crowd with a different promoter: Chicks with Dicks Night featured towering transvestites and pre-ops tottering around on high heels to house and techno; Soul Kitchen featured pre-disco '70s funk, with early blaxploitation films playing silently on the big screen and 40-ouncers and chicken wings for sale; Giant Step had acid jazz and fusion; Café Con Leche nights had salsa nueva and Latin funk;

Funkmaster Flex attracted a hip-hop crowd; Noel Ashman attracted Eurotrash and the face-lifted, well-dressed crowd . . . you never knew, there was every variety of nightlife madness as each night people lined up down the street and around the corner onto Eighth Avenue, waiting to get past our metal detectors and our thirteen burly security goons so they could rip up our bathrooms, crowd around our three bars, smoke weed, snort coke and copulate like bunnies in every nook and cranny of our cavernous pleasure palace.

Jimmy brought me in as an overpaid garde-manger man – 120 smacks a night to plate salads and squirt whipped cream on desserts. But Jimmy was not, at that time, an organizational mastermind. I am. Jimmy spent much of his time roller-blading around the city schmoozing; he had a second job, cooking for Mariah Carey and Tommy Mottola; he was secretly working out a deal for his triumphant return to the Hamptons; and of course he was poking everything in a skirt. By the time he'd swing by the Supper Club, little things like ordering, scheduling, rotating food and organizing menus were afterthoughts. I quickly found that doing it myself was easier than waiting for Jimmy to show up and do it for us, and in no time at all I was running the nuts-and-bolts end of the kitchen: making sure that we had the food, the prep, the bodies and information needed to crank out the enormous volume of parties, buffets, hors d'oeuvres and regular menu items the business required. Jimmy's food, as always, was magnificent, but Jimmy himself seldom seemed to be around. After a few months, I was de facto sous-chef, or kitchen manager – the guy everyone came to to find out what the hell was going on – and when I came back after another brief vacation in the Caribbean, Jimmy, though still nominally the chef, was secretly and simultaneously employed as the chef at The Inn at Quogue out in the Hamptons, and Steven Tempel was working in the Supper Club kitchen.

I guess it was a historic moment.

He showed up looking for a sauté position, his even more degenerate friend Adam Real-Last-Name-Unknown in tow. I had a few weeks to watch these two in action before Sears slipped off to the Hamptons and his even more reduced 'summer schedule', and I begged, pleaded and implored him not to saddle me with these two coke-snorting, thieving, fire-starting, whoring, boozing and troublemaking miscreants. Jimmy ignored my entreaties.

When Steven and Adam were in the kitchen together, I couldn't turn my back for a second. They were hyperactive and destructive, two evil Energizer bunnies who, when they weren't squabbling and throwing food at each other, seemed always to be dodging out of the kitchen on various criminal errands. They were loud, larcenous, relentlessly curious – Steven can't *look* at a desk without rifling its contents; they played practical jokes, and set up whole networks of like-minded co-workers. A few weeks after he arrived, Steven already had the whole club wired from top to bottom: the office help would tell him what everyone else was getting paid, security would give him a cut of whatever drugs they impounded at the door, and the techies let him play with the computers so that when an order for, say, swordfish came in, the dupe would also say, 'Fuck Me Hard'. Maintenance gave him a share of the lost-and-found and split the leftover booty from the promotional events – goody bags filled with cosmetics, CDs, T-shirts, bomber jackets, wrist-watches, etc.; the chief of maintenance even gave Steven the key to a disused office on the Supper Club's neglected third floor, an old janitor's storage room that, unbeknownst to management, had been converted to a carpeted, furnished and fully decorated pleasure pit, complete with working phone. It was a space suitable for small gatherings, drug deals and empire-building. The room was decorated with posters of Latina women penetrating themselves with vegetables, and it had been done up with pilfered carpet remnants and furniture from the adjoining Edison Hotel. As the space was located up a long flight of garbage-strewn back stairs, behind the reeking locker-rooms, down a dark, unlit hall where spare china was stored, management never visited – and a young man could be secure in the knowledge that whatever dark business he was conducting, no matter how loud, unruly or felonious, he was unlikely to be disturbed.

When management finally got wind of the fact that Jimmy was getting paid for *not* working at the Supper Club, I was made the chef. Unfortunately, Steven had already carved out his own invisible empire within my own.

It made things difficult.

The boy could *cook*, though.

The Club, particularly during the winter party season, when we regularly did banquets and sit-downs for hundreds and hundreds of people, required strength, skill and endurance, and an ability to improvise *fast* of its cooks. The bulletin board on my office wall was clogged with party sheets; sit-down meals for 300 would lead directly into four buffets and a cocktail reception for 700 – often on the same day. The logistics involved in buying the food, preparing it and moving it around for so many people were staggering – the invasion of Normandy every day of the week. Having an enterprising and capable little bastard like Steven around was a powerful asset. Here was a guy who could stay up all night snorting coke and drinking Long Island iced teas, getting into trouble of the most lurid kind, and *still* show up the next morning and knock out a thousand meals. I may have spent way too much time investigating the criminal activities of the Steven and Adam crime family, always calling one or the other into my office for a tune-up or an interrogation (I must have fired them both at least three times), but they, particularly Steven, always found a way to weasel their way back into my good graces and make themselves invaluable.

Steven, for a while, it seemed, saw the light (to whatever extent that's possible with Steven). One night, Nancy and I bumped into him at a bar in Westhampton. He'd been moonlighting (typical of Steven) for Sears, and when I saw him, he was slurring his words, his jaw twitching from cocaine, his eyes scrambling around in his sockets like caged spider monkeys, and he slapped an arm around my shoulders and announced that he was going to start showing up to work *on time*, that he was going to start behaving *responsibly*, that he was going to turn over a *new leaf*.

I remember Nancy looking at me as if to say, 'Yeah, *riiight* . . .'

He was, of course, promising much more than he could ever deliver. Life with Steven over the last five or six years has been notable for one hideous outrage after another. But he *did* begin showing up at work on time. He stopped disappearing on two- and three-day benders. He tried, as best he could, to refrain from bringing shame and disgrace upon my house and kitchen.

Most important, Steven, suddenly and inexplicably, became the sort of person who, when he says he's going to do a thing, does it. This, more than anything else, is the essence of sous-chefdom. With Steven around, I no longer had to come in in the morning and say, 'Did you take care of that thing?' The thing was always taken care of.

I like that. I made him my sous-chef.

Let's revisit, reconstructing from an untrustworthy and incomplete record, the checkered career of Steven Tempel: he grew up on Long Island, attended Johnson and Wales culinary school where, unsurprisingly, he ran into trouble (something about an assault) and was nearly expelled. He worked in a diner in Providence while he was at J and W (Steven, for all his faults, likes money and was never afraid to work), did time at Big Barry's out on the Island, bounced around a progression of knucklehead jobs and eventually migrated to Northern California, ending up at a joint called La Casa Nostra, where he encountered the uncontrollable idiot-savant and baking genius Adam Real-Last-Name-Unknown (nobody knows – as far as the Government is concerned, he doesn't even *exist*). Like Hunt and Liddy, these are two guys who should *never* have been allowed in a room together. When they're together, a sort of supernova of stupidity occurs, a critical mass of bad behavior. They like to reminisce about this California idyll period of their lives: snorting coke through uncooked penne, projectile vomiting in the parking lots of strip clubs, driving their owner into insolvency, soliciting, pandering, stealing and in every way leaving a trail of destruction and bodily fluids in their wake. Steven returned to New York, probably one step ahead of the law, and worked brief stints at Mathew's with Mathew Kenney ('Asshole' says Steven), Carmine's, the Plaza Hotel, and some other very decent restaurants for brief periods of time. Along the way, he managed to pick up a very respectable set of line-cooking chops, as well as that peculiar variety of less legitimate skills that continue to serve him well to this day. He remains a remarkable font of knowledge about the inner workings of the restaurant business, the real cogs and wheels. He can fix a broken compressor, repair appliances, pick locks, jury-rig electrical power where there was none before, unclog a grease trap, find a breaker, fix a refrigerator door. And he is a close observer of every detail of human and mechanical activity in the workplace – a guy who *notices* things – probably a result of all those years looking for opportunities for criminality. Little gets by him. If somebody's running a scam, Steven knows all about it. The idea, more than likely, occurred to him first.

As we battled through party season at the Supper Club, Steven and I did a lot of after-work drinking together, sitting around reviewing the events of the evening, planning our moves for the next day, pondering the mysteries of This Life We Live. I came to rely on him more and more, to find out what was going on, to fix things, to help me in the crushing, relentless routine of serving hundreds and hundreds of meals, different menus every day, hors d'oeuvres, à la carte meals, managing a staff of cooks that would swell into double digits for big events then shrink back to a core group of about eight for regular service.

Buying 10,000 dollars-worth of meat a day gave me a strange and terrible thrill, like riding a roller-coaster, and the simple act of moving ceiling-high piles of perishable fish and produce through my kitchen every day was a puzzle, a challenge I enjoyed. I liked being a general again: deploying forces where needed, sending out flying squads of cooks to put out brush fires on the buffet stations, arranging reconnaissance, forward observers, communicating by walkie-talkie with the various corners of the club:

'More filet on buffet six,' would come the call. 'More salmon on buffet four!' 'This is security at the door. I got a body count of three hundred and climbing! They're really coming in!' Amusingly, we shared a radio band with a nearby undercover unit from the street crimes division of the NYPD. They were always trying to get us to change frequency, which we couldn't, as we used them all: one for managers, one for kitchen, and a security band. After threats and shouts didn't work, the cops got clever; they listened, got to know our lingo and our locations and would play games with us, calling for 'More roast beef on buffet one!' when none was needed, or creating notional emergencies that would cause security to gang-rush the 'mezz bathroom' to break up a non-existent fight. It was a wild-style life. It wasn't unusual to see naked women hosing ice cream off their bodies in the kitchen pot sink (the Howard Stern event); sinister Moroccan food tasters packing heat (Royal Air Maroc party); Ted Kennedy in a kitchen walk-through eerily reminiscent of RFK's last moments; our drunken crew, in a hostile mood, bullying a lost Mike Myers into 'doing that Wayne's World *Ex*-cel-lent thing'; Rosie Perez hanging on the sauté end, fitting right in as if she worked with us, sitting on a cutting board, 'What's good to eat in here, boys?'; a clit-piercing on stage (Stern again); Madonna fans trying to sneak through the kitchen from the hotel (she brings her own eggs for Caesar salad); concerts, swimsuit models, hard-core hip-hoppers, go-go boys. One day there would be a wedding for 100 people where the customer spent 1,000 bucks per person for lobster and truffle ravioli, individual bottles of vodka frozen in blocks of ice, baby wedding cakes for every table, and the next, the whole club would be tented over, filled with dervishes and dancers from North Africa, serving couscous and pigeon pie for a thousand.

Thanks to the Bigfoot Program, I never ran out of food, was always prepared, was never late, and Steven helped enormously. What finally made him a serious character in my eyes was the night he ran a knife through his hand while trying to hack frozen demi-glace out of a bucket. Squirting blood all over the place, he wrapped his hand in an apron and listened to my instructions: 'Get your sorry ass down to Saint Vincent's, they've got a fast emergency room. Get yourself stitched up and *get yourself back here in two fucking hours!* We're gonna be busy as hell tonight and I need you *on the line!*' He returned ninety minutes later and managed to work, one-handed, on the sauté station, very capably cranking out 150 or so à la carte dinners. I was pleased with this demonstration of loyalty. Working through pain and injury counts for a lot with me.

I don't really know what happened to the Supper Club. The general manager, with whom I had a good working relationship, was suddenly gone. Nightclub operations were shut down, possibly in response to neighborhood complaints about noise, unmanageable crowds in the streets, change in ownership. The new management team was an oily duo of ex-waiters from the Waldorf, a Spaniard and an 'I dunno' who liked to pretend they were French. I answered an ad in the paper for a chef and was quickly in the wind.

I took Steven along.

One look at One Five, and I knew the place was doomed. Jerry Kretchmer, with the hugely talented Alfred Portale in tow, had just failed in the same location. The new owners were two very nice matronly middle-aged ladies with little to no restaurant experience. But I fell in love with the kitchen. It was huge, well equipped and loaded with history. I'd even worked there for a day while at CIA, as part of a 'Day in New York' field trip. The dining room was appointed with the salvage from the ocean liner *Normandie*, which had sunk mysteriously in New York harbor. It was an irresistible impulse. My predecessor, a jumped-up megalomaniac boob, had already plowed through most of the partners' dough, insisting on a kitchen staff of thirteen people to serve sixty or so dinners a night, so I figured it wouldn't be too hard to make a difference and do some honest toil for these nice ladies, save them a few bucks.

Hiring crew, post-Supper Club, with Steven as my underboss, was always fun. I felt like Lee Marvin, with Steven as Ernest Borgnine, in *The Dirty Dozen* when they recruit a fighting unit from the dregs of the stockade. Steven and I would meet, and I'd say, 'Who's available?' We'd discuss who was still talking to himself, suffering from paranoid delusions ('But can he still work the line?'), who could be lured away from another job ('Is he happy? How happy? What's he getting paid?'), who was still loyal from the collection of part-timers and freelancers we'd used for party work at the Supper Club, who had evenings free after knocking off at Le Bernardin, who could keep it together, show up on time, keep their mouth shut, and do the right thing – even if he woke up every morning naked and covered with puke on a cold bathroom floor. Steven would scour the lunatic fringe, other chefs' kitchens, flipping through the amazing mental Rolodex he kept in his head, the two of us embarking, again, on a clandestine head-hunt that often stripped rival kitchens bare. I loved those first interviews, laying eyes on old friends, new recruits, a motley collection of psychopathic grill men, alcoholic garde-mangermen, trash-talking chick sauciers, Ecuadorian pasta cooks, deranged pâtissiers, cooks who thought that Sylvester Stallone was keeping them under constant surveillance ('Sly *knows* I wrote *Cliffhanger* – and he knows I know *too much*,' said one cook who'd apparently been communicating telepathically with Stallone while flipping burgers at Planet Hollywood). 'I needa two Heineken, seven o' clock!' said my old friend Chinese Davey, from Bigfoot days, his hand scraped raw from extracting bottles of beer from a chained cooler night after night. 'Every night! Seven o clock! Two Heineken!! No Budwasser! *Heineken*!' He got the job. 'I am there, Chef!' said Manuel, the pasta stud, on the phone from a very busy midtown kitchen. 'I am with you!' He dropped his apron in the middle of pre-theater rush, told the chef to fuck himself, and rushed right over. Always liked that guy. He needed Sundays off, to go to church, he said. No problem. And God help me, I even hired Adam . . . now and again.

'I'm never going to slink home again, knowing I fucked up,' I'd tell Steven in one of our many post-game analysis sessions. 'Things go sour here? It won't be for lack of trying on my part. I ain't never gonna dog it, I'm never going home at the end of the shift feeling ashamed. I don't care if the crackpots we work for deserve it or not, I . . . *we* are gonna give a hundred percent. We're gonna fight Dien Bien Phu over and over again every night. I don't care if we lose the war – we're *professionals*, man. We're the motherfuckin' *A-Team*, the pros from Dover, cool breeze . . . and ain't *nobody ever* gonna say we dropped the ball, let the side down, let things slide . . .'

One Five tanked. The 'entertainment' didn't help. We featured musical attractions so pathetic it would have made Joe Franklin blush: one-armed piano players, octogenarian cabaret singers, aspiring Broadway ingénues whose nasal-inflected warbling could shatter glass, haplessly incompetent yodelers . . . customers would wander through our magnificent revolving doors, clap eyes on one of these creatures belting out 'New York, New York' with a Yugoslavian accent, and turn on their heels and run. Like a lot of restaurants in trouble, we got shaken down by every sleazebag publicist ('I got Joey Buttafuoco to come in tonight; make sure to comp him!') and corrupt gossip columnist ('My husband is at loose ends tonight; can you take care of him?'). The press we got from such largesse usually amounted to something like: 'Seen canoodling at One Five, John Wayne Bobbit and Joey Buttafuoco' – not a mention likely to inspire a gang-rush of dining public.

But Steven and I were happy. We had the cooks we wanted. We were making nice food.

When I was hired by Pino Luongo to open up Coco Pazzo Teatro, my brief Tuscan interlude, I took Steven along. And after that, Sullivan's. We were a traveling roadshow, and when we moved to another kitchen, we peeled the best of the cooks we'd left behind with us. Steven, as I said, is my kind of sous-chef. He loves cooking, and he loves cooks. He doesn't yearn for a better, different life than the one he has – because he knows he's got a home in this one. He gets along with just about anyone at any time, total strangers tending to forgive him his most egregious excesses, whatever he says or does. He's an ingratiating bastard – totally without pretense, and you *cannot* embarrass, shame or insult him. He *knows* how bad he is. The Mexican line cooks at Les Halles love him, and his tortured, completely useless command of kitchen Spanish amuses the hell out of them – as do his habits of singing Elton John and Madonna tunes in a high-pitched, atonal voice, prancing shamelessly around the kitchen like some spastic breakdancer, taping over his sensitive nipples with Band-Aids (to avoid chafe, he insists), powdering his balls on the line with cornstarch, and showing anyone who's interested his latest cold sore, the boil on his ass, an incipient zit. He truly loves the technical aspects of cooking, works fast, clean, and makes pretty plates. He likes to step into other stations when other cooks get in the weeds, chiding them in his horrible Spanish. He loves dishwashing when not busy on *his* station, finds no task too low or too demeaning to take an interest in and help. He's a remarkably thoughtful guy – mention you like Gummi Bears and Steven will show up the next day with a bag. If he stops off at a burger stand for a mayo and mustard and ketchup-slathered grease-burger for breakfast, he'll bring a couple extra so everyone can have some. Alone among cooks I've met, he actually enjoys cooking for the floor staff, insisting on making them food that's actually edible. He jokes around with the waiters, managers, flirts with *any* woman, no matter her age, rank, background, and amazingly, they seem to *like* it. Mexican cooks I worked with for a year without hearing them peep a single word in English *or* Spanish were chattering happily away with Steven after only a few hours of meeting him. '*Chuletita loca*', they call him, 'crazy little pork chop'.

He has a tattoo of a cartoon cat wearing a chef's toque on his crotch, and he's all too ready to drop his pants should you express interest in seeing it. In hot months, he works in sandals, no socks, the cuffs of his checks rolled up like clam-diggers (a daring fashion statement in a kitchen, where a dropped knife or spilled duck fat can be a career ender). He wears, with defiantly prole-pride, a dishwasher's snap-front short-sleeve shirt, shunning the traditional chef's jacket. He refuses to wear an apron. He eats his meals smashed together in bite-sized chunks – meat, starch and vegetable mixed into an ugly but apparently edible slurry – and he's always trying out new flavor combinations. Middle of the rush, Steven is holding down his end brilliantly *and*, somehow, making little potato crisp and caviar snackies for the other cooks to try. There's always enough to go around.

Bartenders, waiters, managers, cooks, dishwashers, porters tell him *everything*. Somehow he induces, without even trying, total strangers to tell him their most shameful and intimate secrets. They'll do anything for him, putting up cheerfully with his practical joking, his groping, his annoying practice of trying to throw petits pois into their ears, his horribly frank anecdotes about the previous evening's sexual adventures.

I learned never to try to compete with Steven in the practical joke department. He'll make a life's work out of getting you back. Leave a potato in his shoes and he'll freeze your street clothes. Put a sticker on his back, he'll take your locker door off the hinges and stack it full of porno magazines.

On his birthday, I once arranged for him to receive a free trial pair of adult diapers. The next day, all the cooks were waiting for his reaction. He thanked me sincerely. 'You know? Those things are pretty cool! I sat around the couch, eating nachos and watching TV in my diaper, and it was great. I didn't even have to *get up* to go to the bathroom! It was great! And you know, it feels kinda neat!'

Our clean-living, deeply religious Ecuadorian pasta man at Sullivan's, Manuel, would receive 4A.M. phone calls every night for weeks – Steven mid-coitus with his girlfriend: 'Manuel . . . grunt . . . plorp . . . it's Steven . . . grunt . . . guess what I'm doing?'

And, like everyone in Steven's life, Manuel played along.

'Oh, Chef . . . Chef . . .' he'd say, shaking his head, the next day. '*Chuletita* call me again lass night!' and then he'd burst into giggles.

I don't get it. Still.

If I did half the things that Steven does regularly – and I'm not even talking about the felonies, just the brutish misbehavior, the bad taste, the remarks, the exhibitionism, the conniving – I'd end up in court defending myself against a host of sexual harassment lawsuits. And yet, I can't think of anyone, except the owner of Sullivan's (but that's another story) who *doesn't* like Steven, who doesn't find him adorable, who doesn't confide in him, go to him when they're confused or in trouble . . . an amazing accomplishment for a guy who shows up to work with sperm on his shoes ('Stopped at a peep booth to toss off,' he explains casually. 'Hey! I was *horny!*'), who behaves like an utter pig at times, freely discusses his every digestive, dermatological and sexual manifestation with anyone within hearing.

And this . . . *this*, dear reader, is my closest and most trusted friend and associate.

THE LEVEL OF DISCOURSE

THERE WAS A LULL in service the other night, one of those all-too-brief periods of about ten minutes when the floor staff is busy trying to turn tables, and even though the bar is packed three deep with waiting customers and there's a line out the door, the kitchen is quiet. While busboys stripped and reset tables outside the kitchen door, the cooks, runners and sous-chef swilled bottled water, wiped down their stations and bullshitted.

I stood in the doorway to the cellar prep kitchen and smoked a cigarette nervously. We were in that eerie, eye-of-the-hurricane calm. In ten minutes, when the next wave of hungry public had been seated and breaded and watered, there'd be a punishing rush – the slide filling up with orders all at once, the action swinging from station to station, boiling up the line like a Drano enema. First, the salad guy would get hit, then the sauté station and finally the grill, until everything came down at once – the whole bunch of us in the cramped kitchen struggling and sweating and cursing to move orders out without falling in the weeds. We had only a few moments of peace to go, and I smoked and fidgeted and half-listened to what my crew was talking about.

The tone of the repartee was familiar, as was the subject matter, a strangely comfortable background music to most of my waking hours over the last two decades or so – and I realized that, my *God* . . . I've been listening to the *same* conversation for *twenty-five years*!

Who's the bigger homo? Who takes it in the ass? Who, exactly, at this particular moment, is a *pédé*, a *maricón*, a *finocchio*, a *puta* a *pato*? It's all about dick, you see. It's *chupa mis huevos* time, time for *mama la pinga*, take it in your *culo* time, motherfucker, you *pinche baboso*, crying little woman. And your *vierga*? It looks like a fucking half-order of merguez – *muy, muy, muy chica* . . . like an *insecto*.

This is the real international language of cuisine, I realized, watching my French sous-chef, American pâtissier, Mexican grill, salad and fry guy exchange playful insults with the Bengali runner and the Dominican dishwasher. It's been, for twenty-five years, one long, never-ending game of the dozens, played out in four or five languages.

As an art form, cooktalk is, like haiku or kabuki, defined by established rules, with a rigid, traditional framework in which one may operate. All comments *must*, out of historical necessity, concern involuntary rectal penetration, penis size, physical flaws or annoying mannerisms or defects.

The rules can be confusing. *Cabrón*, for instance, which translates roughly to 'Your wife/girlfriend is getting fucked by another guy right now – and you're too much of a pussy to do anything about it' can also mean 'my brother', depending on inflection and tone. The word 'fuck' is used principally as a comma. 'Suck my dick' means 'Hang on a second' or 'Could you please wait a moment?' And 'Get your shit together with your fucking *meez*, or I come back there and fuck you in the *culo*' means 'Pardon me, comrade, but I am concerned with your state of readiness for the coming rush. Is your mise-en-place properly restocked, my brother?'

Pinche wey means 'fucking guy', but can also mean 'you adorable scamp' or 'pal'. But if you use the word 'pal' – or worse, 'my friend' in my kitchen, it'll make people paranoid. 'My friend' famously means 'asshole' in the worst and most sincere sense of that word. And start being too nice to a cook on the line and he might think he's getting canned tomorrow. My *vato locos* are, like most line cooks, practitioners of that centuries-old oral tradition in which we – all of us – try to find new and amusing ways to talk about dick.

Homophobic, you say? Sub-mental? Insensitive to gender preference, and the gorgeous mosaic of an ethnically diverse work force? Gee . . . you might be right. Does a locker-room environment like this make it tougher for women, for instance? Yep. Most women, sadly. But what the system seeks, what it requires, is someone, *anyone*, who can hold up their station, play the game without getting bent out of shape and taking things personally. If you are easily offended by direct aspersions on your lineage, the circumstances of your birth, your sexuality, your appearance, the mention of your parents possibly commingling with livestock, then the world of professional cooking is *not* for you.

But let's say you *do* suck dick, you *do* 'take it in the twins', it's no impediment to survival. No one really cares about that. We're too busy, and too close, and we spend too much time together as an extended, dysfunctional family to care about sex, gender preference, race or national origin. After level of skills, it's how *sensitive* you are to criticism and perceived insult – and how well you can give it right back – that determines your place in the food chain. You can cover your ears all you want, pretend they're *not* calling you *chino* or *morena* or *indio* or *gordo* or *cachundo* . . . but they are. Like it or not, that's your name, your street tag, whether you chose it or not. I've been *flaco* and *cadavro*, probably *borracho*. That's just the way it is. I call down to my prep kitchen on the intercom – calling for butter or more sauce – and that little gangster who keeps my stock rotated and makes that lovely chiffonaded parsley for me is going to reply (after I'm out of hearing), '*Fuuck YOUU!!*' before giving me exactly what I asked for. Better I say it first: 'Gimme my fucking *mantequilla* and sauce, motherfucker. *A horita* . . . and . . . fuuuck YOU!' And I love that little thug, too – the headband-sporting, baggy-pantsed, top button-buttoned, bottom button open, moon boot-shod, half Puerto Rican, half *cholo vato loco*, with his crude prison-style tats and his butterfly knife tucked in his wristband. I have, on many occasions, pondered adopting him. He's everything I'd want in a son.

Why do I, a fairly educated sort of a swine, take such unseemly pleasure in the guttural utterances of my largely uneducated, foul-mouthed crews? Why, over the years, have my own language skills become so crude and offensive that at family Christmas I have to struggle to *not* say, 'Pass the fuckin' turkey, cocksucker'?

I dunno.

But I *do* love it.

I wallow in it. Just like all the other sounds in my life: the hiss and clatter and spray of the dishwasher, the sizzle as a fillet of fish hits a hot pan, the loud, yelping noise – almost a shriek – as a glowing sizzle-platter is dropped into a full pot sink, the pounding of the meat mallet on a côte de boeuf, the smack as finished plates hit the 'window'. The goads, curses, insults and taunts of my wildly profane crew are like poetry to me, beautiful at times, each tiny variation on a classic theme like some Beat era jazz riff: Coltrane doing 'My Favorite Things' over and over again, but making it new and different each time. There are, it turns out, a million ways to say 'suck my dick'. Most of the people in *my* kitchen can do it in Spanish, French, Italian, Arabic, Bengali and English. Like all great performances, it's about timing, tone and delivery – kind of like cooking.

There are also the terms of the trade, the jargon. Every trade has one. You already know some of our terms. '86' is the best known. A dish is 86'ed when there's no more. But you can use the term for someone who's just been fired, or about to be fired, or for a bar customer who's no longer welcome.

One doesn't refer to a table of six or a table of eight; it's a *six-top* or an *eight-top*. Two customers at a table are simply a *deuce*.

'*Weeded*' means 'in the weeds', 'behind', 'in the shit' or '*dans la merde* – a close cousin and possible outcome of being 'slammed', 'buried' or 'hit'.

A *waitron* or *waitron unit* is an old-school '70s term – gender non-specific – for floor personnel, who are also, at staff mealtime, referred to as the *floor* or the *family* or simply *scum*. And the meal itself becomes – particularly if it's the usual trinity of chicken, pasta and salad – the *shaft meal* or the *gruel*.

Then there's the equipment. Since the introduction of the Cuisinart, *any* food processor can be referred to as *the Queez*; the square and oblong metal sauce containers are *six-pans* or *eight-pans* depending on size, and the long, shallow ones *hotels*. The cook's spoons with holes or slots are, unsurprisingly, *female*, and the unslotted ones, *male*.

Meez is mise-en-place: your set up, your station prep, your assembled ingredients and, to some extent, your state of mind. *A la minute* is made-to-order from start to finish. *Order!*, when yelled at a cook means 'Make initial preparations' such as searing, half-cooking, setting up for finishing. *Fire!* means 'Finish cooking' and get ready for 'pick up'. Food ready to be picked up is put in the *window* or *en la ventana* – also called the *pass*, the *slide* or the *shelf*. The 'slide' refers to the slotted rack where *dupes* or *tickets* containing orders *hang*. So one could say, 'What orders do I have hanging?' and the reply could be, 'You got two steak' on order for the deuce on five, three soles are fired.' A cook might ask for *an all-day*, a total number of a particular item both ordered and fired, with *temperatures*, meaning degrees of doneness. And *on the fly* means *Rush!*

A *wipe* means just what it sounds like: a last-minute plate-cleaning. *Marijuana* or *mota* or *chronic* is chopped parsley. *Jiz* is any reduced liquid, like demi-glace. When one adds whole butter to jiz, one is *mounting*, as in *monter-au-beurre*. *Cook well-done* translates to 'Burn it!' or 'Murder it!' or 'Kill it!' When one finds oneself waiting too long for a well-done steak to finish cooking, and it's holding up the rest of the order, one can suggest throwing it in the *jukebox*, or giving it a little *radar love* in the *micro* or microwave.

The latex surgical gloves we rarely wear are *anal research gloves*, and one usually puts them on with some theatrical flourish, snapping and grinning menacingly, accompanied by suggestions to 'Turn left and cough' or 'Grab your ankles, 'cause here comes *papi chulo*'. Those paper toques are *coffee filters* or *clown hats*, the checked pants we all wear, simply *checks*, our jackets and aprons, *whites*.

When the boss arrives, it's 'Elvis is in the building' or 'Pssst, *desastre es aquí!* And the usual nicknames apply to any and all: cooks, waiters, busboys and runners alike. Crude irony abounds. *Cachundo*, meaning 'piece of ass', might be applied to a particularly homely runner. *Caliman*, meaning 'strong man', is reserved for a weak cook, *Rayo*, or 'flash' to a slow-poke; *Baboso*, or 'drooling idiot' to, well, any drooling idiot. Any blond, well-scrubbed waiter can become 'Opie', 'Richie Cunningham' or 'Doogie Howser Motherfucker'. Stocky busboy? Sounds like *Burro* to me. When referring to themselves collectively, my Mexican *carnales* like *La Raza* or *La M* (pronounced *la emaayy*), or *La Mafia*. Externs from culinary school, working for free as a 'learning experience' – which by itself translates to 'lots of work and no money' – are quickly tagged as *FNG* (Fucking New Guy), or *Mel* for *mal carne* (bad meat). *Army*, short for 'army cook', or the classic but elegant *shoe*, short for 'shoemaker', are the perennial insults for a lousy or 'slophouse' cook.

There are the usual terms of endearment, all perfectly acceptable in casual conversation between cooks: *motherfucker* (a compliment), *cocksucker*, *sunofbeech*, *dipshit*, *scumbag*, *scumsucker*, *dumb-fuck*, *rat-bastard*, *slackjaw*, *idiota*, *bruto*, *animale*, *asesino*, *mentiroso*, *whining little bed-wetter*, *turd*, *tortuga*, *strunze*, *salaud*, *salopard*, *chocha podrida*, *pendejo*, *silly cunt*, *seso de pollo*, *spazz*, *goofball*, *bucket-head*, *chucho*, *papi-chulo*, *sweet-cheeks*, *cupcakes*, *love-chunks*, *culero*, *shit-stain*, *cum-gargler*, and so on. *Asshole*, strangely, is serious, to be used only when genuinely angry, and any expression involving a person's wife/mother/girlfriend/boyfriend or family member directly (with the notable exception of *motherfucker*) is strictly off-limits. You may well have seen your grill man's wife jacking off motorists for spare change on West Street – but you don't talk about it. Ever.

A lot of cook talk is transplanted from the fringes of military jargon. One doesn't carry, one *humps*. To be set up is to be *squared away*. He *sucks it up* and endures, *digs in for the rush*, takes a *bad hit* if one station is disproportionately busy – is simply *fucked* or *fucked in the ass* when things go badly . . . at which point, one's buddy hopefully steps in and *bails you out*, *covers your ass*, *saves your bacon*.

Aspirins are called *crunchies* because we eat them like candy. Finger cots are *condoms*, pronounced with Spanish inflection. The nail on which completed orders are spindled is the *spike*. Any round metal container placed in a water bath is a *bain* (pronounced *bayn*) from *bain-marie* pronounced *baahn maree*), or simply a *crock*. The life we live is *la puta vida*, 'this bitch of a life', and one might well bemoan a sorry state of affairs with a cry of *Porca miseria!* (Pig of misery!) or *Qué doloré!*, 'What pain!'

The slide, when full of dupes, is called the *board*, as in, 'The board is full'. Food currently being loaded by a runner or waiter is *My hand*, as in 'Where's that fucking steak?' Reply: 'My hand, Chef!' A *hot nut* is used when an expeditor wants something *now*: 'I gotta hot nut for that sole on table six'. This is often for a VIP, or 'Very Important Pendejo' or PPX, or *soigneee mutha-fucka* – meaning friend of the owner, or the man himself. So make sure to move that food out *rush* or STAT.

Applying what we've learned to a battlefield situation, one might find oneself saying: 'I gotta hot nut for that six-top on seven, *Cabrón*! It's been fired for ten fucking *minutos, pinche tortuga*. What? You don't got yer *meez* together, *asesino*? Get that shit in the window, you *seso de pollo pinche* grill man – throw it in the fucking jukebox if you have to. The rest of the order my hand! And don't forget to give it a wipe and some *mota* and a squirt of that red jiz on the way out, I got shit hanging here and you're falling in the fucking weeds!'

'Working,' might come the reply. 'I getting buried here. How come the sauté no getting slammed like me? I take it in the ass all night! How' bout table *ocho*? *Fire*? I can go on eight?'

Which might inspire this: 'Eight my hand, *baboso*! Eight fucking *gone*! Eight fucking dying *en la ventana* waiting for Doogie Howser Motherfucker to pick up! You got dead dupes back there, *idiota* – what the fuck are you doing? You *are* in the shit! Hey, Rayo! Step in and bail the *culero* out!'

OTHER BODIES

RUNNERS ARE THE CHEF's Imperial Guard: half-breeds who dress like waiters, are paid out of front-of-the-house payroll, but whose loyalties lie (ideally) with the chef and the kitchen. Usually ex-busboys or exiled waiters, they must choose sides early, especially as they will be called upon to perform tasks that might be interpreted as contrary to the aims of their former comrades.

I like wide-bodied, highly motivated runners. My runners, particularly in busy pre-theater operations, where the entire dining room has to be served during a thirty-to-forty-minute period, are generally whipped into such a frenzy of enthusiasm, fear and naked aggression that I am constantly being asked to tell them to refrain from bowling over the waiters on their missile-like progress to and from the kitchen. It takes unusual skills to be a runner. Language skills are not important. I want dedication, speed, the ability to gauge quickly what the hell is going on in a busy and hectic situation, pick out the next order from a busy array of outgoing orders, carry multiple plates at one time without dropping them, remember position numbers and donenesses at the table, and prioritize sensibly. Runners usually get a full cut of waiters' tips – with the advantage that they don't have to deal with the general public in order to get paid. Their job is to shuttle food, in the proper order, out of the kitchen and to the customer, and to get back to the kitchen quickly. Their job is also to do the chef's bidding – whatever that might entail. Other, more nebulous tasks might include intelligence gathering, like a forward artillery observer, reporting back to the chef/expeditor such cogent bits of data like the answer to 'What's going on on table one? Are they ready for their food? How's the special going over?' and so on. Fetching drinks for the chef might be a regular duty as well, or taking his jacket to the cleaner's, running to the store for emergency supplies, maintaining a clean 'window' and service area, arranging garnishes, even occasional expediting duties. Most of my runners may not know how to speak English, but they know every dish on my menu, and how to pronounce it.

A runner should be able to pick out a medium-rare steak from a group of other donenesses, read a 'board' as well as the chef, and maintain that rabid, pregame, caged-animal mentality one looks for in a professional fullback. I want my runners hyperventilating like Marines about to take a hill before the rush comes. As far as I'm concerned, I am General Patton when it comes to questions of judgment or strategy. Their mission? Get that food out there and get back here *fast*. I have my beautiful food dying under the heat lamps? I don't want my runner stopping off to decrumb a table or empty an ashtray.

And it's useful if my wide-bodied runners can be utilized as enforcers, dealing subtly, if forcefully, with interlopers who would invade my domain and impede the serious business of cooking and serving my food. Some 'friend' of the owner, salesman or chatty waiter is blocking the lane in my kitchen? He's gonna get an elbow in the kidney every time one of my chunky runners passes him by. After a few of these 'inadvertent' bumps and elbow-checks, people usually get the message that they're in the way.

A really good runner is a rare and beautiful find. In the best cases, there is a near-telepathic relationship between chef and runner, requiring only a glance or a facial expression to communicate scads of information. A really good runner will read the dupes over the shoulder of his master, between orders, immediately identifying what will likely come next and where it's going. Some diplomatic skills are nice, too, as my cooks are likely to take umbrage if asked to refire a steak or rush an order in a tone of voice they find grating.

A runner who's willing to snitch on his old pals out on the floor is useful as well. I always like to know if there's some pocket of dissidence welling up there. If some jumped-up maître d' is bad-mouthing me or my specials I'll probably have to deal with it somewhere down the road, so I'd rather know sooner than later. Early warning is always a good thing. Did a busload of tourists just pull up outside the restaurant, all of them planning on jamming a quick three-course meal into their maws before curtain goes up for *Miss Saigon*? If my runner doesn't tell me, who will? The waiters and hosts will be too busy shoving tables together and arguing about whether to tack 18 or 20 percent on their bill.

Though nominally floor staff, in time, as runners become comfortable with the customs and practices of the kitchen, they begin to acquire the same unique world-view: that xenophobic, slightly paranoid perspective of everything that exists outside the kitchen doors, the same ghoulish sense of humor and suspicion of non-kitchen personnel. I like to encourage this, making sure my runners are fed better, flattering them on occasion, taking an interest in their personal lives and finances. I will, when necessary, put the full weight of my strange and terrible power behind them should they need it. Those part-time actors on the floor are holding out on one of my runners, shorting him on his cut? God help them.

The Night Porter

I wish I didn't need a night porter. But I do. Somebody has to clean the restaurant after service, take out the garbage, clean and scrub the insides of the ovens, toss out the dead mice, kill the dying ones, empty the grease traps, hose down the kitchen – all the tasks that no one else in his right mind would do for love or money. The problem is, you have the sort of person who is willing to do this kind of work *alone* and unsupervised in your restaurant all night long. It's thankless, dirty work – dragging leaking, smelly garbage bags out to the dumpster – and as the night porter is all by himself, he might well feel justified in taking full advantage of certain fringe benefits. He could call his family in Mexico on the house phone. He could eat whatever he finds available and not likely to be missed. He could, perhaps, take a drink from those bottles he's dusting. And best yet, he can keep whatever he finds in the dining room. Let's face it, the guy who sweeps and mops a busy restaurant's dining room after a packed Saturday night is going to find some interesting stuff: wallets, jewelry, credit cards, cellphones, handbags, umbrellas, drugs, cash – these kinds of things are regularly left behind by customers. The night porter is probably coming up with some interesting goodies in the employee locker-room as well, fallen from hastily removed uniforms, so an enterprising fellow can supplement his income in all sorts of ways.

As no one else wants the job, or even wants to stay up all night watching him *do* the job, or wants to train someone *else* to do the job, he's got a pretty secure position – even if suspected of occasional petty thievery. Even a known sneak-thief porter is a valued employee, as long as he knows what he *can* steal and what he *can't*. There are, I'm sure, many apartments in the outer reaches of Queens that are fully furnished with the glassware, utensils and kitchen equipment of many a restaurant. And a guy who knows where to buy a Green Card and a Social Security number for thirty bucks probably knows what to do with a hot credit card or where to fence a used Burberry raincoat. Nobody minds – much. Besides, the guy is probably stealing less than the bartender.

The Bartender: The Chef's Friend

There has long been a happy symbiotic relationship between kitchen and bar. Simply put, the kitchen wants booze, and the bartender wants food. The bartender, seeing himself (rightly) as a more exalted creature than the waiters, would like to eat a little better than the employee gruel hardening under the heat lamps between four and five. By the end of his shift, he's hungry, and chicken legs and day-old pasta don't fit with the bartender's image of himself as raconteur, showman and personality. He wants to be treated as special. And he usually is. The chef wants to drink anything he desires, anytime he wants it, without upper management being fully informed of the extent of his alcoholism or his taste for premium liquors. And the bartender is usually happy to help – if handled correctly.

The bartender, being the guy every employee gripes to at one point or another, is also useful for gathering interesting tidbits of intelligence. He is also privy, at times, to the high-level maneuverings of upper management and ownership. He knows – in dollars – how well or how poorly the place did on a given night, who is getting petty cash payouts, and for what purpose. And he's heard plenty. Everyone, sooner or later, forgets that the bartender is *not* really like a doctor or a priest and obliged to keep confidences. They forget that yes, he *is* listening while you bitch about the boss to a friend at the far end of his bar. Hopefully, he's going to tell the chef all about it.

Earlier, I rashly implied that all bartenders are thieves. This is not entirely accurate, though of all restaurant workers, it's the bartender who has the greatest and most varied opportunities for chicanery. The bartenders control the register. They can collude with waiters on dinner checks, they can sell drinks out of their own bottles – I've even heard of a bartender who brought in his own register, ringing a third of the drinks there and simply carrying the whole thing home at night. But the most common bartender hustle is simply the 'buy-back', when he gives out free drinks every second or third round to an appreciative customer. If you're drinking single malt all night long, and only paying for half of them, that's a significant saving. An extra ten-or twenty-dollar tip to the generous barkeep is still a bargain. This kind of freewheeling with the house liquor is also personally good for the bartender; it inspires that most valued phenomenon in a regular bar crowd: a 'following', folks who will actually follow you wherever you work.

Chefs, naturally, love this kind of bartender, and as a rule will not drink anywhere where there *isn't* this kind of 'trade discount'. After work, posses of chefs and cooks will bounce from bar to bar, on a loose, rotating basis, taking full advantage of the liberal pouring policies of bartenders they know from working with them before. They're careful not to 'burn' their favorites – hitting their bar too hard or too often – which is why they tend to move from place to place. The bartender is repaid when he swings by their restaurants with a dinner date and gets treated like a pasha: free snackies, maybe some free desserts, a visit from the chef, fawning, personal service – in short, the kind of warm welcome and name recognition all of us beaten-down, working-class slobs crave when going out to dinner.

ADAM REAL-LAST-NAME-UNKNOWN

THE KITCHEN PHONE RANG, followed by a beep, the little green light indicating that the hostess at the front desk had a call for me.

'Yeah?' I said, covering one ear so I could understand what she was saying over the radio and the clatter of pots and the noise of the dishwasher.

'Call for the chef,' she said. 'Line two.'

I pressed the red flashing light, signaled for Steven at the grill to turn down the radio.

'*Feed the bitch!*' said the voice on the phone. '*Feed the bitch or she'll die!*'

It was Adam.

What he wanted me to do – what he was telling me – was that he was too drunk, too tired, too lazy, too involved in some squalid personal circumstances to come in and feed his starter: a massive, foaming, barely contained heap of fermenting grapes, flour, water, sugar and yeast which even now was pushing up the weighted-down lid of a 35-gallon Lexan container and spilling over on the work table where it was stored.

'Adam, we're *busy* here!' I protested.

'Tell him I'm not doing it,' yelled Steven from the line. He'd been expecting this call. 'Tell him I'm letting her die if he doesn't get his ass in here!'

'*Dude* . . . I've got like . . . a situation here, man. And like . . .

235

I just *can't*. Please. Do me a favor. I promise . . . I'll bake tomorrow night. Please . . . feed . . . the . . . bitch.'

'What's so important? What's so important you can't come in here?' I asked, knowingly soliciting an untruth.

'*Dude*. They're trying to evict me from my apartment and like . . . I gotta be here. I have to be here when my lawyer calls, man.'

'They're *always* trying to evict you from your apartment, Adam,' I said. 'So what else is new?'

'Yeah . . . yeah. But this time, it's *serious*,' said Adam, slurring his words slightly. 'I gotta wait for my lawyer to call; otherwise I'm fucked, you know?'

'What lawyers call at eight fucking *thirty* on a Friday night, Adam?'

'Well, he's not really a *lawyer*, per se. He's more like a *guy* who's like helping me.'

I could picture the scene on the other end of the phone: Adam Real-Last-Name-Unknown, the psychotic bread baker, alone in his small, filthy Upper West Side apartment, his eyes two different sizes after a thirty-six-hour coke and liquor jag, white crust accumulated at the corners of his mouth, a two-day growth of whiskers – standing there in a shirt and no pants amongst the porno mags, the empty Chinese take-out containers, as the Spice Channel flickers silently on the TV, throwing blue light on a can of Dinty Moore beef stew by an unmade bed. He's been snorting coke and smoking weed and drinking vodka from a half-gallon jug of Wolfschmidt's or Fleischman's (if he's drinking a better brand, he probably stole it from the restaurant) and now he's out of money. He doesn't have enough for a cab and he's too lazy and incoherent to hump twenty blocks down and feed the bitch.

I pondered the situation, looking first at the 250-pound blob of starter, and then at Steven.

'I'm *not* doing it!' said Steven (his voice gets high and squeaky when he gets indignant). 'Tell Vinnie to go fuck himself!' (Steven calls Adam 'Vinnie'. I don't know why. Maybe it's his real name.)

I kept Adam waiting.

'I'll help you feed her, man,' I told Steven. 'I don't want to *look* at the guy, the way he sounds. You really want to *see* him? The condition he's in? *You* know how he gets.'

'All right, all right,' said Steven, grumbling under his breath as he slapped a steak on the grill. 'This is the last time, though. Tell him. Tell him that next time I'm going to let her die. I'm going to throw her in the trash. We can *buy* bread.'

'We'll feed her,' I told Adam.

I was now committed to wrestling a back-breakingly heavy, ungainly blob out of the plastic Lexan, heaping it in stages into the big Hobart mixer and 'feeding' it with a mix of warm water and fresh flour and yeast. Then I'd have to scrape it *back* into the Lexan, haul *that* back up onto its resting place, stack sheet pans and potato sacks on top of it. It was a two-man job, one that would leave flour and goop all over my clean kitchen, leave dough under my fingernails and clinging to my clogs. But anything was preferable to having Adam Real-Last-Name-Unknown in my kitchen right now. *Anything*.

Why did God, in all his wisdom, choose *Adam* to be the recipient of greatness?

Why, of all his creatures, did He choose this loud, dirty, unkempt, obnoxious, uncontrollable, megalomaniacal madman to be His personal bread baker? How was it that this disgrace as an employee, as a citizen, as a human being – this undocumented, untrained, uneducated and unwashed mental case who's been employed (for about ten minutes) by every kitchen in New York – could throw together a little flour and water and make magic happen?

And I'm talking *real magic* here, people. I may have wanted Adam dead a thousand times over. I may have imagined, even planned his demise – torn apart by rabid dogs, his entrails snapped at by ravenous dachshunds, chained to a pillory post and flogged with chains and barbed wire before being drawn and quartered – but his bread and his pizza crust are simply divine. To see his bread coming out of the oven, to *smell* it, that deeply satisfying, spiritually comforting waft of yeasty goodness, to tear into it, breaking apart that floury, dusty crust and into the ethereally textured interior . . . to *taste* it is to experience real genius. His peasant-style boules are the perfect objects, an arrangement of atoms unimprovable by God or man, pleasing to all the senses at once. Cézanne would have wanted to paint them – but might not have considered himself up to the job.

Adam Real-Last-Name-Unknown may be the enemy of polite society, a menace to any happy kitchen, a security risk and a potential serial killer, but the man can *bake*. He's an idiot-savant with whom God has serious, frequent and intimate conversations. I just can't imagine what He's telling him – or whether the message is getting garbled during transmission.

The crusaders of yore, it is said, used to stop off at the local church or monastery before heading off to war; where they were allowed to purchase indulgences. This was sort of like a secured, pre-paid credit card from heaven, I imagine, and negotiations probably went something like this.

'Bless me, father, for I am *about* to sin. I plan on raping, pillaging and disemboweling my way across Southern Europe and North Africa, taking the Lord's name in vain, committing sodomy with all and sundry, looting the holy places of Islam, killing women and children and animals and leaving them in smoking heaps . . . as well, of course, as getting up to the usual soldierly hijinks of casual eye-gougings, dismemberment, bear-baiting and arson. Given this sinful agenda, padre, how much is this gonna cost me?'

'That'll be a new roof for the vestry, my son, perhaps a few carpets from down there. I understand they make a lovely carpet where you'll be goin' . . . and shall we say fifteen percent off the top, as a tithe?'

'Deal.'

'Go in peace, my son.'

Adam gets right with God with every proof rack of sourdough bread he pulls out of the oven: every crispy, crunchy, deliciously blistered pizza. It's God's little joke on all of us. Especially me.

I've hired him three or four times, and fired and rehired him again on countless occasions. He's in his late twenties to early thirties, I think, though he looks older. He's of medium height, with lank black hair, thinning at the crown. He's barrel-chested, with the huge shoulders and upper arms of a guy who's been balling dough for years. His eyes are brown but they look coal-black, at once menacing and pathetic, set into a mischievous baby face whose expression can change in an instant from huggably endearing and childlike to slaveringly insane.

To sign on Adam to your crew is to buy, for a time, the best bread I've ever tasted. It ensures that your customers, when examining their bread baskets, will exclaim, 'Where did you get this *bread*?' and 'Where can I *buy* this bread?' It also means that your life will be a waking nightmare, that every corner of your walk-ins and kitchen shelving will be likely to contain various sinister-looking and foul-smelling science experiments: rotting grapes, fermenting red peppers, soggy buckets of mushroom trimmings – the gills and stems decomposing into noxious, black sludge – all of them destined for 'the bitch' or one of her many offspring, smaller batches of starter that have been flavored with, or 'started' by one of these primordial oozes. Walk-ins will contain buckets of slowed-down starter and forgotten batches of dead starter. Freezers will be loaded with half-baked boules, frozen sour mix, the floors sticky with dough. Like some virulent snail, Adam leaves tracks.

But, he also leaves the 'stuff': the most amazing olive and herb breads, pepper bread, mushroom bread, focaccias, pizzas, garlic twists, breadsticks and brioches. He *claims* to be of Sicilian heritage, affecting the mannerisms and gestures and expressions of the street guinea from some Scorsese-inspired Brooklyn – but is he, actually of Italian lineage? No one knows for sure. Steven claims to have seen his birth certificate – the *real one*, mind you – and that his real last name is Turkish or Arab. But who knows? Documentation from Adam is always of dubious provenance. His cooking background is certainly Italian, no question there, he is not to be relied on for baguettes. If you believe him – which you shouldn't – he was taught to bake by Lydia Bastianich (he's fond of showing off a tattered and dog-eared copy of one of her books, inscribed to one of his many known aliases).

He's worked, to my direct knowledge, as a cook, chef, consultant, pie man at pizzerias, deli help, pâtissier and baker. Half of what comes out of his mouth is utter bullshit – the rest, suspicious at best. He is perpetually broke and in debt. The corner deli, says Steven, gives him credit, as does his local bar, and Adam pays them during the good times and stiffs them in the bad. He's always headed off to Little Italy to pay off some shady character, cop weed, or settle his rent problems. He used to sue everyone he worked for – claiming harassment, breach of contract, theft of services, unfair labor practices, even sexual harassment – and has had surprisingly good luck with his second career as professional litigator. Many of his victims, I suspect, were willing to pony up a few dollars – just to make him go *away*.

Jimmy Sears, who first brought Adam Real-Last-Name-Unknown into my circle of acquaintances (the notorious Steven and Adam acquisition of the '92 season), is another reluctant admirer. Like me, Jimmy should know better than to let this savage beast wander free in his kitchen, but he keeps doing it, keeps hiring him, for the 'stuff'. The Sears/Adam relationship has been a legendarily contentious one, coming to blows on more than one occasion.

They have been both arch-enemies and close associates, rolling around trying to kill each other on the lawns at the Inn at Quogue, having wrestling matches at 13 Barrow and screaming contests at the Supper Club. Steven, who's known Adam longest, has had many adventures with him, both here in New York and in California – episodes of such nauseating stupidity, self-indulgence, cruelty and horror that even *I* find them unprintable. Adam has threatened to sue me many times. He *has* sued Sears, I believe, a number of times, as his assessment of what he is owed is frequently at odds with reality. (To be fair, Jimmy's assessments of what he *owes* is sometimes at variance with established fact as well.) There is a photo, taken years ago for a magazine article that was never printed, showing Adam, covered from head to toe in flour, holding Jimmy in a head-lock, pretending to bash his skull in with a rolling-pin. It was the perfect re-creation of their relationship.

Just recently, after many years, I stopped by to see Jimmy Sears at his new place, a swank nightclub/supper club in the Gramercy area. I sat down at a table, ordered some food (Jimmy's food is always excellent) and when the bread basket arrived, I looked up from the table at Jimmy with a horrible sense of recognition.

'You *didn't*?' I rasped, scarcely able to believe it.

'I did,' said Jimmy, sighing. 'I have Adam making my bread and my pizza.'

The last I'd heard, Adam was bragging about getting the marshals to yank out Sears's stoves and equipment to pay off his claim of non-payment, claiming he was going to bash Jimmy's skull into red paste this time, make him cry like a little girl, destroy his life. The previous year, Adam had had to be delivered to the Westhampton train station under police escort after one of the famous Quogue incidents: the Hamptons' first forced deportation. Jimmy was Adam's favorite obsession, a ready-to-go revenge scenario, his number one topic of conversation. Now? Like so many relationships in the restaurant business, everything old was new again.

To endure Adam as an employee was to become a full-time cop, psychiatrist, moneylender, friend and antagonist, though he *does* have his sweet side.

Steven, Nancy and I went skiing with him one time. Adam was thrilled to be doing something *normal*. Dr Hervey Cleckley, in his groundbreaking work on serial killers, *The Mask of Sanity*, discusses this phenomonon, where the career sociopath, vestigially aware of his character, emulates normalcy by overcompensating – becoming a scoutmaster, a crisis-line counselor, a Republican fund-raiser. In this case, Adam, excited by the prospect of a wholesome activity like 'going skiing with the guys', prepared a bacchanalian picnic lunch for his fellow skiers: two chest coolers filled with homemade caponata, antipasto, sliced cold cuts, freshly baked Italian bread, cheese, marinated artichokes, roasted peppers . . . he must have been up all night getting it ready. And he skied like a hero, though he's the last person in the world who should be allowed. He had his ski boots on the wrong feet for the first hour. He had neglected to bring gloves or mittens. He lost a ski pole. But he soldiered on without complaint. I vividly recall looking down from the ski lift, seeing him fall on his face, then clamber up again, and thinking, 'You know, there *is* something to love about this guy . . . beyond the bread.' He's an extraordinary survivor, a man who has attained some nice highs and endured some truly low lows and always managed to bounce back. Maybe he's calling himself something else this time around. Maybe his paychecks are made out to some fictional company, a third party, his latest alias, but he's still on his feet at the end of the day . . . and still making that incredible bread.

Adam is not a stupid guy, though I sometimes think he aspires to be. His anecdotes are wildly exaggerated, unspeakably crude and graphic adventures – usually involving his penis – but without the earnest and self-deprecating charm of his friend Steven's accounts. Adam's comedy material runs along pretty predictable lines: referring to his dill bread starter, for instance, as 'dildo', accompanied by a maniacal laugh. He has an unusual and frankly terrifying tic; when he eats, one eye rolls up into its socket. I'm told he makes funny faces when he has sex, too, but I try very hard not to picture that. He's a sentimental guy who can take real pride in his work: I've seen him weep when his tiramisù didn't come out as planned, and when a cassata cake he'd made began to slide in the heat. He sulks, wheedles, whines, and bullies when he wants something – which is always – and you can pretty much tell what frame of mind he's in from his appearance. If he hasn't shaved, it's *not* a good time to be around him.

At Sullivan's I'd schedule his baking shifts at night, after the kitchen closed. I did not want him interacting with the other cooks. His faux-macho banter with the Ecuadorian and Mexican line cooks invariably caused offense, and he was an incurable slob.

'You will arrive in my kitchen promptly at one A.M. You will bake my bread, and you will be *gone* by the time my first cook arrives in the morning,' were my instructions. I did not want him telling my garde-manger guy that he was going to 'make him his woman', or bragging about some imaginary or real adventure at the '*casa de putas*' or singing witlessly obscene and unfunny Christmas carols to the dishwashers, who saw him as a near-Satanic apparition. Allowing Adam to work unsupervised at night, however, meant that he would lift my reach-in doors off the hinges to help himself to midnight snacks of T-bone steaks, white truffle risotto and tomato salad – washed down, no doubt, with a bottle of pilfered Dom Perignon now and again. But that was to be expected. The bread. It was soooo good.

The first few months of Adam's employment were always the honeymoon. He showed up pretty much on time, producing, one way or the other, what was required. Then, when things were going well – the customers commenting favorably on the product, his masters happy – he'd start to enter a fugue state – 'martyr mode' – where he'd begin sulking, feeling put-upon, sorry for himself. All that work he was doing by himself, all that fine Adam bread, was under-appreciated by his cruel and insensitive overlords. He would begin trying to jack me up for more money, demanding restitution for 'expenses', taxis and 'research'. He'd want new equipment, massive amounts of specialty baking goods, the authorization to phone up companies and spend money autonomously. In short, he'd become insufferable. When his demands weren't met, he'd start slacking and not showing up for work.

The 'feed the bitch' calls would become more frequent.

That's usually when I began buying bread out.

And that's when Adam, not eligible for unemployment benefits, would go back to making sandwiches at the Yankee Doodle Deli, brunch-cooking at West Side saloons, consulting to some crack-brained pizzeria owner or novice restaurateur, freelancing for deadbeat caterers or just lying around his apartment. He'd print up another résumé, another tissue of lies, invariably with another last name, and he'd start all over. And sooner or later, I'd call him again . . . or Sears would, and Adam Real-Last-Name-Unknown would be back in the saddle again.

Adam *can* surprise you. He gets along well with my wife. He's actually polite in stretches. For the last few years (something of a record for Adam), he's been working for a very fine caterer and apparently doing good work there. I turned on public access cable one night to see Adam, in chef's whites, exchanging witty banter with a late-night cable host and guests, holding his own very nicely. He was delightful and funny and fast on his feet, and he had an impressive display of baked goods laid out on a table to sample. He's still making bread and pizzas for Jimmy Sears. For some time, I have heard no tales of violent assaults or thirteen-dollar whorehouses or near overdoses. So maybe he really *has* cleaned up his act.

God knows, a man who can make those perfect rough-slashed boules of sourdough and Tuscan country bread deserves his place in the sun. Somewhere.

He's the best at what he does, after all. The finest bread I've ever had. And the most expensive: in human cost, aggravation and worry. Hiring Adam Real-Last-Name-Unknown was always a trade-off – with God or Satan, I don't know – but it was usually worth it. Bread *is* the staff of life. And Adam, the unlikely source.

Something *else* God has to answer for.

DEPARTMENT OF HUMAN RESOURCES

A GOOD FRIEND OF mine, about a year into his first chef's job, had a problem with one of his cooks. This particularly rotten bastard had been giving my friend a ride for quite a while: showing up late, not showing up, getting high at work, behaving insolently and fomenting dissent among his co-workers. Convinced that the whole kitchen revolved around his station, *his* mood swings and *his* toil, he felt free to become a raving, snarling, angry lunatic – a dangerously loose cannon rolling around on deck, just *daring* his chef and his co-workers to press the wrong button.

After a no-show and a late arrival and yet another ugly, histrionic incident of insubordination, my friend had no choice but to fire his cocaine-stoked and deranged employee, telling him, in classic style, to 'Clean out your locker and get the fuck out!'

The cook went home, made a few phone calls, and then hanged himself.

It's a measure of what we do for a living that this kind of a thing could happen – and that my friend, on his next visit to my kitchen, was greeted with gestures of mimed strangulation, cooks and waiters holding a hand over their heads, sticking their tongues out and rolling their eyes up, tagging my friend, to his face, as 'serial killer' and remorselessly teasing him. My friend had worked for me for years, and had, at various times, caused me much grief and frustration. Since becoming a chef in his own right, however, he'd taken to calling me at intervals – to apologize for his past bad acts, telling me that when faced with managerial problems of his own involving personnel, or 'human resource difficulties', he'd seriously regretted all the pain and worry he'd caused me.

Now he *knew*, you see. He *knew* what it was like to be a leader of cooks, a wrangler of psychopaths, the captain of his own pirate ship, and he wasn't liking that part of the job very much. Now somebody was dead and there was, inarguably, a causal relationship between the event of the troublesome cook's firing and his death by his own hand.

'The guy was fucked up anyway, it's not your fault,' was the standard conciliatory remark. It was about as sympathetic as any of us could get.

'Guy would have done it sooner or later, man. If not with you, some other chef.'

That didn't quite cut it either.

'The guy had to go,' is what I said, the kind of cold-blooded statement not unusual for me when in chef-mode. 'What? Are you gonna keep the guy *on*? Let him talk shit to you in front of your crew? Let him show up late, fuck up service . . . because you're afraid he's gonna *off himself*? Fuck him. We're on a lifeboat, baby. The weak? The dangerous? The infirm? They go *over the side.*'

Typically, I was overstating the case. I've coddled plenty of dangerously unstable characters over the years; I've kept on plenty of people who I *knew* in the end would make me look bad and become more trouble than they were worth. I'm not saying I'm Mister Rogers, a softie – okay, maybe I *am* saying that . . . a little bit. I appreciate people who show up every day and do the best they *can*, in spite of borderline person-alities, substance abuse problems and anti-social tendencies; and I am often inclined to give them every opportunity to change their trajectories, to help them to arrive at a different outcome than the predictable one when they begin visibly to unravel.

But once gone – quit, fired or dead – I move on to the next problem. There always is one.

There have been a lot of success stories out of my kitchens over the last two decades. Mostly Mexicans and Ecuadorians who now own homes, have careers, enjoy the respect of their peers and their neighbors. They support families, drive their own cars, speak English fluently – all things *I* can barely do. I care about my crew and their problems.

I go home Saturday night with a sulking cook getting crispy around the edges on my mind? Someone in my kitchen talking about going AWOL, exhibiting symptoms of the dreaded martyr mode? My weekend is ruined. All I'm going to be thinking about for every waking moment is that cook and what I can do to fix the situation. I'll lie there on the bed, staring into space, paying scant attention to the TV, or what my wife is talking about, or the everyday tasks of bill paying, maintaining a home, behaving like a normal person.

I don't *know*, you see, how a normal person acts. I don't know how to behave outside my kitchen. I don't know the rules. I'm *aware* of them, sure, but I don't care to observe them anymore – because I haven't *had* to for so many years.

Okay, I can put on a jacket, go out for dinner and a movie, and I can eat with a knife and fork without embarrassing my hosts. But can I really behave? I don't know.

I have *responsibilities*, I tell myself and my wife. I've got things on my mind. I'm in charge of people's lives . . . and it can weigh heavily on me.

In my world, you see, my friend *is* a killer.

No, he's not, you say. How could he have predicted what this drug-addled maniac was going to do? How can what some cokehead cook has done to himself and to his family be laid at *his* door?

Because it can. Because when you look somebody in the eyes and can them, there's no telling what terrible result might ensue. He might come at you with a meat cleaver or a boning knife. He might, like Adam Real-Last-Name-Unknown, drag you into court, on whatever specious yet embarrassing grounds. He might turn tail and simply leave the business, move to Arizona and sell insurance – as one talented cook of my acquaintance did. On the other hand, he could simply suck it up, move on to the next kitchen and make a smashing success of himself; ten years in the future, you might find yourself standing next to him at the James Beard Awards dinner, where he's just picked up his award for Best New Chef, and resplendent in his tux he turns and pees smilingly on your pants leg. These are all considerations when peering down the line at some troubled and troubling employee and pondering his fate.

Survival has its costs.

I took a fateful cab ride many years ago. Rolling back from the Lower East Side with a bunch of close friends, all of us fresh from scoring dope, I jokingly remarked on an article I'd seen, detailing the statistical likelihood of successfully detoxing.

'Only one in four has a chance at making it. Ha, ha, ha,' I said, my words ringing immediately painful and hollow as soon as I'd said them. I counted our number in the back of that rattling Checker Marathon. Four. And right there, I knew that if one of us was getting off dope, and staying off dope, it was going to be *me*. I wasn't going to let these guys drag me down. I didn't care what it took, how long I'd known them, what we'd been through together or how close we'd been. *I* was going to live. *I* was the guy.

I made it. They didn't.

I don't feel guilty about that.

'We're in a lifeboat . . .' begins one of my standard inspirationals to new sous-chefs. 'We're four days out to sea, with no rescue in sight. There are two Snickers bars and a tiny hunk of salt pork left in our stores, and that fat bastard by the stern is getting crazier with every hour, becoming more and more irrational and demanding, giving that Snickers bar long, lingering looks – even though he's too weak to help with the rowing or the bailing any more. He presents a clear and present danger to the rest of us, what with his leering at the food and his recently acquired conviction that we're plotting against him. What do we do?'

We kick fat boy over the side, I say. Maybe we even carve a nice chunk of rumpsteak off his thigh before letting him go. Is that wrong?

Yah, yah, yah, tough guy. *Sure* you'd do that. To which I'd say, 'You don't *know me very well.*' Insurrection? A direct challenge to my authority? Treasonous dereliction of duty? The time will come, my friend, when it's gonna be *you* going over the side. I will – and I tell my cooks this *ahead of time* – contrive, conspire, manipulate, maneuver and betray in order to get you out of my kitchen, *whatever* the outcome to you personally. If an unexpected period of unemployment inspires you to leap off a bridge, hang yourself from a tree or chug-a-lug a quart of drain cleaner, that's too bad.

The *absolutes* first attracted me to this business (along with that food thing). The black and white of it. The knowledge that there are some things you *must* do – and some things you absolutely *must not*. What little order there has been in my life is directly related to this belief in clear right and clear wrong: maybe not moral distinctions, but practical ones.

Another cook has to cover for you? Wrong.

Chef spending too much time kissing your boo-boos, stroking your ego, solving your conflicts with co-workers? Wrong.

Talking back to your leader? Wrong.

You will soon become dead to me.

My friend the novice 'killer', feeling truly awful about what happened, said, 'Tony. I'm *different* than you – '*I* have a heart!' I laughed and took that for a compliment – which it kind of was – if a backhanded one.

I do have heart, you see. I've got plenty of heart. I'm a fucking sentimental guy – once you get to know me. Show me a hurt puppy, or a long-distance telephone service commercial, or a film retrospective of Ali fights or Lou Gehrig's last speech and I'll weep real tears. I *am* a bastard when crossed, though, no question. I bully my waiters but at least I comfort myself afterward, when I wonder if maybe I went a little too far – at least I don't bite them on the nose, as one chef I know did. I don't throw plates . . . much. I don't blame others for my mistakes. I am attentive to the weak but willing, if merciless to the strong who are not so eager to please. Though slothful to a fault in my off-hours, I am not lazy at work, and I am fiercely protective of my crew, of my chain of command, of my turf. I have perjured myself on a cook's behalf. I *will* cut my nose off to spite my face – if a favored cook's well-being is at stake – meaning I will quit a job rather than let management, ownership or anybody else toy with *any* member of my crew. I *will* walk out of a perfectly good situation if someone insists on squeezing my cooks for unreasonable amounts of extra work at no additional recompense. I'm not bluffing when I threaten to quit over principle. My loyalty, such as it is, is to my restaurant – if that loyalty is not to the detriment of dedicated underlings. The ones who've hung with me, endured what I think should be reasonably endured, have done the right thing.

Everything else is just noise.

Isn't it?

COFFEE
AND A CIGARETTE

THE LIFE OF BRYAN

THERE ARE BETTER CHEFS in the world. One comes reluctantly, yet undeniably, to that conclusion early in one's career. There's always some old master or new hotshot who's doing things with food you never would have thought of – if they hadn't done it first. And of course, in the thin air at the peak of the culinary Mount Olympus, where the three- and four-star demi-gods dwell – guys like Eric Ripert, Grey Kunz, Bouley, Palladin, Keller, you *know* the names, I don't have to tell you – they have the added advantage of not only being geniuses or near-geniuses, but they tend to command crews that are larger, better trained, and more single-minded in their zeal. This didn't just happen, mind you. These guys don't get hundreds of hungry young culinarians banging on their kitchen doors, begging for the privilege of mopping their brows and peeling their shallots just because they have their names stitched on their jackets. Nobody is building million-dollar kitchen facilities around their chef, shelling out for combi-steamers, induction burners, fine china, Jade ranges, crystal snifters and fistfuls of white truffles because the guy can sling steaks faster than the other guy, or because he has a cute accent. Cream rises. Excellence does have its rewards. For every schlockmeister with a catch-phrase and his own line of prepared seasonings who manages to hold American television audiences enthralled, there are scores more who manage to show up at work every day in a real kitchen and produce brilliantly executed, innovatively presented, top-quality food. I am, naturally, pissed off by the former, and hugely impressed by the latter.

But for my money, the guy I know who embodies the culinary ideal? A no-bullshit, no muss, no fuss, old-school ass-kicking *cook* of the first order?

That would have to be Scott Bryan, down the street at Veritas.

I'd been hearing about this guy for years – significantly, from other chefs and cooks.

'Scott says this . . .' and 'Scott says that . . .' and 'Scott doesn't make veal stock; he's roasting *chicken* bones! Buys fresh killed . . . in, like, *Chinatown*!'

Someone would mention his name in passing, and other chefs would get this curious expression on their faces, like the runner of Satchel Paige's admonition: 'Don't look back – someone might be gaining on you.' They'd look worried, as if, examining their own hearts and souls and abilities, they were aware that not only *couldn't* they do what Scott does, but they *wouldn't*.

He was a cult figure, it seemed, among cooks of my acquaintance. Over time, I developed an idea of him as some sort of hair-shirt ascetic, a mad monk, a publicity-shy perfectionist who'd rather do *no* business at all – die in obscurity – than *ever* serve a bad meal.

The whole world of cooking is not my world, contrary to what impression I might have given you in the preceding pages. Truth be told, I bring a lot of it with me. Hang out in the Veritas kitchen, take a hard look at Scott Bryan's operation, and you will find that everything I've told you so far is wrong, that all my sweeping generalities, rules of thumb, preconceptions and general principles are utter bullshit.

In my kitchens, I'm in charge, it's always *my* ship, and the tenor, tone and hierarchy – even the background music – are largely my doing. A chef who plays old Sex Pistols songs while he breaks down chickens for coq au vin is sending a message to his crew, regardless of his adherence to any Escoffier era merit system.

A guy who employs, year after year, a sous-chef like Steven Tempel is clearly *not* Robuchon – or likely to emulate his successes. It is no coincidence that all my kitchens over time come to resemble one another and are reminiscent of the kitchens I grew up in: noisy, debauched and overloaded with faux testosterone – an effective kitchen, but a family affair, and a dysfunctional one, at that. I coddle my hooligans when I'm not bullying them. I'm visibly charmed by their extra-curricular excesses and their anti-social tendencies. My love for chaos, conspiracy and the dark side of human nature colors the behavior of my charges, most of whom are already living near the fringes of acceptable conduct.

So, there *are* different kinds of kitchens than the kinds I run. Not *all* kitchens are the press-gang-crewed pressure cookers I'm used to. There are islands of reason and calm, where the pace is steady, where quality always takes precedence over the demands of volume, and where it's not always about dick dick dick.

As we close in on hotel-motel time, let's compare and contrast. Let's take a look at a three-star chef who runs a very different kind of kitchen than mine, who makes food at a higher level, has had a nearly unblemished track record of working with the best in the business, a guy who has always kept his eye on the ball – which is to say, the food. If I suffer by comparison, so be it. I think I said earlier that I was going to tell you the truth. This is part of it.

Scott Bryan, like me, happily refers to himself as a 'marginal' character. When he says 'marginal', you can hear his hometown of Brookline, Massachusetts, in his voice, the same accent you hear in body shops and Irish bars in 'Woostah', 'New Bedfahd,' 'Glahsta,' and Framingham. Scott uses the term 'dude' a lot, though, which leads one to believe there might be surf in Boston. When I dropped by to see him recently, passing first through his stylishly sparse sixty-five-seat dining room, past his four sommeliers – count them, *four* – through a kitchen staffed by serious-looking young Americans in buttoned-up Bragard jackets with the Veritas logo stitched on their breasts and chefwear MC Hammer pants, down a flight of stairs, I found him wrapping a howitzer-sized log of foie gras in cheesecloth. He was wearing a short-sleeved dishwasher shirt, snaps done up to the collar, Alice In Chains blaring in the background. I took inordinate comfort from this, thinking, 'I do that! Maybe we're not so different!' But, of course, we *are* very different, as you shall see.

Scott grew up in what he calls a 'housing development – a project, really', unlike me, who grew up in a leafy green wonderland of brick colonial homes, distant lawn-mowers, backyard croquet games, gurgling goldfish ponds and Cheever-esque cocktail parties. Scott went to Brookline High, a public school where the emphasis seems to have been on technical skills; they had a culinary program and a restaurant open to the public. I went to private school, a tweedy institution where kids wore Brooks Brothers jackets with the school seal and Latin motto (*Veritas fortissima*) on the breast pocket. Scott learned early that he might have to actually *work* for a living, whereas I, a product of the New Frontier and Great Society, honestly believed that the world pretty much owed me a living – all *I* had to do was wait around in order to live better than my parents.

At an age when I was helping to rack up my friends' parents' expensive automobiles and puking up Boone's Farm on Persian carpets, Scott was already working – for Henry Kinison at the Brookline High restaurant. He was doing it for money. Junior year, he took a job in a 'Hungarian Continental' joint, and as a fishmonger at Boston's Legal Seafood. One worked, and that was it. Scott, though still unmoved by the glories of food, found that he preferred cooking to his other imagined career option: electrical engineer or electrician.

His early mentor, Kinison, urged him to attend Johnson and Wales' culinary program in Providence, and along the lines of 'Why not?' he went along.

He hated it.

While studying, he began working for Bob Kinkead at the

much-vaunted Harvest restaurant in Cambridge, and if there is a single epiphany in Scott Bryan's life, a single moment when he decided what it was he was going to do for the rest of his life, it was there – when he first tasted Kinkead's lobster salad with foie gras and truffle vinaigrette. His reaction was immediate. He decided to leave Johnson and Wales.

'I'm not going back,' he said, abandoning culinary school for life in the real world.

He was good. He had to be. Kinkead clearly knew he was on to something. With Scott barely out of high school, Kinkead packed him off to France with the one-word instruction: 'Eat!'

Like me, Scott is conflicted on the issue of the French. We like to minimize their importance, make fun of their idiosyncrasies. 'It's a different system over there,' he said, talking about the work habits of the surrender-monkey. 'You start young. For the first ten years of your career, you get your ass kicked. They work you like a dog. So, when you finally get to be a sous-chef, or a chef, your working life is pretty much over. You walk around and point.' Putting a last twist on his foie gras torpedo, he shrugged. 'Socialism, man. It's not good for cooks.'

But when he sees bad technique, technique that's *not* French, it's torture. As Scott well knows – and would be the first to admit – as soon as you pick up a chef's knife and approach food, you're already in debt to the French. Talking about one of the lowest points in his career, a kitchen in California, he described going home every night 'ashamed, and a little bit angry', because 'the technique was bad . . . it wasn't *French*!'

They may owe us a big one for Omaha Beach, but let's face it, without my stinky ancestors we'd still be eating ham steak with pineapple ring. Scott knows this better than anybody.

Back from France, he rejoined Kinkead, opening 21 Federal with him on Nantucket.

Now here, exactly, is where our career paths divide.

Scott had some chops now. He was good on the line. He had a

résumé, some notable names and recommendations, working experience, exposure to France and French food.

So did I, at that point in my career. *I* was good! *I'*d been to France. *I* had a CIA diploma – at a time when that was a pretty rare and impressive credential. So, what the hell happened? How come *I'*m not a three-star chef? Why don't *I* have four somme-liers?

Well, there are lots of reasons, but one reason is that I went for the money. The first chef's job that came along I grabbed. And the one after that and the one after that. Used to a certain quality of life – as divorcees like to call it, living in the style to which I'd grown accustomed – I was unwilling to take a step back and maybe *learn* a thing or two.

Scott was smarter and more serious. He was more single-minded about what he wanted to do, and *how well he wanted to do it*. He began a sort of wandering apprenticeship, sensibly designed to build experience over a bank account. He came to New York and went to work for Brendan Walsh.

Brendan Walsh and Arizona 206 are names that seem to pop up in the résumés of almost every '80s-era American chef. John Tesar, Kerry Heffernan, Pat Williams, Jeff Kent, Maurice Rodriguez, Herb Wilson, Donnie Masterton – *everyone*, it seemed passed through those kitchen doors at some point in their early careers. And for Scott, it was his version of 'the happy time', a period where 'everyone knew what we were doing was impor-tant. It was a *team* of cooks.' From this early petri-dish of culinary talent, Scott moved onwards and upwards, parlaying one once-in-a-lifetime gig into another, racking up a box score of famous chefs and heavyweight talents that would make any ambitious young cookie jerk to attention just at the mention of their names.

The Gotham with Alfred Portale. Back with Kinkead at 21 Federal in DC. Square One in California. Back to New York with David Bouley. A Hamptons interlude with Jimmy Sears. (Pause for breath here.) Sous-chef for *Eric Ripert at Le Bernar-din* (!)

As if his career wasn't going swimmingly enough for a guy who only a few years earlier had been considering a life installing light sockets and fuse-boxes, he then opened Lespinasse with Grey Kunz.

And if this isn't a rich enough meal for you, to round out his skills and ensure his usefulness as an all-around major league player, he crossed the line from à la carte cuisine to *pastry* – a nearly unthinkable act – and went to work with the awesome überpâtissier, Richard Leach, at Mondrian.

See what I mean?

I would never have done that.

If I had a well-disposed Eric Ripert and Grey Kunz in *my* background, I'd be endorsing blenders, committing unnatural acts in the pool near the Vegas outpost of my not-very-good-anymore restaurant chain, and pickling my liver in Louis Treize. At that point in my career, I wouldn't be shutting down the whole gravy train so I could learn pastry! I'd be mugging it up on the Food Network, schmoozing at the Beard Awards dinner, and contemplating a future where I'd never have to get out of my pajamas!

Just goes to show you.

Scott hates all that stuff. His partner, Gino Diaferia, says, 'I have to drag him kicking and screaming,' to do a guest shot on Letterman, appear on the Food Network, or do the dog and pony act at Beard House. 'I told him, he could get *four* stars someday' he says. 'He doesn't *want it!*' Gino shakes his head and smiles. 'He says he won't play with his food that much.'

Is it all about the food with this guy? I don't know. Scott likes to refer to himself as a cook, and when he says, about another chef, 'He's a good cook,' it's the highest praise he can offer.

Sopping up free martinis at the Veritas bar, I asked Gino whether he thought Scott was in it for the food or for the lifestyle. It gave him pause.

'I don't know.' He seemed clearly troubled by the question. 'I mean, I think he likes the lifestyle. A guy who comes in and hangs around on his day off, you *know* he's got to like the lifestyle. And he loves going out after work with cooks and chefs for drinks . . . *you* know.' He paused and thought about the question again. 'But . . .'

Gino is another example of 'everything I just told you is wrong'. Here's a guy who was in the home fuel oil business, with *zero* restaurant experience, who became partners with a couple of guys for a lark at the then vegetarian Chelsea bistro, Luma. When things began to lose their charm, he bought out the partners and began spending all his time at the restaurant, learning the business from the ground up. 'I was supposed to be a *silent* partner!' Looking around for a chef, a waiter who had worked for fishmongers-to-the-stars, Wild Edibles, told him, 'Scott Bryan is available.'

'I met with him at a coffee shop. He looked at the menu and said, "No vegetarian. That's gotta go." I said, "Fine!" Scott said maybe he'd consult.'

'He came in, started working, changing things, months go by . . . six months! I look at my wife and she looks at me: "Is he consulting? Is he *staying*?" I kept asking him: "Scott, can we make a deal?" Finally, one day he says, "Well . . . I think I *will* stay."'

The rest, as they say, is history. Luma got a quick two stars from Ruth Reichl at the *New York Times* and lots of buzz. Restaurants that change their entire approach midstream *never* succeed – remember I told you that? Wrong! Restaurants owned by guys in the fuel business don't succeed. I might have said something like that, too. Wrong. Operations that expand into multi-units often dilute the qualities that made them good in the first place. Not this time.

Time passed, Luma did well, and Gino and Scott opened Indigo, on West 10th Street, in a spot so poisonous, so reeking of failure that eight or nine restaurants had come and gone in my memory alone. Remember all that yammer about cancerous locations? Sites so cursed that any and all who seek to follow are doomed? Wrong again, jerk.

Indigo was located only a few blocks away from One Five. I'd been hearing quite enough about Scott Bryan, so when the place opened, I remember trudging over in the middle of a blizzard, sitting at the bar and scarfing up free tastings. I thought it was mind-bogglingly good and I told people so. I dragged my crew over, one by one, to try the mushroom strudel, the Manilla clams. We marvelled at Scott's menu, the perfect my-way-or-the-highway document. All the things that conventional wisdom tells a chef he *has* to do, all those must-have crowd pleasers that eat up half your menu before you can sneak in the selections you actually love, – they weren't there! There was no soup. No vegetarian plate. No *steak*! The chicken was not some generic roasted bird with non-threatening seasonings; it was a weird, ballsy, spicy concoction, involving red *curry*, for chrissakes! And *good*. The only beef was braised shoulder – a daube provençale so good that my whole crew at One Five now ran over to Indigo after work. Our two kitchens closed at the same time, so we'd phone ahead to say we were coming over, and start cooking that daube – just put it on the bar, for God's sake! Let it get cold, it's okay! The Indigo seafood selections were admirably unpopular fishes – cod and mackerel – and exciting. This was food for *cooks*. This was food that *we got*. Simple, straightforward and absolutely pretense-free. Like Scott.

Tucking into that daube of beef, or Scott's sweetbreads, was fun for me and my appreciative crew. What's he doing, we wanted to know, while examining a particular item we hadn't tried yet. How is he dealing with mackerel? Then we'd find out.

Everything on Scott's plates is edible. It's *food*, first and foremost, to be eaten, not looked at – though his presentations are inspired. Try and imagine the clean, unfussy integrity of Japanese cuisine, with the unrestrained flavors and soul-food heartiness of a well-remembered Grandma's best dish. He was braising economy cuts. He was taking greasy, oily fishes that nobody wanted and making magic. He was presenting it in big bowls in pretty stacks where – if you jammed your fork through all three layers – you got something that combined to actually taste good. He wasn't piling food on top of itself because layer one *looked good* on top of layer two and three. It tasted good that way. And those big bowls? At Indigo, and at Veritas, when something comes in a big bowl it's because there's gonna be sauce left in the bottom; chances are, you're going to be running a crust of bread around in there and mopping it up when the entree has been eaten.

It's why Scott has three stars and I don't.

It's why he probably won't be getting four stars anytime soon. His food is too good – and too much fun to eat. You feel you can put your elbows on the table in a Scott Bryan–Gino Diaferia restaurant and get about the serious business of tasting and smelling and chewing the good stuff.

I asked Scott if he thinks about food after work. When he's lying in bed in the dark, is he thinking about what he's going to run for special tomorrow? He said no. 'I come in, see what's on the market. I wing it,' he replied. I didn't believe him.

'Does Scott think about food? When he's not working?' I asked Gino, out of Scott's hearing. He smiled.

'He thinks about food,' Gino said. 'A lot.'

Scott is thirty-four years old. He's got dark, boyish good looks, with an eccentric nose that looks right on a chef. There are dark blue rings under his eyes and he has the skin pallor of a man who's spent too many hours toiling under fluorescent kitchen lighting. He wears the bemused expression of a guy who *knows* how bad it can get, who's always looking and waiting for the other shoe to drop. He's not so much a screamer anymore. 'I used to blow up all the time. I still yell, if there's laziness, sloppiness, someone thinks they're getting over.' Pointed sarcasm seems more the preferred tactic these days. And he does not share my pleasure in handling a pirate crew. 'Someone has a problem with another cook in my kitchen? I tell them work it out amongst themselves. I don't have time for that. I say, "Work it out,' cause if you still have a problem with so-and-so tomorrow? You're gone. Maybe you're *both* gone."' He doesn't bully, harangue or excoriate; the occasional caustic comment seems chillingly effective. I hung out in the Veritas kitchen recently, knocked off work at Les Halles and ran over to see how the other half works. It's a very quiet place.

During the middle of the rush on a Friday night, with a full dining room, the pace was positively relaxing – more a seriously focused waltz than the kind of hard-checking mosh-pit slam-dancing I live with. No one was screaming. Nobody was kicking any oven doors closed, putting any English on the plates, or hurling pots into the sink. Scott, expediting, never raised his voice.

'Go on, entrees. Thirty-two,' he said in a near-whisper. That's all it took for five line cooks to swing into action and start converging on plates. 'Pick up,' he said, 'table twelve.'

Three waiters appeared, each expertly wiping, garnishing and finishing a different plate, squeezing drops of chive oil, lobster oil or thirty-year-old balsamic from eye-dropper-sized squeeze bottles. No one was cursing or sweating. The stove-tops, cutting boards, counter space, cook's whites, even the aprons were spotless – at eight-thirty on a Friday night! Each sauce and salad, each item was tasted by the person preparing it, each and every time. Three orders of veal cheek special came up at the same time; they were absolutely identical.

At Les Halles, I go through a 10-pound bag of shallots every day, so it was truly jarring to see Scott Bryan's mise-en-place. The shallots on station were not chopped. They weren't Robot-Couped either. They were *brunoised* – every tiny little piece uniform, textbook, perfectly squared off and near sub-atomic in dimensions. The chopped chives were the same, not a thread, not a single errant or irregular shred, every one the size of a cloned single-cell organism.

The whole kitchen smelled of truffles. Two thumb-sized knobs of the wildly expensive fungus sat by the garnish tray, where Scott would shave them onto outgoing orders. Truffle oil was being poured into pans like I use olive oil. Sauces were being mounted with foie gras and Normandy butter. And everything – *everything* – was being made to order. Risotto? Out of the box and into the pot. From scratch.

A tiny young woman worked at a corner station, and I made the immediate Neanderthal assumption as I first took in the crew: 'Extern, maybe from Peter Kump or French Culinary, having a learning experience dishing out veggies.' I passed right over her as I swept my eyes down the line looking for the heavy hitters. In time I began, peripherally, to become aware of her movements. I looked again, closer this time, and saw that she was plating fish, cooking risotto, emulsifying sauces, taking on three, then four, then five orders at a time – all the while never changing expression or showing any visible signs of frustration or exasperation (as I would have under similar circumstances). No worries, just smooth, practiced motions, moves you see in twenty-year veterans: no pot grabbed without side-towel, no wasted effort, every sauce getting a quick taste, correcting seasonings, coming up on her stuff at the same time as the rest of the order – generally holding down her end like an ass-kicking, name-taking mercenary of the old school, only cleaner and better. Her station and her uniform were absolutely un-marked by spills, stains or any of the expected Friday-night detritus.

'Where did *she* come from?' I whispered to Scott. Not amazed that a woman could do the job, but that *anyone* other than a thirty-five-year-old Ecuadorian mercenary could do it so stone-cold. (Remember what I said about Americans versus *mis carnales* from points south? Wrong again.)

'Oh, her?' said Scott casually. 'Alain Ducasse.' Mentioning *God*'s name as breezily as I'd say, 'the Hilton' or 'Houlihan's'.

If this sobering revelation wasn't painful enough, if I wasn't choking down enough crow, there was some more humble pie to come: a waiter came in with a half-empty bottle of wine, a 1989 Le Chambertin, and *handed it to the Dominican dishwasher*. At this point, I was ready to answer one of those ads in the paper for

'Learn How To Drive the Big Rigs!', maybe take up mink ranching. Anyway, the grateful dishwasher examined the bottle for sediment, promptly decanted the remains, poured some wine into a stem glass – which he held knowledgeably between two fingers by the stem – and then swirled, examining the ropes with a discerning eye, before taking an airy slurp. I was ready to hit myself hard with the nearest blunt object.

Oh yeah: the food.

Luxurious, but austere. Bluefin tuna tartare with pickled cucumbers, lime, chili and lemon grass was formed by hand. Unlike a lot of his peers, Scott doesn't like torturing food into unnatural shapes so it looks like something else. (Metal rings, remember? You might want to reconsider what I said about *them* too.) Green and white asparagus were spooned with chanterelles and truffle fondue. Chilled lobster was stacked on fava bean purée and drizzled with Ligurian olive oil. Even the green salads were hand picked, one leaf after the other piled gently on the plate, the garde-manger guy tasting the occasional piece. A filet mignon came up in the window with a medallion of bone marrow looking pretty and pink under a thin veneer of sauce.

And Scott still doesn't make veal stock. There was tête de porc en crépinette, monkfish with white beans, lardons, roasted tomato and picholines, diver scallops with pea shoots, black truffle vinaigrette and truffle/chive/potato purée, Scottish salmon hit the pass-through with chestnut honey-glazed onions, old sherry wine vinegar and chicken jus.

Not a damn thing to sneer at. That I do more meals at Les Halles in forty-five minutes than Scott does all night was cold comfort. The food was all so dead-bang *honest*. No bogus wild-weed infusions, cookie-cutter piles of pre-made garnishes, no paper collars used to force food into tumescence. Garnishes, such as they were, were edible; the food looked good without them. And the plates were white, no SB logo, no multicolored spirals, baroque patterns, oddball novelty shapes, football field sizes or ozone layer-puncturing space needles of verticality. The pâtissier whacked off a hunk of Morbier for a cheese plate – a daring selection, touch that stuff and you'll be sniffing your fingers for a week. Bread was from Amy's, along with a rustic ciabatta.

When orders came in faster, the pace quickened slightly, but nobody ran. Nobody seemed hurried. Scott jumped from station to station as his mood dictated: fish, sauté, garde-manger, even pastry. In his absence, waiters wordlessly stepped in and did the expediting and plate finishing, with imperceptible change in product. (Waiters shouldn't touch food. Did I say that? Wrong again.)

Is everybody getting their food on time, I wondered. Everyone was so damned calm and collected in here that maybe it's chaos outside, a herd of pissed-off diners glaring silently at their waiters and wondering where their chow is – waiting for that made-to-order risotto so the rest of the order can come up. I decided to see.

No such luck. Outside, the dining room was as relaxed as the kitchen, nothing but happy faces, lingering over appetizers, sipping wine, expressions those of anticipating first-time lovers who just *know* they're going to be good together. The bar was packed with monomaniacal wine aficionados, pouring over the 1,400-strong wine list like Talmudic scholars – beakers, glasses, decanters laid out in front of them making them look like well-dressed Dr Frankensteins. They had a lot to ponder. The Veritas list is an imposing volume with a very reasonable range of wines from 18 to 25,000 dollars. I asked the bartender, hopefully, if any of these wine wonks ever got into it over the relative merits of say, Côtes du Rhône vs. Bordeaux, or '95 vs '98? 'Anybody ever take a poke at another guy, duke it out over grape varieties? Drunken brawls over topsoil, irrigation, drink now or drink later?'

Nope. All is calm. Pleasure rules.

Listening to the customers talking seriously, *really* seriously about wine, I find yet another reason why Scott is a three-star chef and I'm not: I know almost nothing about wine.

I am not immune to the charms of wine. I've lived around it, enjoyed it, cooked with it all my life. I am not entirely ignorant on the subject, nor am I dismissive of its importance. I still remember vividly, heading off to the vintner in Bordeaux with my Oncle Gustav, to get our empty bottles refilled with *vin ordinaire* from those giant casks. I can tell the difference between good wine, bad wine and great wine. I have a pretty good working knowledge of the wine-producing regions of France and Italy. I am vaguely aware that California seems to produce drinkable product these days. But I couldn't tell you grape variety with any more assurance than I could talk about stamp collecting or phrenology. And to be truthful, I've always felt that I've survived *enough* dangerous obsessions in my life; the knowledgeable appreciation of fine wine has always seemed to me to hold potential for becoming yet another consuming habit – an expensive one. When you know what it's like to squat on a blanket on upper Broadway in the snow, selling off a lifetime's accumulation of rare books, records and comic books for drugs, the idea of spending next week's paycheck on a bottle of red seems like, well, something that I probably shouldn't be doing.

So, even though I've been gushing here about Veritas and all things Bryan, I'm really doing the place a disservice. The menu, the business, the whole concept of Veritas is built around the wine – a formidable cellar put together by two of the premium collector/connoisseurs in the universe. It should be pointed out that Scott's food at Veritas is designed to complement that wine. I can only imagine that it does. The fish dishes are unusually hearty, drinkable with red for the most part, I believe (don't trust me on this), and the meat and poultry dishes are constructed and refined to match up nicely with the list. Some of the Asian seasonings and ingredients of Early Bryan have been dispensed with in order best to accomplish that mission.

As for me, I drink beer and vodka when I eat at Veritas, preferring to spend my lucre on what I *know* to be good – namely the food. I know that's a lot like going to Egypt and not bothering to look at the pyramids, but hey, I'm just an old-time cookie with a chip on his shoulder and a heart full of envy.

Problem is, Scott's an old-time cookie, too. After the kitchen closed (at ten forty-five they were talking about getting the last orders in!), I took him up to the Siberia Bar, down the subway steps, through the platform-level bar and into the downstairs annex. I was hoping to get him drunk, find something to dislike about the miserable bastard who's so much better than me. Maybe I could get him sloshed, he'd start venting, make injudicious comments about some of those culinary heroes he'd worked for in the past.

I mentioned I'd eaten at Le Bernardin recently, the full-bore chef tasting. An eyebrow went up. 'Oh yeah? What did you have?'

When I told him, he looked happy, like I get when describing my first oyster.

'You have the mackerel tartare, dude?' he asked.

'Yeah,' I said, hesitating. 'It was good . . . really good.'

'Yeah,' said Scott. 'It is good, isn't it? What else did you have?'

I told him, the two of us talking about menus like some people talk about the Miracle Mets or the Koufax-era Dodgers.

'Who's making food these days that interests you,' I asked.

'Oh, let's see . . . Tom. Tom Collicchio at Gramercy Tavern. Tom makes really good food . . . and Rocco di Spirito at Union Pacific is doing interesting stuff.'

'Have you seen this foam guy's shit?' I asked, talking about Ferran Adrià's restaurant of the minute, El Bulli, in Spain.

'That foam guy is bogus,' he smirked, 'I *ate* there, dude – and it's like . . . shock value. I had seawater sorbet!'

That was about as much bad-mouthing as I could get out of him. I wanted to know what he likes to eat, 'You know, after hours, you're half in the bag and you get hungry. What do you want to eat?'

'Beef bourguignon,' he said right away.

I've found common ground. Red wine, beef, some button mushrooms and a few pearled onions, bouquet garni, maybe some broad noodles or a simple boiled potato or two to go with it. A crust of bread to soak up the sauce. Maybe I'm not wrong about everything.

All cooks *are* sentimental fools.

And in the end, maybe it *is* all about the food.

MISSION TO TOKYO

IF THERE WAS ANY justice in this world, I would have been a dead man at least two times over.

By this, I mean simply that many times in my life the statistical probabilities of a fatal outcome have been overwhelming – thanks to my sins of excess and poor judgment and my inability to say no to *anything* that sounded as if it might have been fun. By all rights I should have been, at various times: shot to death, stabbed to death, imprisoned for a significant period of time, or at very least, victimized by a casaba-sized tumor.

I often use the hypothetical out-of-control ice-cream truck. What would happen if you were walking across the street and were suddenly hit by a careening Mister Softee truck? As you lie there, in your last few moments of consciousness, what kind of final regrets flash through your mind? 'I should have had a last cigarette!' might be one. Or, 'I should have dropped acid with everybody else back in '74!' Maybe: 'I should have done that hostess after all!' Something along the lines of: 'I should have had more *fun* in my life! I should have *relaxed* a little more, *enjoyed* myself a little more . . .'

That was never my problem. When they're yanking a fender out of my chest cavity, I will decidedly *not* be regretting missed opportunities for a good time. My regrets will be more along the lines of a sad list of people hurt, people let down, assets wasted and advantages squandered.

I'm still here. And I'm surprised by that. Every day.

So in the spring of 1999, I really and truly thought that I had *had* all my great adventures, that the entertainment and excitement segment of the program was long over. Been there and done that was more than an assumption for me, it was a defensive stance, and one that kept me – and keeps me – from repeating the stupid mistakes of the past. Sure, there were things to learn. I learn things all the time. But I'm talking about eye-opening, revelatory, perspective-altering life experiences: the exotic, the frightening, the totally new. I wasn't about to sample any new experimental hallucinogens at age forty-three. I wasn't going to submerge myself in some new criminal sub-culture, steeping myself in the customs and practices of professional gamblers, heroin seekers or sexual adventurers – though at one time it would have greatly appealed to me. I didn't think I'd be shipping out on a great big clipper ship (as Lou Reed puts it), wandering the back streets of Peshawar or sampling live monkey brain in the Golden Triangle. My personal journey, I thought, was pretty much over. I was comfortably ensconced in secure digs, with a wife who still – remarkably – found me to be amusing on occasion. I had a job I loved, in a *successful* restaurant . . . and I was *alive*, for chrissakes! I was still *around*! Though the game had long since gone into overtime, I still had a few moves left in me, and I was content to play them out where I'd started – New York City, the place I believed, heart and soul, to be the center of the world.

So it came as a surprise when one of the two partners at Les Halles, Philippe LaJaunie – a man I'd barely conversed with up to that time – approached me one spring afternoon and said, 'Chef, we'd like you to go to Tokyo. Make the food look and taste like it does in New York.'

Now, Brasserie Les Halles is a much-loved New York institution, serving authentic French workingman's fare to hordes of diners each night. I'm an American, whatever my lineage, so it threw me off-guard to be asked if I'd care to go halfway around the world to consult and advise a French chef – in Japan – on the fine points of cassoulet, navarin d'agneau, frisée aux lardons and boudin noir at Les Halles Tokyo.

But my masters, Philippe (a Frenchman) and José de Meireilles (a Portuguese francophile), seemed convinced enough of my mystical connection to the food they clearly adore to pack me on to a plane and send me jetting off to Tokyo for a week. It was a daunting and unusual assignment and I was going alone – my wife would not be joining me.

My biggest concern was the flight: *fourteen hours* in the air, and *no smoking*(!) I scored some Valium before leaving for the airport, thinking maybe I could knock myself out and sleep through the ordeal. Unfortunately, as my Israeli-navigated town car swung into the Kennedy Airport environs, I couldn't find the damn pills. I tore frantically through my pockets and carry-on luggage, near tears, cursing myself, my wife, God and everybody else who might be responsible for this hideous situation.

I checked my knives through, not wanting to carry them on, and was soon dug in, at 11 A.M., at the bar by the departure gate: last stop for degenerate smokers. My companions were a very unhappy-looking bunch of Asia veterans. Like me, they were chain-smoking and drinking beer with grim, determined expressions on their faces. A Chinese gentleman next to me, apropos of nothing, shook his head, blew smoke out of his nose and said, 'Sleeping pill. Only thing to do is sleep. Fourteen hour to Narita. Long time.' This did not improve my mood. Another bar customer, an MP headed to South Korea to pick up a prisoner, slammed back another draft and described the horror of business class to the other side of the world. He too shook his head, lips pursed, resigned to his fate. A red-faced Aussie with a five-hour layover waiting for him on the Tokyo end, advised me to have another beer – *at least*. 'Or three, mate. Nothing to do but bloody *sleep*.' Yeah, right, I thought. Got any Demerol?

As a back-up, I had acquired a few nicotine patches. I rolled up my left sleeve and slapped one directly over a vein, hoping for the best as they sounded final boarding.

The flight was endless. The in-flight movie was a slight

improvement over looking out the window: a Japanese film about, as best as I could gather, fly-fishing. Guys standing around in waders, philosophizing about carp in a language I couldn't understand, had a pleasantly somnolent effect and I managed, with the help of many more beers, to pass out for a few hours.

I should point out, by the way, that I know *nothing* about Japan. Oh, sure, I've seen *The Seven Samurai* and *Rashomon* and *Yojimbo* and the Kurosawa *policiers*, and Sonny Chiba and *Gidrah versus Mecha-Godzilla* for that matter, but I was in every significant way ignorant of all things Japanese. I knew only enough about Japanese culture and history to know that I knew nothing. I spoke not a word of Japanese. I had, with only a week's warning before my trip, not even acquired a guidebook or a street map for the city of Tokyo. But I *did* like sushi and sashimi.

The city of Tokyo is an amazing sprawl – something out of William Gibson or Philip Dick – seeming to go on forever. The bus from the airport wound over bridges, down through tunnels, up fly-overs that wrapped around the upper floors of apartment and office buildings. I passed canals, industrial parks, factories, residential areas, business districts, carp ponds, austere temples, indoor ski slopes, rooftop driving ranges. As I got closer to my destination, it was getting dark, with giant, screaming video screens advertising beverages and cellphones and recording artists, garish signs in English and Japanese, lines of cars, crowds of people – row after row after row of them, surging through intersections in orderly fashion. This was *not* America or any-place remotely like it. Things on the other side of the world were very, very *different*.

The bus unloaded at a hotel in Roppongi district, and a helpful dispatcher in a uniform hailed me a cab. The rear passenger door swung open for me, operated by the driver by lever, and I slid on to a clean, white slip-covered back seat. Dispatcher and driver examined the Les Halles business card with address, debating route and destination. When the matter was decided, the door swung closed and we were off. The driver wore white gloves.

Roppongi district is international in character – like an Asian Georgetown – and Les Halles Tokyo, located in the shadow of the Eiffel-like Tokyo Tower, and across the street from a pachinko parlor, looked much like its older brother in New York, though spanking new and impeccably, surgically clean. Les Halles New York is loved for its smoke-stained walls, creaky chairs, weathered wooden bar – the fact that it resembles what it is: a familiar, worn, old-school brasserie of the Parisian model. Les Halles Tokyo, on the other hand, though accurate to the model down to the tiniest design detail, was shiny and undamaged, and apparently kept that way.

It was a warm night when I arrived, and the French doors to the café were open. Philippe saw me from the bar. He'd arrived a day earlier. He came out to greet me.

'Welcome to Tokyo, Chef,' he said.

I had been provided with an apartment nearby, and Philippe helped load my luggage on the handlebars of two borrowed bicycles for the short trip over. My first close-up look at Tokyo was from the seat of a rickety three-gear as I pedaled furiously to keep up with Philippe. He took off at a good pace down Roppongi's very crowded streets. You're *supposed* to ride on the sidewalks, I later learned, though I don't know how that's even possible. Traffic runs the wrong way over there, so heading straight into it, I picked and wove my way between cars and vans, dodging pedestrians, trying to keep my 50-pound duffel bag on the handlebars and not get dragged backwards off the seat by the other bag hanging around my neck. Roppongi Crossing, though by no means Tokyo's largest or busiest intersection, is where thousands of teenagers meet before heading off to the bars and clubs. The streets were unbelievably dense with pedestrians, people hanging around, flashing neon, flapping banners, more screaming signs, pimpy-looking young men in suits and patent leather shoes, surrounded by dyed-blond Asian women in thigh-high boots and micro-mini skirts. Philippe took a hard turn and we were heading down a hill, through twisting, narrow and decidedly quieter streets. Things became stranger and even more unfamiliar, the smell of something good to eat issuing from every building we passed.

The organization kept a few apartments in a kind of residential hotel. It looked like a hotel, felt like a hotel, but had no visible employees. Comfortable, spacious by my imagined Tokyo standards, and equipped with cable TV, phone, fax, kitchenette and ingeniously designed bathroom, I was soon unpacked and agreeably installed, my mysterious French boss staying next door.

'I'm sure you want to shower, maybe rest for a while,' said Philippe, before heading back to Les Halles. 'Can you find your way to the restaurant?' I was pretty sure I could.

After a long shower in the short, deep apartment bathtub, I managed to find my way back to Les Halles, where I was shown around and introduced. Frédéric Mardel was the chef, from Aquitaine by way of Bora-Bora. His chefs de partie, Hiroyoshi Baba of Japan, Delma Sumeda Elpitiya of Sri Lanka and Mo Ko Ko of Myanmar were gracious in the extreme. Fortunately, the common language in the kitchen was French, which I found, to my surprise, that I could still speak and understand.

I had been worried about this moment; I'd been apprehensive about invading another chef's kitchen. We tend to get our backs up with the arrival of interlopers, and though it may have been nice to be held up as some sort of benchmark for the Les Halles organization, I knew how *I'd* have felt if the chef from say, the Washington or Miami branch came swanning into *my* kitchen, wanting to show me how the big boys do it. Frédéric was a friendly and gracious host, however, and like the rest of the crew, had never been to New York. I was a curiosity, as strange to them as they were to me.

The kitchen was small and spotless, with dangerously low range hoods for a 6-foot-4 guy like me. A grate-covered canal ran around the floor beneath each station, with a current of constantly flowing water washing away any detritus that might fall from cutting boards. Containers were all space-saving square in shape, and the counters were low to the ground. I put on my whites, unwrapped my knives and hung around the kitchen for a while, watching food go out, taking it all in, making small talk with the crew, aware of a persistent throbbing behind my eyes, an unpleasant constriction around my temples, a feeling that I was somehow not getting enough oxygen.

Beat from the flight, I only stayed a few hours that night, until at 10 P.M. Tokyo time, my brain thoroughly poached with jet lag, I slunk back to the apartment to collapse.

I woke up at 5 A.M., hungry, put on a pullover, long-sleeved T-shirt, jeans, black elk-skin cowboy boots that had seen better days, and a suit-cut leather jacket that Steven had picked up used for me at a flea market. I was ready for adventure.

Breakfast.

At first, I didn't have the nerve. I wandered Roppongi's early-morning streets, tortured by the delicious smells emanating from the many businessmen's noodle shops, intimidated by the crowds. Japanese salarymen sat cheek-to-jowl, happily slurping down bowls of soba. I didn't want to stare. I didn't want to offend. I was acutely aware of how freakish and un-Japanese I looked, with my height, in my boots and leather jacket. The prospect of pushing aside the banner to one of these places, sliding back the door and stepping inside, then squeezing on to a stool at a packed counter and trying to figure out how and what to order was a little frightening. One couldn't enter a place, change one's mind and then creep away. The prospect of being the center of attention at this tender hour, with the capillaries in my brain shriveled from all the beers on the flight, and the jet lag even worse than it had been the day before – I just couldn't handle it. I wandered the streets, gaping, my stomach growling, looking for somewhere, anywhere to sit down and have coffee, something to eat.

God help me, I settled for Starbucks. At least, I saw from the street, they allowed smoking. It was drizzling outside by now, and I was grateful for the refuge, if ashamed of myself. I sipped coffee (when I ordered it, the counter help repeated the order to one another at ear-splitting volume: 'Trippa latte!! *Hai! One trippa latte!*'

I sat by the window, head pounding, smoking and sipping, summoning the courage for another pass at a soba joint. There was no way, I told myself, that I was gonna eat my first Tokyo meal in *Starbucks*! Pinned under the wheels of that hypothetical Mister Softee truck, I *would* have something to regret. Muttering to myself, I charged out of Starbucks, found the narrowest, most uninviting-looking street, pushed aside the banner of the first soba shop I encountered, slid back the door and plopped myself down on a stool. When greeted, I simply pointed a thumb at the guy next to me and said, 'Dozo. I'll have what he's having.'

Things worked out well. I was soon slurping happily away at a big, steaming bowl of noodles, pork, rice and pickles. This method of ordering would become my modus operandi over the following days and nights. I can tell you that I felt a lot better about myself after my breakfast. I spent a few hours at the restaurant before hailing a cab for Chiyoda-ku district. I had an engagement.

If you didn't already know, a few years back I wrote a satirical thriller *policier*, set, predictably, in the restaurant business. Based loosely on my experiences at Work Progress and with the 'Italian fraternal organization' I mentioned earlier, it was acquired for translation by the eminent Japanese publishing house, Hayakawa. Being the hustler that I am, upon learning I was headed for Tokyo I immediately contacted my Japanese publisher, volunteering, a bit disingenuously, to do 'anything I could' to help promote the book over there. I don't know how nice or how welcome a thing to do it was. The book had been out for a while – and clearly had not set the world on fire. David Hasselhoff might have hit it big over there; *Airwolf* reruns were once huge on the Pacific Rim; but my little book had not, I think, caused my publishers to send for me to satisfy public demand for a closer look. What a responsibility, I now realized, what a situation I had saddled Hayakawa with, giving them an alarming *one week*'s notice of my arrival.

However horrified they might privately have been, they responded with enormous tact and hospitality. An event was organized. A reception committee was formed. Cars were laid on. Lunches arranged. Copies of my book were found and quickly displayed in the ground-floor bookstore of their corporate offices. So, I found myself headed off to the Chiyoda-ku district to meet the chef of La Rivière, a restaurant adjacent to and owned by my publisher. I was to cook a meal evocative of my earlier work of fiction for the benefit of the press, provide a few bons mots at a press conference, appear on Japanese cable TV (network also owned by my publisher) and in every way cause inconvenience to strangers who had been nothing but generous to me from afar.

The chef of La Rivière, Suzuki-san, must have been thrilled to have me show up in his kitchen. Bad enough some big, hairy gaijin was getting rammed down his throat, making use of his staff, rummaging through his reach-ins – but I was cooking *Italian*. The menu for the event was minestra toscana, followed by a paillard of veal with roasted red pepper coulis and basil oil, and a salad of arugula, endive and radicchio. Chef Suzuki was polite, as I was ushered into his kitchen with the requisite bowing and greeting. He was helpful and polite in every way, as was his crew. But he must have been simmering with rage and disgust. Suzuki-san and I communicated through a translator and gestures, my gift of a Yankee World Series Champs baseball cap going only a short way to ameliorating the chef's molar-grinding distaste for what I was about to do to his kitchen. My simple Italian lunch, re-creating a home-cooked meal prepared by a gangster character in the book, must have looked to the chef like roadkill. And the portions! I thought I'd scaled them down nicely, but after serving the meal to a roomful of bowing, chain-smoking and very genial Hayakawa executives and a few press-ganged members of the fourth estate, I found myself repeatedly asked, 'Bourdain-san, the portions at Les Halles, how many grams of meat in each order?' When I replied, the reaction was giggling and head-shaking – an indication, I came to believe, of abject terror. The prospect of returning a partially eaten entree, of not finishing, is a terrifying one. And the proper Japanese will avoid causing such offense at all costs. So the thought of tucking into a 2½-pound côte de boeuf, or a full order of cassoulet toulousaine, must have seemed to my hosts like scaling a mountain of dung.

Still, the Hayakawa people were extremely kind. I was driven around by two senior editors, invited to lunch – with Chef Suzuki cooking this time. My second book was, I believe, rushed into print; it might otherwise have been forgotten had I not turned up on their doorstep. I got to see myself on Japanese TV and in the press; I was shown how to use the subways by Hayakawa hosts; I experienced the not unpleasant occasion of having a whole room of people bowing to me in near unison; I got to meet the elegant, shrewd and impressive Mr Hayakawa himself; and I signed a lot of books for persons no longer living – a first for me. Apparently this is not an unusual practice, a commemorative signed copy for the deceased.

I wasn't doing too badly by day three. My head still felt as if someone was tightening a vise around it, and I'd probably offended many at Hayakawa with my inadvertently boorish behavior, but I had been out on my own and around town. I'd cooked in not one, but two Japanese kitchens. I was comfortably taking cabs, ordering food and drink, using mass transit and exploring at will. I was having a good time. I was learning.

Back at Les Halles, I used my recent experience at La Rivière to scale down the portions and pretty up the presentations. Working with Frédéric and his crew, I rearranged plates to resemble smaller versions of what we were doing in New York: going more vertical, applying some new garnishes, and then observing customer reactions. I looked for and found ways to get more color contrast on the plates, moved the salads off to separate receptacles, stuck sprigs of herb here and there. With

Frédéric, I tried to develop a repertoire of specials – trying to make sense of the arcane system of supplies in Japan.

Things were different here. What was ordered was not always what arrived. My inquiries about foodstuffs were often met with blank stares and shrugs. When the problem was finally identified, the answer was most often, 'Too expensive.' The supply situation really was a problem. Onglet (hanger), côte du boeuf (rib section), and faux filet (sirloin) were all shipped from our central boucherie in New York, so that was fine. But the bright red filet was Japanese product and wildly expensive. Fish and produce were objects of religious sanctity – particularly fish – and the price reflected that. A gift of a melon in Japan implies a life of obligation. Frites are taken very seriously in our organization, but Japanese potatoes have an unusual starch/sugar content and require blanching in water. I suggested peanut oil instead of canola, like we use in New York, and was informed that one could rent a small apartment for what it cost to fill a deep-fryer with it. I'd brought along some white truffle oil and some truffles and the crew gazed at them like Martian artifacts.

There was no runner or expeditor at Les Halles Tokyo. After food was plated, it was hand-carried to the outer service bar where it was picked up by the waiters. The garde-manger, who also doubled as pâtissier and worked in an open area, visible to the dining room, was required out of custom, to shriek 'Welcome!' in Japanese, along with waiters, bartender and manager, to all arriving guests. This was somewhat alarming to a jet-lagged newcomer like myself. The process was repeated on departure, as it was almost everywhere I went, the ubiquitous scream of '*Arigato gozaimashiTAAAA!*' making me want to leap out of my skin.

Frédéric was beat. He worked seven days a week, fourteen-plus hours a day, as did the general manager. It was early days for our new outpost – not yet busy enough to require a full staff – and total commitment was required. The GM's eyes seemed to float around in his skull in pools of fatigue. The cooks worked split shifts, arriving at the last possible second before service, working through lunch, then they were cut loose to wander idly around Roppongi – far from their residences – before returning for dinner. The carping and grumbling an arrangement like this would inspire back in New York would lead invariably to mutiny and open revolt. Here? People went about their tasks with considerable good cheer and dedication.

The proletarian chic of Les Halles New York was something new to the Japanese. They don't really get the humble working-man's fare. They *adore* the higher-end stuff, though, and there were unintentionally hilarious re-creations of haute and nouvelle classics (fettucine *and* rice on the same plate, for instance). There was and is a heartfelt desire to learn about French cuisine, to enjoy it. Though business has picked up enormously since my trip, at the time I was there, eating at Les Halles – with its Flintstones-sized portions and funky attitude about blood, fat and organ meat – was still a bold adventure. Still, I suspected it was just a matter of time.

An unusual number of single women would show up for lunch, sitting alone and looking shiftily, even guiltily, about before tucking into their steaks and nibbling their frites. The female office workers looked pleasantly secretive about their brasserie encounters, as if they were involved in some deliciously dirty and forbidden conspiracy – like meeting a lover. Watching a group of Japanese salarymen tear into a côte de boeuf for two I got the impression of a kind of gleeful social disobedience, an almost revolutionary act of convention breaking. It was my first experience of the proper Japanese cutting loose. I would see more.

I went out exploring all the time by now. The jet lag wouldn't let me sleep, so I crashed late and rose early, plunging blindly down dark streets at all hours. There is, apparently, no street crime in Tokyo. The most menacing looking bunch of Elvis-coiffed pimps and touts would move aside wordlessly at my approach. Gaining on a group of leather-jacketed punks with silver hair and motorcycle jackets from behind, one of them would detect me and make an almost imperceptible sound – a cough or a clearing of the throat – meaning, apparently, '*Gaijin* coming through', and the crowd would part to make way. No one, and I mean no one, would meet my eye with a direct gaze. Whether standing outside a whorehouse at four in the morning, or examining their pinky rings by an idling Yakuza limo, no one ever said, 'What are *you* looking at?', as might have been the case in American cities under similar circumstances. Barkers for hostess bars and strip clubs and whorehouses – even the ones that accepted Westerners – never solicited me directly; I passed through them like a ghost. I walked. And walked. Streets full . . . streets empty . . . day and night, aimlessly in wide concentric circles, using a visible landmark to navigate around. I took subways to stops where I had no idea where I was and walked more. I ate sushi. I slurped soba noodles. I ate food off conveyor-belt buffets where every imaginable dish rolled by and one simply grabbed what one wanted. I entered bars populated by only Japanese, bars for expatriates and the women who love them. Booze was affordable and there was no tipping anywhere. I was the Quiet American, the Ugly American, the Hungry Ghost . . . searching and searching for whatever came next.

One night at Les Halles, Philippe invited me out for what turned out to be the most incredible meal of my life.

He'd seen, by now, how I was digging Tokyo. He knew from my arrival and departure times about my nocturnal wanderings, so I guess he figured I was ready. He grinned mischievously all the way.

As usual, I had no idea where we were going. Philippe led me across Roppongi, crossing to the skankier, glitzier side where the streets were choked with touts and barkers, whores and shills, video arcades, hostess bars and love hotels. We passed by the poodle-cut pimpy boys and the heavily made-up Thai, Filipina and Malaysian women in their platform boots and crotch-high dresses, past enormous and eerily empty Yakuza-run nightclubs, karaoke bars, restaurants. It became darker as we walked farther and farther from the neon and screaming video signs – yet still, not a rude comment or hostile stare. Finally, Philippe stopped, sniffed the air like a hunting dog, turned suddenly and headed for a dimly lit stairwell in a deserted courtyard, a single pictogram of a leaping fish the only indicator of activity below. Down a flight of steps, not a sound, to a bare sliding door. He pushed it aside and we were standing in a small, well-lit sushi bar. Three young sushi chefs in headbands and two older men in chefs' coats manned an unfinished blond-wood bar, packed with somewhat inebriated-looking businessmen and their dates. We were ushered to the only two open seats, directly in front of a slowly melting monolith of carved ice, surrounded by fish and shellfish so fresh, so good-looking, it took my breath away.

My chef friends in New York would have gouged out an eye or given up five years of their lives for the meal I was about to have.

First, hot towels. Then the condiments: freshly grated wasabi, some dipping sauce. We were brought frozen sake, thick, cloudy, utterly delicious. The first sip seemed to worm its way directly into my brain like an intoxicating ice-cream headache. I had many more sips, Philippe all too anxious to pour more and more. The first tiny plate, tentacles of baby octopus, arrived, the chef standing there while we ate, examining our reactions – which were, of course, moans, smiles, bows of appreciation and thanks. Already feeling the sake, we thanked him in French, English and bad Japanese – covering all bases. More bows. The chef removed the plates.

His hands moved, a few motions with a knife, and we were presented with the internal parts of a giant clam, still pulsating with life as it died slowly on our plates. Again, the chef watched as we ate. And again, we were a good audience, closing our eyes, transported. Next came abalone with what might have been the roe and liver of something – who cared? It was *good*.

More sake. Snapper came next. Then bass. Then mackerel, fresh and squeaky and lovely to look at.

We went on, calling for more, our appetites beginning to attract notice from the other chefs and some of the customers who'd never it seemed, seen anyone – especially Westerners –

with our kind of appetites. Each time the chef put another item down in front of us, I detected almost a dare, as if he didn't expect us to like what he was giving us, as if any time now he'd find something too much for our barbarian tastes and crude, unsophisticated palates.

No way. We went on. Calling for more, more, Philippe telling the chef, in halting Japanese, that we were ready for anything he had – we wanted *his choice*, give us your best shot, motherfucker (though I'm sure he phrased it more elegantly). The other customers began to melt away, and our hosts, the chef joined by an assistant now, seemed impressed with our zeal, the blissed-out looks on our faces, our endless capacity for more, more, *more*. Another clam arrived, this one tiny, more roes, some baby flounder – it kept coming, accompanied by pickled wasabi stem, seaweed so fresh I could taste deep ocean water. Another tiny moist towel was provided in a little basket and Philippe informed me that custom allowed us to eat with our hands at this point in the meal. Tuna arrived, from the belly, from the loin. We kept grinning, kept bowing, kept eating.

Our sakes were refilled, the chef openly smiling now. These crazy gaijin wanted it all, baby! The best course yet arrived: a quickly grilled, halved fish head. The chef watched us, curious, I imagine, to see how we'd deal with this new development.

It was unbelievable: every crevice, every scrap of this sweet, delicate dorade or Chilean pompano (I didn't know from looking at the partly charred face, and by now didn't much care) had responded differently to the heat of the grill. From the fully cooked remnant of body behind the head to the crispy skin and cartilage, the tender, translucently rare cheeks, it was a mosaic of distinct flavors and textures. And the *eye*! Oh, yeah! We dug out the orbs, slurped down the gelatinous matter behind it, deep in the socket, we gnawed the eyeball down to a hard white core. When we were done with this collage of good stuff, when we'd fully picked over every tiny flake and scrap, there was nothing left but teeth and a few bones. Were we finished? No way!

More sashimi, more sushi, some tiger shrimp, what looked

like herring – so fresh it crunched. I didn't care what they put in front of me any more, I trusted the smiling chef and his crew, I was going along for the full ride. More frozen sake . . . more food. The last few customers got up and lurched to the door – like us, red-faced and perspiring from the booze. We continued. There had to be *something* we hadn't tried yet! I was beginning to think that some of the cooks were calling their homes by now, telling their families *get in here and get a load of these gaijins!! They're eating everything in the store!*

After course twenty or so, the chef slit, brushed, dabbed and formed the final course: a piece of raw sea eel. Earthenware cups of green tea were delivered. Finally, we were done.

We left to the usual bows and screams of '*Arigato gozaima-shiTAAA!!!*' and picked our way carefully, *very* carefully, up the stairs, back to the physical world.

I left Philippe at Les Halles, had a couple of cocktails at an empty faux-Irish pub and staggered back to my apartment. I had to get up early for the fish market.

Tsukiji, Tokyo's central fish market, puts New York's Fulton Street to shame. It's bigger, better, and unlike its counterpart in Manhattan a destination worth visiting if only to gape.

I arrived by taxi at four-thirty in the morning. The colors of the market alone seemed to burn my retinas. The variety, the strangeness, the sheer *volume* of seafood available at Tsukiji amounted to a colossal Terrordome of mind-boggling dimensions. The simple awareness that the seafood-crazy Japanese were raking, dredging, netting and hooking *that much stuff* out of the sea each day gave me pause.

A Himalayan-sized mountain of discarded styrofoam fish boxes announced my arrival, as well as a surrounding rabbit warren of shops, breakfast joints and merchants servicing the market. The market itself was enclosed, stretching seemingly into infinity under a hangar-type roof, and I will tell you that my life as a chef will never be the same again after spending the morning – and subsequent mornings – there. Scallops in snow-shoe-sized black shells lay atop crushed ice, fish, still flopping, twitching and struggling in pans of water, spitting at me as I walked down the first of many narrow corridors between the vendors' stands. Things were different here in that the Japanese market workers had no compunction about looking you in the eye, even nudging you out of the way. They were *busy*, space was limited, and moving product around, in between sellers, buyers, dangerously careening forklifts, gawking tourists and about a million tons of seafood was tough. The scene was riotous: eels, pinned to boards by a spike through the head, were filleted alive, workers cut loins of tuna off the bone in two-man teams, lopping off perfect hunks with truly terrifying-looking swords and saws which, mishandled, could easily have halved their partners. Periwinkles, cockles, encyclopedic selections of roes – salted, pickled, cured and fresh – were everywhere, fish still bent from rigor mortis, porgy, sardines, swordfish, abalone, spiny lobsters, giant lobsters, blowfish, bonito, bluefin, yellowfin. Tuna was sold like gems – displayed in light-boxes and illuminated from below, little labels indicating grade and price. Tuna was king. There was fresh, dried, cut, number one, number two, vendors who specialized in the less lovely bits. There were hundreds, maybe thousands of gigantic bluefin and bonito, blast-frozen on faraway factory ships. Frost-covered 200–300-pounders were stacked everywhere, like stone figures on Easter Island, a single slice taken from near the tail so quality could be examined. They were laid out in rows, built up into heaps, sawed into redwood-like sections, still frozen, hauled about on forklifts. There were sea urchins, egg sacs, fish from all over the world. Giant squid as long as an arm and baby squid the size of a thumbnail shared space with whitebait, smelts, what looked like worms, slugs, snails, crabs, mussels, shrimp and everything else that grew, swam, skittered, clawed, crawled, snaked or clung near the ocean floor.

Unlike the low-tide reek of Fulton, Tsukiji smelled hardly at all. What scent it had was not of fish, but of seawater and the cigarettes of the fishmongers, I had never seen, or even imagined, many of the creatures I saw.

Hungry, I pushed into a nearby stall, the Japanese version of Rosie's diner: a place packed with rubber-booted market workers eating breakfast. The signs were entirely in Japanese, with no helpful pictures, but a friendly fishmonger took charge. What arrived was, of course, flawless. Here I was in the Tokyo version of a greasy spoon, surrounded by a mob of tough-looking bastards in dripping boots and the requisite New York-style rude waitress, and the food was on a par with the best of my hometown: fresh, clean, beautifully, if simply, presented. Soon, I was wolfing down sushi, miso soup, a tail section of braised fish in sauce, and an impressive array of pickles. Beats two eggs over.

I loaded up with cockles and squid for the restaurant, bought some knives for my sous-chef back in New York and, head aching, stopped off at Akasuka Temple where the ailing apparently waft incense smoke over their afflicted parts. The smoke did nothing for my head. I bought aspirin – which incongruously came with free candy and pamphlets advertising patent medicines – and took a taxi to Kappabashi, Tokyo's Bowery.

It was the perfect metaphor for Tokyo: ringing up some wine glasses, cocktail shakers, tablecloth clips and cake molds, the clerk at the restaurant supply store added up my bill on an abacus – but computed the tax on a calculator.

I was really beginning to worry about my head when I finally bumped into Philippe again at the restaurant. Can this still be jet lag, I asked him. The pain seemed to be aspirin-proof. Am I dying?

'Oh, you mean "the helmet"?' he asked, circling his own head with his fingers to indicate the exact location of the pain. He shrugged, '*C'est normal.*'

It's never a good thing when a Frenchman says '*C'est normal.*'

I knew he'd been up early too; I'd heard him knocking around his room as I left for the fish market. Here it was, seven at night, as usual I was starting to fade, my English degenerating into monosyllables, experiencing hot flashes, sweats, and chills. I asked Philippe, hopefully, if he'd had a nap since the morning. He looked so damn fresh, crisp and debonair in a smartly cut suit, positively rosy-cheeked, and in the middle of some Byzantine accounting and scheduling problem which would have caused me difficulty when my faculties were at their peak.

'Oh, no,' he said, cheerfully. 'When I am in Tokyo I don't sleep much. I just take my vitamins and *go*.'

The following night was my last in Tokyo. Philippe took me out to a shabu-shabu joint in Shibuya, Tokyo's Times Square. It was Friday night and all the painstakingly observed customs and practices of the workday went out the window. The streets were packed with herds of insanely drunk businessmen and teenagers. In Tokyo, it's apparently okay, even de rigueur, to go out with the boss and the boys from the office and get completely, stuttering, out-of-control drunk. In such circumstances, after a night of drinking and karaoke, it's okay to vomit on your boss's shoes, take a swing at him, call him an asshole. He'll probably throw you over his shoulders and carry you home. Everybody was drunk. Everywhere, lovely young women brushed the hair out of their violently heaving boyfriends' faces as they leaned on all fours into the gutters. Suit-and-tied salary-men projectile vomited, lurched, sang, caroused and staggered like bumper cars down the humanity-clogged streets. Mobs of people surged in never-ending waves toward Shibuya station to meet friends and lovers by the statue of a dog. The dog, it was explained to me, had continued to show up every day at the station, long after its master had died. That kind of dedication impresses the Japanese and a statue was erected in the pooch's honor; it's one of the most popular meeting places in the city. Nearby the narrow, neon-lit streets swam with more nightclubs, bars, restaurants, screaming, building-high video screens whose exhortations made my molars shake like tuning forks.

We found a shabu-shabu joint, a crowded tatami room where there were no other Westerners, and managed to contort our limbs under and around the low table. A big wok filled with broth was heated up for us, and a uniformed attendant arrived with an Everest-high heap of meat, vegetables, seafood and noodles. We kicked off the meal with hot sake, heated with grilled fish bones. The fish oil that collected on the top was ignited before drinking, and the flavor was heavily aromatic, with fumes that seemed to penetrate brain tissue immediately. Item by item, according to cooking time, the food was added to the oil – like a giant fondue. When everything had been deposited into the wok, we were left to our own devices, save frequent refills of chilled sake.

I did *not* want to leave. I had only begun to eat. There were a million restaurants, bars, temples, back alleys, nightclubs, neighborhoods and markets to explore. Fully feeling the effects of the sake, I was seriously considering burning my passport, trading my jeans and leather jacket for a dirty seersucker suit and disappearing into the exotic East. This . . . this was excitement, romance, adventure – and there was so much more of it, *too* much more of it for even another month, another year, another *decade* to adequately contain my investigations. I *knew* I could live here now. I'd learned a few things, not much, but enough to negotiate traffic, feed myself, get drunk, get around town. I pictured myself as a character like Greene's Scobie in Africa, or the narrator of *The Quiet American* in Saigon, even Kurtz in *Heart of Darkness*, my head swimming with all sorts of romantically squalid notions. At two o'clock in the morning, the streets still swarming with young Japanese in American sports cars, girls sitting on the back of convertibles, gangsters and whores emerging from nightclubs, moving on to the next place, shirtless gaijins howling at the moon from upstairs whorehouses, I staggered down dark back streets, hit some more bars and, finding myself incongruously hungry again, and wanting to soak up some of the sea of alcohol in my stomach, committed the ultimate in Tokyo faux pas – I ate a McDonald's hamburger while I walked. The trains shut down at eleven-thirty, and most of Tokyo, it seemed, preferred to stay out all night to taking a taxi. One could, Philippe had explained before leaving me off at Roppongi Crossing, borrow money to get home from almost any policeman if drunk and unexpectedly short of funds. The idea of *not* returning the next day to repay the debt was, in typically Japanese thinking, unthinkable.

I walked, unsteadily, for hours, stopped off for a final drink, managed, somehow, to get back to my apartment and call Nancy.

She'd laid on some fresh bialys from Columbia Bagels, and some Krispy Kreme donuts for my return. I began packing.

SO YOU WANT TO BE A CHEF?

A COMMENCEMENT ADDRESS

FOR CULINARY STUDENTS, LINE cooks looking to move up in the world, newcomers to the business – and the otherwise unemployables who make up so much of our workforce – I have a few nuggets of advice, the boiled-down wisdom of twenty-five years of doing right and doing wrong in the restaurant industry.

For the growing number of people who are considering becoming a professional chef as a second career I have some advice, too. In fact, let's dispose of you first:

So you want to be a chef? You *really, really, really* want to be a chef? If you've been working in another line of business, have been accustomed to working eight-to-nine-hour days, weekends and evenings off, holidays with the family, regular sex with your significant other; if you are used to being treated with some modicum of dignity, spoken to and interacted with as a human being, seen as an equal – a sensitive, multidimensional entity with hopes, dreams, aspirations and opinions, the sort of qualities you'd expect of most working persons – then maybe you should reconsider what you'll be facing when you graduate from whatever six-month course put this nonsense in your head to start with.

I wasn't kidding when I said earlier that, at least in the beginning, you *have no rights*, are not entitled to an opinion or a personality, and can fully expect to be treated as cattle –

only less useful. Believe it. I wish I had a dollar for every well-meaning career changer who attended a six-month course and showed up to be an extern in my kitchen. More often than not, one look at what they would really be spending their first few months doing, one look at what their schedule would be, and they ran away in terror.

To those serious ones who *know* what it is they are entering, who are fully prepared, ready, willing and able, and committed to a career path like, say, Scott Bryan's – who want to be chefs, *must* be chefs, whatever the personal costs and physical demands – then I have this to say to you:

Welcome to my world!

And consider these suggestions as to your conduct, attitude and preparation for the path you intend to follow.

1. Be fully committed.   Don't be a fence-sitter or a waffler. If you're going to be a chef some day, be *sure* about it, single-minded in your determination to achieve victory at all costs. If you think you might find yourself standing in a cellar prep kitchen one day, after tournéeing 200 potatoes, wondering if you made the right move, or some busy night on a grill station, find yourself doubting the wisdom of your chosen path, then you will be a liability to yourself and others. You are, for all intents and purposes, entering the military. Ready yourself to follow orders, give orders when necessary, and live with the outcome of those orders without complaint. Be ready to lead, follow, or get out of the way.

2. Learn Spanish!   I can't stress this enough. Much of the workforce in the industry you are about to enter is Spanish-speaking. The very backbone of the industry, whether you like it or not, is inexpensive Mexican, Dominican, Salvadorian and Ecuadorian labor – most of whom could cook you under the table without breaking a sweat. If you can't communicate, develop relationships, understand instructions and pass them along, then you are at a tremendous disadvantage.

Should you become a leader, Spanish is absolutely *essential*.

Also, learn as much as you can about the distinct cultures, histories and geographies of Mexico, El Salvador, Ecuador and the Dominican Republic. A cook from Puebla is different in background from a cook from Mexico City. Someone who fled El Salvador to get away from the Mano Blanco is not likely to get along with the right-wing Cuban working next to him. These are your co-workers, your friends, the people you will be counting on, leaning on for much of your career, and they in turn will be looking to you to hold up *your* end. Show them some respect by bothering to know them. Learn their language. Eat their food. It will be personally rewarding and professionally invaluable.

3. Don't steal. In fact, don't do *anything* that you couldn't take a polygraph test over. If you're a chef who drinks too many freebies at the bar, takes home the occasional steak for the wife, or smokes Hawaiian bud in the off hours, be fully prepared to admit this unapologetically to any and all. Presumably, your idiosyncrasies will – on balance – make you no less a chef to your employers and employees. If you're a sneak and a liar, however, it will follow you forever. This is a small business; everybody knows everybody else. You will do yourself immeasurable harm.

Don't *ever* take kickbacks or bribes from a purveyor. They'll end up owning you, and you will have sold off your best assets as a chef – your honesty, reliability and *integrity* – in a business where these are frequently rare and valuable qualities.

Temptation, of course, is everywhere. When you're a hungry, underpaid line cook, those filet mignons you're searing off by the dozens look mighty good. Pilfer one and you're bent. Ask for one, for chrissakes! You'll probably get one. If they won't let you have one, you're probably working in the wrong place.

Faking petty cash vouchers, stealing food, colluding with a purveyor or a co-worker is extraordinarily easy. Avoid it. Really.

I was bent for the first half of my career, meaning, I pilfered food, turned in the occasional inflated petty cash slip, nicked beer for the kitchen. It didn't feel good. Slinking home at the end of the night, knowing that you're a thief, whatever your excuse ('My boss is a thief' . . . 'I need the money' . . . 'They'll never notice') feels lousy. And it can come back to bite you later in your career.

Recently, I agreed to meet with the representative from a major seafood wholesaler. I met him at the empty bar of my restaurant, during the slow time between lunch and dinner, and told him that I'd done business with his company at another restaurant. I was inclined to like the company. The products and services had, in my experience so far, been first rate, and what he needed to do to get my business was simply provide the same or better-quality fish as my other purveyors – and do so at a lower price. I meant it, too. I am absolutely tone-deaf to criminal solicitation. It bores me. And for all my misbehavior over the years, I have never – and I mean *never* – taken money or a thing of value from a purveyor in return for my master's business.

'Junior' (that was his name), from X Seafood, seemed puzzled by my apparent obtuseness that day. Thick-necked, crew-cutted, but oh-so-friendly, 'Junior' seemed to think that maybe we were talking about sex, when in fact all the while we were discussing the internal combustion engine. There were long silences as his gentle, cheerful probings and expressions of non-specific good will were left dangling in the air. After a while of this – me wanting only to know how much he was charging for Norwegian salmon today, and resisting his unspoken entreaties suddenly to muse aloud about how, maybe, it would be nice if I could afford a hot tub for my apartment – he gave up in frustration and left.

Minutes later, a waiter drew my attention to a plain white envelope on the floor. Opening it, I found a stack of 100-dollar bills and a list of nearby hotels and restaurants with some names checked off. 'Junior' had apparently dropped it. I have to tell you, I felt pretty damn good calling up 'Senior' down at X Seafood and breezily informing him that his son seemed to have left something behind by mistake at my restaurant: could they please send someone to come pick it up? A red-faced functionary picked the envelope up within minutes, and I never heard from that company again.

All sorts of scumbags will offer you every variety of free stuff if you entertain the prospect of doing business with them, slipping them food, or looking the other way. Screw them all. Don't even play footsie with them, meaning, 'I'll take the case of Dom – but I don't know if I can always do business with you.' Don't even do that. There are a *lot* of scumbags in the restaurant business, people who *will* let the Gambino Family decide who gets the fish order or the liquor order in return for Knicks tickets or a lap dance, and these are people who you will have to deal with, sometimes adversarially. How can you win an argument with one of these people when *you*'re a scumbag too?

4. Always be on time.

5. Never make excuses or blame others.

6. Never call in sick. *Except* in cases of dismemberment, arterial bleeding, sucking chest wounds or the death of an *immediate* family member. Granny died? Bury her on your day off.

7. Lazy, sloppy and slow are bad. Enterprising, crafty and hyperactive are good.

8. Be prepared to witness every variety of human folly and injustice. Without it screwing up your head or poisoning your attitude. You will simply *have* to endure the contradictions and inequities of this life. 'Why does that brain-damaged, lazy-assed busboy take home more money than me, *the goddamn sous-chef*?' should not be a question that drives you to tears of rage and frustration. It will just be like that sometimes. Accept it.

'Why is he/she treated better than me?'

'How come the chef gets to loiter in the dining room, playing kissy-face with [insert minor celebrity here] while *I*'m working my ass off?'

'Why is my hard work and dedication not sufficiently *appreciated*?'

These are all questions best left unasked. The answers will drive you insane eventually. If you keep asking yourself questions like these, you will find yourself slipping into martyr mode, unemployment, alcoholism, drug addiction and death.

9. Assume the worst. About everybody. But don't let this poisoned outlook affect your job performance. Let it all roll off your back. Ignore it. Be *amused* by what you see and suspect. Just because someone you work with is a miserable, treacherous, self-serving, capricious and corrupt asshole shouldn't prevent you from enjoying their company, working with them or finding them entertaining. This business *grows* assholes: it's our principal export. *I*'m an asshole. You should probably be an asshole too.

10. Try not to lie. Remember, this is the restaurant business. No matter how bad it is, everybody probably has heard worse. Forgot to place the produce order? Don't lie about it. You made a mistake. Admit it and move on. Just don't do it again. Ever.

11. Avoid restaurants where the owner's name is over the door. Avoid restaurants that smell bad. Avoid restaurants with names that will look funny or pathetic on your résumé.

12. Think about that résumé! How will it look to the chef weeding through a stack of faxes if you've never worked in one place longer than six months? If the years '95 to '97 are unaccounted for? If you worked as sandwich chef at Happy Malone's Cheerful Chicken, maybe you shouldn't mention that. And please, if you appeared as 'Bud' in a daytime soap opera, played the Narrator in a summer stock production of '*Our Town*', leave it off the résumé. Nobody cares – except the chef, who won't be hiring anyone with delusions of thespian greatness. Under 'Reasons for Leaving Last Job', never give the real reason, unless it's money or ambition.

13. Read! Read cookbooks, trade magazines – I recommend *Food Arts, Saveur, Restaurant Business* magazines. They are useful for staying abreast of industry trends, and for pinching recipes and concepts. Some awareness of the history of your business is useful, too. It allows you to put your own miserable circumstances in perspective when you've examined and appreciated the full sweep of culinary history. Orwell's *Down and Out in Paris and London* is invaluable. As are Nicolas Freeling's *The Kitchen*, David Blum's *Flash in the Pan*, the Batterberrys' fine account of American restaurant history, *On the Town in New York*, and Joseph Mitchell's *Up in the Old Hotel*. Read the old masters: Escoffier, Bocuse et al as well as the Young Turks: Keller, Marco-Pierre White, and more recent generations of innovators and craftsmen.

14. Have a sense of humor about things. You'll need it.

KITCHEN'S CLOSED

MY HANDS HURT.

My feet hurt too, sticking out from under the covers, radiating pain up to the knees.

Sunday morning at eight o'clock and I'm lying in bed after a king-hell, bone-crushing Saturday night at Les Halles, making noises no human should ever make. Just getting my Zippo to light takes three tries with unresponsive fingers, a few muttered curses. I'm psyching myself up for the long walk to the bathroom, an exercise I will no doubt execute with all the grace and ease of a Red Foxx, and the further challenge of the child-proof cap on the aspirin bottle.

I tend to get philosophical on Sunday mornings; it's an activity well suited to my current physical condition, when even lighting cigarettes is difficult, and the chamber-pots my brother and I would see in the old house in La Teste de Buch seem like an attractive and sensible option.

I got, finally, the hands I always wanted. Hands just like the ones Tyrone taunted me with all those years ago. Okay, there are no huge water-filled blisters – not this weekend anyway. But the scars are there, and as I lie in bed, I take stock of my extremities, idly examining the burns, old and new, checking the condition of my calluses, noting with some unhappiness the effects of age and hot metal.

At the base of my right forefinger is an inch-and-a-half diagonal callus, yellowish-brown in color, where the heels of all the knives I've ever owned have rested, the skin softened by constant immersions in water. I'm proud of this one. It distinguishes me immediately as a cook, as someone who's been on the job for a long time. You can feel it when you shake my hand, just as I feel it on others of my profession. It's a secret sign, sort of a Masonic handshake without the silliness, a way that we in the life recognize one another, the thickness and roughness of that piece of flesh, a résumé of sorts, telling others how long and how hard it's been. My pinky finger on the same hand is permanently deformed, twisted and bent at the tip – a result of poor whisk handling. Making hollandaise and béarnaise every day for Bigfoot, I'd keep the whisk handle between pinky and third finger, and apparently the little finger slipped out of joint unnoticed and was allowed to build up calcium deposits, until it became what it is today, freakish-looking and arthritic.

There are some recent scrapes and tiny punctures, a few little dings here and there on the backs of my hands – the result of rummaging at high speed through crowded reach-in boxes, hauling milk crates filled with meat upstairs, busting open boxes and counting cans on Saturday inventory – and a few shiny spots where I must have spattered myself with hot oil or simply grabbed a pot handle or pair of kitchen tongs that was too hot. My nails, such as they are – I gnaw them in the taxi home from work – are filthy; there's dried animal blood under the cuticles, and crushed black pepper, beef fat and sea salt. A large black bruise under the left thumbnail is working its way slowly out over time; it looks as though I've dipped the thumb in India ink. There's a beveled-off fingertip on the left; I lopped off that fingertip while trying to cut poblano peppers many years back. Jesus, I remember *that* one: the face on the emergency room intern as he crunched the curved sewing needle right through the nail, trying vainly to re-attach a flap of skin that was clearly destined to become necrotic and fall off. I remember looking up at him as I twisted and writhed on the table, hoping to see the cool, calm, somehow reassuring expression of a Marcus Welby looking back at me. Instead, I saw the face of an overextended fry cook – a kid, really – and he looked pained, even grossed-out as he pulled through another loop of filament.

There's a raised semi-circular scar on the left palm where I had a close encounter with the jagged edge of a can of Dijon mustard. Almost passed out from that one – that terrible few seconds before the blood came, me looking at my injured paw and it not looking like my hand at all, just some terribly violated slab of very pale meat. When the blood came it was almost a relief.

There are some centimeter-long ridges in the webbing of my left hand, between thumb and forefinger, from the Dreadnaught, when I would regularly lose control of the oyster knife, the dull blade hopping out of or breaking through the shell to bury itself in my hand. The knuckle wounds are so numerous, and have been opened and reopened so frequently, that I can no longer recall, in the layer upon layer of white scar tissue, where or when I got any of them. I know that one of them is the result of boiling duck fat at the Supper Club, but other insults to the flesh have come and gone; it's like the layers of an ancient city now, evidence of one kitchen after another piled up on top of each other. The middle finger of my left hand, at the first joint, where the finger guides the knife blade, has been nicked so many times it's a raised hump of dead flesh, which tends to get in the way of the blade if I'm whacking vegetables in a hurry. I have to be careful. My fingerprints are stained with beet juice (hot borscht as soupe du jour yesterday), and if I hold my fingers to my nose, I can still smell smoked salmon, chopped shallots and a hint of Morbier rind.

I'm not even going to talk about my feet.

It's been twenty-seven years since I walked into the Dreadnaught kitchen with my hair halfway down my back, a bad attitude, and a marginal desire to maybe do a little work in return for money. Twenty-six years since my humiliation at Mario's when I looked up at Tyrone's mightily abused claws and decided I wanted a pair like that. I don't know who said that every man, at fifty, gets the face he deserves, but I certainly got the hands I deserve. And I've got a few years to go yet.

How much longer am I going to do this?

I don't know. I *love* it, you see.

I love heating duck confit, saucisson de canard, confit gizzards, saucisson de Toulouse, poitrine and duck fat with those wonderful tarbais beans, spooning it into an earthenware crock and sprinkling it with breadcrumbs. I love making those little mountains of chive-mashed potatoes, wild mushrooms, ris de veau, a nice, tall micro-green salad as garnish, drizzling a perfectly reduced sauce around the plate with my favorite spoon. I enjoy the look on the face of my boss when I do a pot-au-feu special – the look of sheer delight as he takes the massive bowl of braised hooves, shoulders and tails in, the simple boiled turnips, potatoes and carrots looking just right, just the way it should be. I love that look, as I loved the look on Pino's face when he gazed upon a perfect bowl of spaghetti alla chitarra, the same look I get when I approach a Scott Bryan daube of beef, a plate of perfect oysters. It's a gaze of wonder: the same look you see on small children's faces when their fathers take them into deep water at the beach, and it's always a beautiful thing. For a moment, or a second, the pinched expressions of the cynical, world-weary, throat-cutting, miserable bastards we've all had to become disappears, when we're confronted with something as simple as a plate of food. When we remember what it was that moved us down this road in the first place.

Lying in bed and smoking my sixth or seventh cigarette of the morning, I'm wondering what the hell I'm going to do today. Oh yeah, I gotta write *this* thing. But that's not *work*, really, is it? It feels somehow shifty and . . . dishonest, making a buck *writing*. Writing *anything* is a treason of sorts. Even the cold recitation of facts – which is hardly what I've been up to – is never the thing itself. And the events described are somehow diminished in the telling. A perfect bowl of bouillabaisse, that first, all-important oyster, plucked from the Bassin d'Arcachon, both are made cheaper, less distinct in my memory, once I've written about them. Whether I missed a few other things, or described them inadaquately, like the adventures of the Amazing Steven Tempel, or my Day in the Life, are less important. Our movements through time and space seem somehow trivial compared to a heap of boiled meat in broth, the smell of saffron, garlic, fish-bones and Pernod.

Though I've spent half my life watching people, guiding them, trying to anticipate their moods, motivations and actions, running from them, manipulating and being manipulated by them, they remain a mystery to me. People confuse me.

Food doesn't. I *know* what I'm looking at when I see a perfect loin of number one tuna. I can *understand* why millions of Japanese are driven to near bloodlust by the firm, almost iridescent flesh. I *get* why my boss grows teary-eyed when he sees a flawlessly executed choucroute garnie. Color, flavor, texture, composition . . . and personal history. Who knows what circumstances, what events in his long ago past so inspire this rare display of emotion? And who needs to know? I just know what I see. And I understand it. It makes perfect sense.

'*Là voilà!*' my old Tante Jeanne used to shout, as she limped out to the garden picnic table bearing a rustic salade de tomates, a fresh baguette, and that cheesy butter I had long since come to love. And every once in a while, I'll remember, in my very spine, what those days felt like, smelled like, even sounded like: the faraway neee-nawww, neee-nawww sounds of a distant Black Maria, the rooster's call from the neighbor's yard, the feel of sand between my toes, the draft up the leg of my too-short shorts. All it takes, sometimes, is the sight of a sliced red tomato and some rough-cut parsley. I might find myself humming 'These Boots Were Made for Walking' or 'Whiter Shade of Pale', and thinking about those canned chives on the *Queen Mary*, how they crunched between my teeth, the blissful shock as I realized the soup was actually cold.

I've left a lot of destruction in my wake, and closed a hell of a lot of restaurants. I don't know what happened to many of my early owners, whether they're back pulling teeth for a living, or whether they still cling to the dream, trying to get some other operation off the ground, trying to stay ahead of their latest creditors, the latest unforgiving developments of market forces and broken equipment, unreliable cooks and menacing money-lenders. I don't know. I know I didn't do the best job for some of them, though I did the best I could have done – at the time.

The cooks who've passed through my kitchens? I *know* where most of them have gone; I'm more likely to keep in touch, as I might need some of them again. The brilliant Dimitri has been out of the life for years – and doesn't return my phone calls. I don't recall doing anything too bad to Dimitri, other than dragging him to New York. But I suspect he doesn't want to get tempted should I call with an unusual offer. 'Hey, Dimitri! This gig would be *perfect* for you! It'll be just like old times.' They make movies about that, the old bank robbers getting together for one final score. Dimitri knows better than that. He must.

My old friend from high school, Sam, is still in the business. He's still bouncing around. He does very nicely catering and doing part-time mercenary work at various bistros around town, married now to a lovely and hugely talented pastry chef. I see him often.

Adam Real-Last-Name-Unknown has held a steady job at a prestigious caterer for almost two years now, and seems to be doing very well. Patti Jackson (from my Pino interlude) works down the street, with a hunky-looking assistant I can well picture her referring to by saying, 'Have him washed and oiled and delivered to my chambers!' Beth the Grill Bitch works for private clients now, feeding Atkins Diet to wealthy jumbos. She eats at Les Halles often and is considered to be a visiting celebrity in my kitchen – especially when she demonstrates some new karate moves and sleeper holds for my awed crew.

Manuel, the pasta cook I stole from Pino, and who worked with me at Sullivan's, enduring the late night sounds of Steven penetrating his girlfriend, is back in Ecuador, finishing work for his degree in engineering.

At Les Halles, life goes on as always. The same crew showing up, on time, every day: Franck and Eddy, Carlos and Omar, Isidoro and Angel, Gerardo, Miguel, Arturo, the two Jaimes, Ramón and Janine. They're still with me, and I hope they stay with me. My bosses, however, when they read *this*, will *really* prove themselves patrons of the arts if they don't can me right away.

My wife, blessedly, has stayed with me through all of it, the late nights, the coming home drunk, my less than charming tendency not to pay any attention at all to her when mulling over prep lists and labor deployment and daily specials and food costs. A few months back, in a moment of admittedly misguided solidarity with my heavily decorated kitchen crew, I got a tattoo, a reasonably tasteful headhunter's band around my upper arm. Nancy, however, was on record as finding skin art about as attractive as ringworm; she took it, not unreasonably, as a personal affront. She was mightily pissed off, and still is, for that matter . . . but she still wakes up next to me every morning, laughs at my jokes on occasion, and helpfully points out when I'm being an asshole. The few days a year we spend in Saint Martin have been the only times I've ever *not* been a chef since she's been with me. Squatting under a palm tree, gnawing on barbequed chicken legs and drinking Red Stripes, there's *nothing* more important on my mind than what we're having for dinner – the stuffed crab backs or the spiny lobster – and I imagine that for once I behave in some approximate way like a normal person.

Tragically, inexplicably, my old sous-chef and director of covert operations, Steven, has chosen to leave New York for Florida with his girlfriend, pulling up stakes, giving up his apartment, even bringing along his goldfish. So it doesn't look like he'll be coming back anytime soon. I can't imagine life without him. My doppelgänger, my evil twin, my action arm and best friend – I just can't imagine *not* being able, at any time, to pick up the phone and call him on his cell, enlist his help in whatever dark plans I'm hatching at the moment. Plus, I'll need somebody strong to work my grill on Saturday nights. He'll be calling of course. 'Guess where I am . . . right now?' He'll let me listen for a few seconds to the sounds of waves lapping against the beach, or of the car with its top down, cruising down the main drag in South Beach. The bastard.

I'll be right here. Until they drag me off the line. I'm not going anywhere. I hope. It's been an adventure. We took some casualties over the years. Things got broken. Things got lost.

But I wouldn't have missed it for the world.